Law and Providence
in Joseph Bellamy's
New England

RELIGION IN AMERICA SERIES
Harry S. Stout, General Editor

Law and Providence
in Joseph Bellamy's
New England

*The Origins of the New Divinity
in Revolutionary America*

MARK VALERI

New York   Oxford
OXFORD UNIVERSITY PRESS
1994

Oxford University Press

Oxford   New York   Toronto
Delhi   Bombay   Calcutta   Madras   Karachi
Kuala Lumpur   Singapore   Hong Kong   Tokyo
Nairobi   Dar es Salaam   Cape Town
Melbourne   Auckland   Madrid

and associated companies in
Berlin   Ibadan

Copyright © 1994 by Mark Valeri

Published by Oxford University Press, Inc.
200 Madison Avenue, New York, New York 10016

Oxford is a registered trademark of Oxford University Press, Inc.

Library of Congress Cataloging-in-Publication Data
Valeri, Mark R.
Law and providence in Joseph Bellamy's New England :
the origins of the New Divinity
in revolutionary America / Mark Valeri.
p. cm.—(Religion in America series)
Includes bibliographical references and index.
ISBN 0-19-508601-5
1. New Divinity (Movement)—History.
2. New England—Church history—18th century.
3. Bellamy, Joseph, 1719–1790.
4. Providence and government of God—History of
doctrines—18th century.
I. Title.
II. Series: Religion in America series (Oxford University Press)
BX7250.V35   1994   285'.0974'09033—dc20   94-8629

2 4 6 8 9 7 5 3 1

Printed in the United States of America
on acid-free paper

For
Lynn MacKinnon Valeri

Acknowledgments

One of the few unmixed pleasures of writing a book is to acknowledge those who befriended the writer and his project. This book concerns Joseph Bellamy, an eighteenth-century Connecticut preacher who was one of the originators of an American brand of Calvinism known as the New Divinity. I offer it as at least some payment for the many debts of friendship accrued in its making. I express my gratitude to the following institutions and people in particular.

The National Endowment for the Humanities, the Oregon Council for the Humanities, and Lewis and Clark College awarded me several grants for research and travel. The National Endowment for the Humanities also funded a year's fellowship at the American Antiquarian Society, where I benefited enormously from the hospitality and expertise of John Hench, Joanne Chaison, and Marie Lamoureux. Each of the research institutions and archives listed in the bibliography has given generous access to its manuscripts.

Ed and Barbie Danks and Don and Marion MacKinnon provided friendship and hospitality on numerous research trips to Connecticut. They always dispelled the thought, which came on me every July, that it was a cruel fate to have to trade Oregon's summers for New England's.

From its inception as a doctoral dissertation, this project has had many kind readers. John Murrin, Albert Raboteau, and the late Paul Ramsey provided critical insight at an early stage. Chris Grasso and Steve Bullock made helpful suggestions at a later stage. Philip Gura pressed me to make Bellamy more interesting than I had in my dissertation; William Freehling helped me to do so (I hope) by chastening my prose. A newly organized group of American historians in the Portland area—Joel Bernard, Jackie Dirks, Jane Hunter, David Johnson, Chris Lowe, and Larry Lipin—commented on drafts of several chapters. Larry has been especially patient in critiquing the social analyses of an instinctively intellectual historian. At Lewis and Clark, Dick Rohrbaugh has given encouragement; John Callahan has given that, and his wisdom on words. Michael McGiffert edited (as only he can) an earlier version of Chapter 5, which contains material from an article in *The William and Mary Quarterly*. This material is reprinted with permission. I would be remiss if I did not also mention R. Fenton Duvall, Jim Hunt, and William Slottman, who at an early stage in my career led me to appreciate the study of history.

To my good fortune, my fellow students of the New Divinity are highly talented and generous scholars. Mark Noll, who writes about much more than the New Divinity, may not count himself a student of that movement, but he has frequently expressed an interest in Bellamy. He gave me confidence that this project was worthy of publication, even with its many faults. Joseph Conforti, whose book was the first I read on the topic, has offered many acute historiographical and bibliographical suggestions. William Breitenbach has edited my work with consummate skill and precision. I have been amused by the coincidence that Bill teaches at a nearby institution; this may make the Pacific Northwest, an unlikely candidate, the latest outpost of the New Divinity.

My scholarly debts are deepest to two other historians of American religion who have given their time and encouragement with remarkable grace. Harry Stout of Yale University guided this manuscript to Oxford University Press. His cheer and energy lifted my spirits on many a sultry summer day in New Haven. John Wilson of Princeton University advised my doctoral work, introduced me to Jonathan Edwards, suggested Bellamy as a dissertation topic, and invited me to coauthor an essay with him— my first foray into print. John's gifts as an interpreter of American religion are matched only by his kindness and wisdom. Over the past decade I have said "thank you" to him more times than I can count. This makes one more.

The one to whom this book is dedicated has read this study many times, commented on it perceptively, and talked about it with interest and enthusiasm. She knows far too much about Joseph Bellamy. I can only hope to return the measure of friendship that she has so steadily bestowed on me.

Contents

Abbreviations

Anderson   Glenn Paul Anderson, "Joseph Bellamy (1719–1790): The Man and his Work." Ph.D. diss., Boston University, 1971

CA   Connecticut Archives, Ecclesiastical Series, Connecticut State Library, Hartford, Connecticut

CHS   Joseph Bellamy Papers, Connecticut Historical Society, Hartford, Connecticut

CR   J. Hammond Trumbull and Charles J. Hoadly, eds., *Public Records of the Colony of Connecticut, 1636–1776.* 15 vols., Hartford, Connecticut, 1850–1890

HS   Joseph Bellamy Papers, Boxes 187–190, Folders 2929–2964, Case Memorial Library, Hartford Seminary, Hartford, Connecticut

HSP   Simon Gratz Collection, Historical Society of Pennsylvania, Philadelphia, Pennsylvania

HW   William Cothren, *History of Ancient Woodbury, Connecticut, from the First Indian Deed in 1659 to 1854.* 2 vols., Waterbury, Connecticut, 1854–1872

PHS   Joseph Bellamy Correspondence, transcribed by Richard Webster, Presbyterian Historical Society, Philadelphia, Pennsylvania

WLR   Woodbury Land Records, Woodbury Town Hall, Woodbury, Connecticut

WMQ   *The William and Mary Quarterly*, Third Series

Works   Joseph Bellamy, *The Works of the Rev. Joseph Bellamy, D.D., Late of Bethlem, Connecticut.* 3 vols., New York, 1811–1812

WPR   Woodbury District Probate Records, Woodbury Town Hall, Woodbury, Connecticut

WTR   Woodbury Town Records, Volume I (1731–1773) of List Records, Woodbury Town Hall, Woodbury, Connecticut

YS   Joseph Bellamy Papers, Group 609, Box 1, Sterling Memorial Library, Yale University, New Haven, Connecticut

Law and Providence
in Joseph Bellamy's
New England

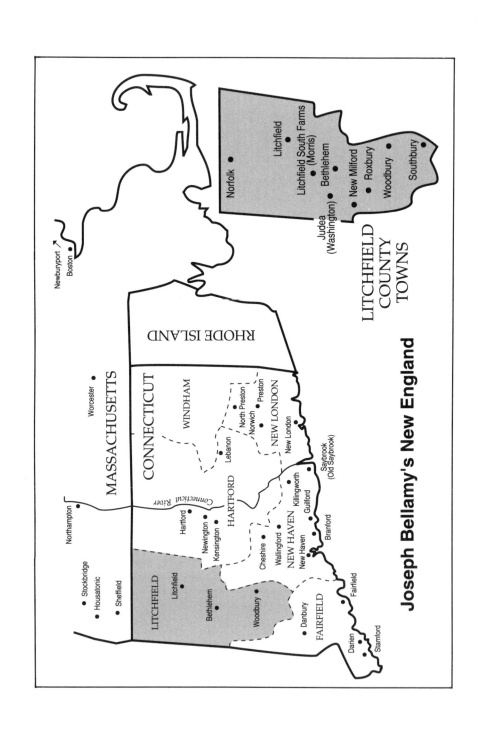

Joseph Bellamy's New England

Introduction

> My grandmother's blue book was published and recommended to the
> attention of New England . . . just twenty-six years before the Decla-
> ration of Independence. . . . There is not the slightest doubt that it
> was heedfully and earnestly read in every good family of New En-
> gland; and its propositions were discussed everywhere and by every-
> body. This is one undoubted fact; the other is, that it was this genera-
> tion who fought through the Revolutionary war.
>
> HARRIET BEECHER STOWE, *Oldtown Folks* (1869)

The "serious" and "puzzling subjects" under consideration in Harriet Beecher
Stowe's 1869 novel *Oldtown Folks* were the dogmas of Calvinism, recalled
through the story of Grandmother Badger and her "blue book." An old-
style New Englander, Grandmother allowed herself one diversion from "the
daily battle of existence." She read her favorite volume, "by the Rev. Dr.
Bellamy of Connecticut, called 'True Religion delineated, and distinguished
from all Counterfeits.'" As described by Stowe's fictional narrator, Joseph
Bellamy's book "was written in a strong, nervous, condensed, popular style,
such as is fallen into by a practical man speaking to a practical people, by a
man thoroughly in earnest to men as deeply in earnest, and lastly, by a
man who believed without the shadow of a doubt, and without even the
comprehension of the possibility of a doubt." Those who first subscribed to
True Religion Delineated (Boston, 1750), marveled Stowe, were rationalists
and revivalists, merchants and ministers, magistrates and otherwise unknown citizens; "almost every good old Massachusetts or Connecticut family," as well as more common folk, knew Bellamy's theological speculations.[1] The farmers and shopkeepers in Grandmother's day were "practical
people." Yet, as metaphysically driven as they were pragmatic, they craved
knowledge of "the WHENCE, the WHY, and the WHITHER of mankind." Bellamy's
theology answered the whence and the whither with one central Calvinist
dogma: God decreed all that was—creation and the Fall, holiness and sin,
the salvation of the elect and the damnation of the rest.

Stowe thus wrote of Joseph Bellamy's appeal nearly eighty years after
his death. New Englanders readily embraced Calvinism, she explained,
because its dark and cold doctrines seemed to reflect reality; "nothing in

their experience of life" had ever predisposed them to "find the truth agree-able." They learned firsthand of original sin, human depravity, and the unmitigated necessity of divine grace. More important, the "doctrine of Divine sovereignty" (Stowe's catchphrase for Calvinism) explained and imputed meaning to a tragic existence, giving "great rest to the human mind in those days." The assertion of God's reasons for allowing evil, cen-tral to Bellamy's writing, consoled. It also motivated. Stowe saw that "strength of mind and strength of will and courage and fortitude and endurance" flowed from such confidence. Joseph Bellamy's "blue book" emboldened Americans especially in a time of social and political revolution; its creed made it "rather a recreation to fight only British officers."[2]

Although Stowe found Calvinism an impossible anachronism in her time, she gave the right impression in *Oldtown Folks*: Bellamy was remark-ably important in his. Born in 1719 in Wallingford, Connecticut, he lived most of his adult life as the pastor in Bethlehem, Litchfield County, until his death in 1790. Always controversial, Bellamy was a popular preacher, a noted revivalist, an influential teacher of ministerial candidates, an au-thority in ecclesiastical politics in New England, and a widely read polemi-cist. Along with Samuel Hopkins (1721–1808), he promoted a variety of Calvinism known as the New Divinity theology, or, more descriptively, "consistent Calvinism." At a time when Yale, Harvard, and the College of New Jersey (Princeton) had no distinct faculties of divinity, he organized in his home an informal institute for theological study, taking in both college-age students and fledgling preachers with bachelor's degrees. From his nearly sixty pupils came most of New England's Calvinist leaders, in-cluding David Austin (1760–1850), Jonathan Edwards, Jr. (1745–1801), Nathaniel Niles (1743–1814), and John Smalley (1734–1808)—who taught Nathanael Emmons (1745–1840). Bellamy also developed adult classes in his parish that were the forerunner of the nineteenth-century Sunday school. He became known throughout the colonies; in 1753 a Presbyte-rian church in New York City offered to make him the highest paid clergy-man in America.[3]

By the end of his career, Bellamy led an immense force among Con-necticut's Congregational clergymen. Between 1765 and 1783 his fol-lowers took fully half of New England's pulpit appointments; by 1790 self-proclaimed New Divinity pastors controlled New England churches in and west of the Connecticut River Valley (especially in Litchfield and Hartford counties in Connecticut and in Berkshire County in Massachu-setts), were prominent in key regions in the east (particularly in New London County in Connecticut and in Essex, Norfolk, and Plymouth counties in Massachusetts), and were scattered throughout Vermont and Maine and even New York and New Jersey. In 1787, Edwards, Jr., was confident that "a majority of the ministers [in Connecticut] mean to embrace the system of my father and Dr. Bellamy."[4]

Opponents such as Israel Holly (1728–1804) observed that the New Divinity "entangled and ensnared" not only "the literary world" but also "the common people." Bellamy's prominence in Connecticut infuriated Ezra Stiles (1727–1795), who complained that Bellamy was the "Pope of Litchfield County" and the most powerful cleric in western New England. As president of Yale, Stiles feared that the college's best and brightest were enamored of Bellamy and that New Divinity students would overrun Yale, flood Connecticut's pulpits, overwhelm the churches with Bellamy's ideas, and "undoe the Colony."[5]

Just as contemporary opponents could not deny the New Divinity's influence, so later New Englanders could not forget its legacy. Bellamy's stature grew even as liberal theologies spread in the nineteenth century. In 1828 both Nathaniel William Taylor (1786–1858) and Joseph Harvey (1787–1873), Taylor's opponent, appealed to Calvin, Edwards, and Bellamy as the three most eminent Reformed authorities. Lyman Beecher (1775–1863), father of Harriet Beecher Stowe and leader of New England's Second Great Awakening, claimed in 1832 that Jonathan Edwards (1703–1758) and Bellamy were "the authors which contributed to form and settle my faith." In 1833 the founders of Hartford Seminary endorsed "the doctrines which have been held in New England for generations," those of "Edwards and Bellamy," the "glory of New England." In 1848 the trustees of that same institution set down this common version of New England's religious genealogy: Saint Paul to Calvin to Edwards to Bellamy to Timothy Dwight (1752–1817).[6]

Scholars too often have read the genealogy "from Edwards to Dwight," from the First Great Awakening to the Second. Many have passed over Bellamy, New England's leading Calvinist from 1750 to 1780, because his period has been regarded chiefly as prelude to Calvinism's demise in the freewheeling, entrepreneurial, and Arminian culture of the early national era.[7] Yet Bellamy promoted a resurgence of a hardened, aggressive, and socially engaged Calvinism. In the midst of New England's transformation from provincial society to part of a new Republic, the New Divinity rose, flourished, and provided a huge exception to the "epitaphs," as Edmund Morgan once put it, by which we have known the fate of Calvinism in America.[8]

How, among Old Lights, proto-Unitarians, Baptists, radical sects, and sheer atheists, did Bellamy articulate a message so persuasive that it charmed scores of ordinary New Englanders, attracted dozens of students, incited Holly, alarmed Stiles, and commanded the filial respect even of Taylor and Beecher? Bellamy's career, with which the New Divinity originated and gained a widespread appeal, provides answers.

Bellamy's innovations on the theology of Jonathan Edwards made Calvinism significant for the Revolutionary generation. Rather than rehearse Edwards, his mentor and the most sophisticated theologian in eighteenth-century America, Bellamy refashioned evangelical Calvinism.

During the 1730s and 1740s Edwards challenged a society of self-satisfied Arminians. From 1750 through the 1770s Bellamy confronted anything but overconfidence; religious dissent and economic expansion exacerbated social schisms, and war between Britain and France threatened New England's existence. After the Treaty of Paris in 1763 ended the French and Indian War, American patriots faced the prospect of rebellion against the most powerful empire in the world. New England desperately needed theological and ethical vision. Bellamy judged that radical evangelicals minimized the social expression of virtue, and that liberals within the estabished clergy rejected truth as a guide to public policy. Attempting to unite sound doctrine to society, he contended for Calvinism's public voice.

Bellamy found that voice in the rhetoric of law. New England's social crises raised profound questions about the compatibility of a Calvinist doctrine of divine rule and common moral sentiments, which were often expressed in the Enlightenment language of natural law. Bellamy's promotion of Calvinism therefore led him to contemplate the intersection of religious, natural, and moral law. As he went beyond Edwards in defining this connection and its social implications, he embraced universal standards for economic and political equity. He turned a Calvinist doctrine of human nature into a critique of the rising culture of commerce. He also joined a transatlantic debate about the meaning of social calamity, war, and revolution. His emphasis on this deep-rooted problem in western Christianity—the relationship of divine sovereignty, moral justice, and evil—made God's purposes no aloof, metaphysical speculation. He transformed a Calvinist understanding of providence into a weapon against New England's social and political evils. His theology thus yielded socially potent theories about virtue, law, and government. "The generation who fought through the Revolutionary war," as Stowe put it, perceived Bellamy's thought to be vitally pragmatic.

Bellamy's career illuminates not only developments within Calvinism but also Calvinists' role in Anglo-American political culture. Although scholars have debated at length the relation between religion and American independence, they rarely have examined how individual preachers developed explicitly political messages. The following account shows how a leading New Light became dislodged from the apolitical niches of revivalism. Bellamy came to settle on a discourse of law that, as James Kloppenberg and Martyn Thompson remind us, became the common ground for patriots of different philosophical and religious persuasions.[9] Bellamy's use of that discourse, moreover, contributed particularly to the communal impulses of what often has been called republican ideology. He lodged moral authority not in private conscience but in a divine law and polity that regulated common life. His increasing involvement in public affairs during the 1750s, adoption of republican political ideals during the 1760s, and eventual support of the patriot movement provides a case study of Revolutionary thought as it formed in a New England village.[10]

Yet theological impulses lay beneath his social commentary. Bellamy turned to law as an answer to questions about God's relation to the social order. It is ironic, then, that the means by which he popularized the New Divinity—giving it shape as moral and social utterance—have been criticized as an unwitting betrayal of Calvinism, a loss of vital piety and decline into moralism.[11] Some of these criticisms are telling, but most have misconstrued the New Divinity as a sterile and codified abstraction, remote from the lives of common folk. The New Divinity originally spread because of its sensitivity to the human dilemmas of life in late colonial New England.

Bellamy spoke to and with a wide range of people, not merely to other theologians and certainly not just to Calvinists. He engaged liberal American writers, refashioned consistent Calvinism in dialogue with British and European thinkers, and took much of his agenda from pressing social issues. He followed the rules of and thereby furthered a moral discourse that responded to New England's public crises. More important, his new emphases connected Calvinism to other cultural expressions in mid-eighteenth century New England. By uniting moral and civil law to theological discourse, this underestimated cleric informed the very nature of social and political thought in Revolutionary New England.

Notes

1. The subscription list to *True Religion Delineated* (Boston, 1750) reveals a widespread audience, drawn from the Boston area and western Massachusetts and from all over Connecticut, New York, and Long Island. It named distinguished New Lights such as Jonathan Edwards, controversial separatists such as John Cleaveland, celebrated Old Lights such as Samuel Moody, and rationalists such as Ebenezer Gay.

2. Stowe, *Oldtown Folks* (Boston, 1869), 367–70, 373–76, 378. Stowe's sympathetic portrait is all the more remarkable in that she was drawn to Episcopalianism (her maternal grandmother was in fact a member of the Episcopal Church).

3. For Bellamy's students and his school of the prophets, see Joseph Conforti, *Samuel Hopkins and the New Divinity Movement: Calvinism, the Congregational Ministry, and Reform in New England Between the Great Awakenings* (Grand Rapids, Mich., 1981), 33–36, 227–32; Anderson, 402–47; and William Orpheus Shewmaker, "The Training of the Protestant Ministry in the United States of America, before the Establishment of Theological Seminaries," *Papers of the American Society of Church History*, 2d ser., 6 (1921): 71–202. Bellamy's New York salary is cited in Anderson, 470.

4. Edwards, Jr., to John Erskine, Feb. 8, 1787, quoted in Robert L. Ferm, *Jonathan Edwards the Younger, 1745–1801, A Colonial Pastor* (Grand Rapids, Mich., 1976), 65. Statistics compiled by Allen C. Guelzo, *Edwards on the Will: A Century of American Theological Debate* (Middleton, Conn., 1989), 91–93, and Conforti, *Samuel*

Hopkins, 227–32, have been compared to figures given in Harold Field Worthley, *An Inventory of the Records of the Particular (Congregational) Churches of Massachusetts Gathered 1620–1805* (Cambridge, Mass., 1970), and Joseph S. Clark, *A Historical Sketch of the Congregational Churches in Massachusetts, From 1620 to 1858* (Boston, 1858), 191–216.

5. Holly, *Old Divinity Preferable to Modern Novelty* (New Haven, Conn., 1780), 65; Stiles, *The Literary Diary of Ezra Stiles,* ed. Franklin Bowditch Dexter, 3 vols. (New York, 1901), I:129, II:499, and III:463–64; and Stiles, *Extracts from the Itineraries and other Miscellanies of Ezra Stiles,* ed. Franklin Bowditch Dexter (New Haven, Conn., 1916), 451.

6. Taylor, *Concio ad Clerum* (New Haven, 1828), 8; Harvey, *A Review of a Sermon, Delivered in the Chapel of Yale College* (Hartford, Conn., 1829), 5–10; Beecher, *Dependence and Free Agency* (Boston, 1832), 32–33; also Beecher, *Autobiograhy, Correpondence, Etc., of Lyman Beecher, D.D.,* ed. Charles Beecher, 2 vols. (New York, 1865), II:157. Hartford Seminary quotations, taken from the records of Bennett Tyler and the trustees, are given in Curtis Manning Greer, *The Hartford Theological Seminary* (Hartford, Conn., 1934), 64, 67.

7. See, for example, Nathan O. Hatch, *The Democratization of American Christianity* (New Haven, Conn., 1989).

8. Edmund S. Morgan, "The Puritan Ethic and the American Revolution," *WMQ* 24 (1967): 3–43, quotation from 43.

9. James T. Kloppenberg, "The Virtues of Liberalism: Christianity, Republicanism, and Ethics in Early American Political Discourse," *Journal of American History* 74 (1987): 9–33; Martyn P. Thompson, "The History of Fundamental Law in Political Thought from the French Wars of Religion to the American Revolution," *American Historical Review* 91 (1986): 1103–28.

10. In his important work *From Puritan to Yankee: Character and Social Order in Connecticut, 1690–1765* (Cambridge, Mass., 1967), Richard L. Bushman maintained that New Lights were protoliberals. In *Religion and the American Mind: From the Great Awakening to the Revolution* (Cambridge, Mass., 1966), Alan Heimert demonstrated the communalism of evangelicals such as Bellamy but overemphasized the themes of egalitarianism and nationalism. See also Ruth H. Bloch, "Religion and Ideological Change in the American Revolution," in Mark A. Noll, ed., *Religion and American Politics: From the Colonial Period to the 1980s* (New York, 1990), 44–61. For further historiographical comment, with discussion of republicanism, see Chapter 5.

11. Joseph Haroutunian, *Piety to Moralism: The Passing of the New England Theology* (New York, 1932; rep. 1970). For the historiography of the New Divinity, see the Epilogue.

1

Conversion

The earliest autobiographical event that Joseph Bellamy recorded was his conversion. He recalled it some forty-seven years later, in 1783, while urging his daughter Betsey (b. 1759) to seek hers. "This is my comfort," he wrote, "that God Almighty has been my chief joy from the time I was seventeen years old to this day." He explained to Betsey that conversion was an identifiable and sensible moment of humiliation, confession, and faith. "Feel and confess all your guilt," he counseled; "ask his pardon in the name of Christ, and his grace to form you anew." If his advice reflected his own experience, then Bellamy's conversion came also as a release from "the hustle and bustle of life," the search for status and social position; it yielded a sense of security and confidence. Bellamy may well have recollected that his spiritual transformation occurred when he had gone to Northampton, Massachusetts, to reside and study with Jonathan Edwards. He suggested that his daughter obtain "*Mr. Edwards's History of Redemption*," in which she would find "a map of the road to [the heavenly] world, and a glimpse of its glory."[1]

It is telling that Bellamy's self-observations, of which he made only a few, began with 1736—the year that he experienced regeneration, preached his first sermons, and met Jonathan Edwards. Bellamy came of age in the shadow of Edwards and under the force of the spiritual and social tumult known as the Great Awakening. These events shaped his private and public life for the first decade of his career. To be sure, he eventually differed from Edwards in his approach to the social, philosophical, and ethical problems encountered by evangelicals in the aftermath of the revivals; from the mid-1740s through the early 1780s Bellamy's emphasis on the moral law and social application of a rigid Calvinism formed the core of a New Divinity that diverged from the piety of Edwards. The import of Bellamy's later works cannot be understood, however, without an appreciation for his earlier commitment to the Edwardsean-inspired revivals.[2]

We have scant record of his early life, but we know that Joseph Bellamy grew up without wealth, professional standing, or social prestige. He was born on August 20, 1719, the fifth child and fourth son of Matthew Bellamy, Jr., (1677–1752) and Sarah Wood (d. 1721).[3] Matthew's second wife, Mary Johnson, raised Joseph, his five surviving full siblings, and five half-siblings. Like other New Englanders who became evangelicals, and like most leaders of the future New Divinity school, Joseph came from an economically active and geographically mobile family. His forebears repeatedly abandoned the established centers of New England society and moved toward the frontier. His grandfather, Matthew Bellamy, Sr. (d. 1689?), settled in New Haven in 1639 and taught school there for several years. Although he signed New Haven's plantation covenant, the elder Bellamy did not establish himself in a position of social respectability. After the New Haven court censured him as a "new comer" with an "excitable and litigious spirit," he moved west to Stamford and, later, east to Guilford, Saybrook, and, eventually, the small community of Killingworth (north of Saybrook). In 1677 Matthew Bellamy, Jr., was born in Killingworth. The family, still subsisting on the income from the elder Bellamy's school-teaching, moved west again, eventually settling in Fairfield. Sometime in the late 1680s Matthew, Sr., died, presumed lost at sea. Joseph's father moved to Wallingford in 1696, sold the few bits of land that the family had accumulated in its travels, and became an aggressive and somewhat troublesome entrepreneur. He speculated in various ventures, none of which were markedly successful: land, a weaving business, part of a copper mine, and a tavern that served the miners.[4]

Such activities brought the Bellamys neither social prestige nor harmony with the more settled townspeople living in the center of Wallingford. Matthew led the efforts of several families to establish a new parish, Cheshire, outside the town. Joseph Bellamy was born in the midst of five years of squabbles and political maneuverings that culminated when the Connecticut General Assembly granted the petition of Cheshire settlers in 1723. Matthew promptly balked at the taxes that the new church in Cheshire required, requested permission to remain in the Wallingford congregation, and was refused. Disputes over land claims and unpaid debts frequently put Matthew in court. He had none of the social characteristics of the town leaders: aristocratic family ties, long-term residence, education, or professional status. He never became a magistrate or town committeeman. In both court cases of which we have records of decisions, Bellamy lost.[5]

Joseph inherited, then, a rather sketchy and contentious past, and as an adult he rarely associated with his family. His correspondence and probate records show no evidence that he ever visited, corresponded with, or even mentioned his grandfather, father (who lived until 1752), stepmother, or any of his siblings. As the son matured, he came to reject the mobile and entrepreneurial life of the father; Joseph ministered for fifty years in a stable community and there disparaged the very litigiousness, land speculation, indebtedness, and tavernkeeping that had marked his father's career.[6]

At the age of twelve Bellamy left the quarrelsome community in Cheshire to attend Yale, where he found controversy of a different sort. Three factions clashed at the college. The first, which received the label "Old Light" by the end of the century, represented New England's religious establishment. Forming less a distinct party than a broad consensus among the standing ministry, Old Lights upheld the ordinances of Puritanism in churches supported by the government. They believed that God gave to New England a covenant that promised a stable commonwealth and secure church in return for corporate obedience to the laws of God.

Although established Old Light ministers affirmed the necessity of personal faith, they came to emphasize good standing in the social order as a civic and religious duty. One sign of this emphasis was the gradual emergence of territorial patterns of church membership. In theory, Puritan congregationalism required a testimony of one's full conversion for access to church membership, communion, and baptism of one's children. In the 1670s, however, many churches began to practice the Half-way Covenant, which provided baptism for the grandchildren of regenerate, visible saints. By the second quarter of the eighteenth century, even broader policies of church membership gained acceptance. Churches in Connecticut and Massachusetts adopted the theories of Solomon Stoddard (1643–1729), Samuel Willard (1640–1707), and Boston's Brattle Street Church, which held that assent to the creed, conformity to common moral standards, and participation in the sacraments (together called "owning the covenant") were preparatory means of conversion. This so-called Stoddardean pattern required only upright behavior and orthodox beliefs for communicant privileges; it minimized regeneration as a condition for participation in the church. Religious training, in this context, rarely strayed from catechesis and moral discipline. Much of the standard curriculum at Yale, based on the Westminster Confession and on Puritan divines, was taught so as to reinforce these innovations on the "New England way." Of the Old Lights produced at Yale in Bellamy's years there, four became widely known opponents of the revivals and antagonists of Bellamy. William Hart (1713–1784) and Ebenezer Devotion (1714–1771) each wrote several treatises critical of New Light preaching, and Elisha Webster (1713–1788) and Chester Williams (1718–1753) opposed the ecclesiastical positions of Bellamy and other New Lights.[7]

The second faction at Yale, much more controversial, represented Anglicanism and, in the minds of most Calvinists, its necessary corollary—English theology slanted toward intellectualism, Arminianism, and formalism. Shortly before Bellamy entered Yale, the trustees had called upon Elisha Williams (rector from 1726 to 1739) to buttress Reformed orthodoxy at the college in the wake of Timothy Cutler's and Samuel Johnson's 1722 conversions to the Church of England. Despite Williams's efforts, Anglicanism achieved some following in New Haven by the mid-1730s. Several students joined the English Church, while Johnson and Cutler increased the activity of the Anglican mission to America (the Society for the Propagation of the Gospel) in New Haven. The s.p.g. aimed to win New Englanders back to high liturgy and episcopal polity; Anglicans of decidedly more tolerant bent urged New Englanders also to consider the Enlightenment theology favored especially by the elite of the English Church. In 1732 George Berkeley donated to the college nearly a thousand books, most of which were Anglican and liberal. Yale's library now offered its students not only the Puritan tomes of William Ames and Samuel Willard but also deist tracts by William Wollaston, Thomas Sherlock, and Anthony Collins. The theological curriculum expanded accordingly, from catechetical exercises on the Bible and orthodox divinity to disputation on texts from a variety of historical, philosophical, and ethical positions. The presence of rational theology at Yale was all the more notable for its popularity in Boston, where several prominent pastors became enamored of theological liberalism.[8]

Yale's third faction achieved notoriety as the New Light or evangelical party. News of Jonathan Edwards's 1734–1735 Northampton awakening spread to New Haven when Bellamy was an undergraduate. Several of his classmates joined the revival, including Aaron Burr, Sr. (1716–1757), James Davenport (1716–1757), Benjamin Pomeroy (1704–1784), and Eleazar Wheelock (1711–1779). Inspired by Edwards, these evangelicals insisted that only an immediate experience of grace, called regeneration, qualified one to claim true faith and thus membership in the church. This message seemed initially an answer to Rector Williams's prayers—an antidote to the Anglican and liberal Arminianism offered by Berkeley's books. New Lights attacked Arminianism well enough, but many went further than Williams anticipated. They concluded that the established ministry itself espoused Arminianism by confusing the social terms of the covenant with genuine conversion.[9]

Bellamy also learned at Yale that religious polemics mirrored larger social divisions. His position fit the general pattern described by Harry S. Stout and Joseph Conforti, who show that New Lights and New Divinity ministers typically grew up in settlements on the frontier and in families that were geographically mobile and had few ties to the professions.

Bellamy came from a small town that had little access to networks of trade and communication or to printers, schools, and ecclesiastical or political convocations in Boston, Hartford, New Haven, and New London, whereas his more highly cultured classmates came from coastal towns, the Connecticut Valley, and eastern Connecticut. Yale's class orders at that time heavily depended on social status. Most of those in the top half of Bellamy's class came from the families of pastors or other public figures such as magistrates. Most of those in the bottom half came from the families of artisans, farmers, and merchants. They had relatively few ties to the legal profession, the magistracy, or the clergy. Moreover, if they were outlivers such as Bellamy's father, recently settled on the fringes of an established town, they infrequently held local or provincial political positions and often dissented from town oligarchies—local elites who often claimed social and political prerogatives by virtue of long-term residence in the same town. From Bellamy's arrival in New Haven, the college reminded him of his modest origins. The young man from Cheshire ranked twenty-third out of twenty-four on the matriculation list.[10]

Bellamy gradually found his religious identity among Yale New Lights from similar social backgrounds. Most of his classmates in the bottom half of the college's social order became New Lights, whereas most of those in the top half became Old Lights or Anglicans. Led by Old Lights, Connecticut's colony-wide General Association of pastors recognized this division when it noted in 1741 that proponents of the Awakening did not belong to positions of prestige, power, or authority; they were "chiefly of the lower and younger sort." We know little of Bellamy's spiritual biography from this period, but we might surmise that he and his social peers felt marginalized by an Old Light establishment that rewarded prestige and professional pedigree. As Bellamy's future career demonstrated, the revival movement provided him and his fellow evangelicals with a new sense of religious, social, and cultural identity. They came to see themselves as a band of like-minded reformers, the truly converted within a corrupt standing order.[11]

The operative word here is *within*; unlike some evangelicals, Bellamy never abandoned the religious establishment completely. Radical New Lights, led in Connecticut by James Davenport, increasingly despaired of reform. They often separated themselves from existing churches and paid little heed to traditional Calvinist theology, even less to accepted rules for social behavior. Scorning the Congregational hierarchy, standing churches, the state, and Yale alike, they ordained uneducated preachers, pronounced anathemas on other ministers, and encouraged disorderly conduct. Bellamy came to identify with moderate New Lights, or evangelical Calvinists, who intended to operate according to customary sentiments for social order. Although they condoned some separations during the height of the revival in 1741–1742, moderates more generally came to oppose separatist activities that bespoke rejection of Congregationalism altogether.

As evangelicals, they emphasized conversion by faith in, and a personal encounter with, Christ; as Calvinists, they found their normative theological principles within the doctrines and ecclesiastical practices derived from the Reformed tradition and transmitted to New England through English Puritan writers and continental dogmaticians. They upheld an educated and regulated ministry and eschewed disruptive public behavior. These moderates were Bellamy's most intimate associates: Edwards; David Brainerd (1718–1747), with whom Bellamy took several evangelistic tours through Litchfield County; Samuel Hopkins, who, along with Brainerd, frequently preached in Bethlehem; and Wheelock, a long-time confident of Bellamy's.[12]

Bellamy, despite his alienation from the Old Light socioreligious order, prepared for ordination within the church establishment. Candidates for the ministry in New England normally spent the year following college in practical and theological study with an experienced pastor. After an unhappy period with the conservative Old Light Samuel Hall (1695–1776) in Cheshire, Bellamy went to Northampton in 1736 to reside with the leading spirit of the New Lights, Jonathan Edwards, who had a greater influence on him than any other of his associates. Edwards was the elder adviser and the most distinguished theologian of the evangelicals in New England; Bellamy was his first theological pupil. In the same year that Bellamy underwent conversion and studied with Edwards, Edwards produced the first major exposition of New Light theology, sermons on "Justification by Faith Alone," and began to write a widely read account of the early revivals, *A Faithful Narrative of the Surprising Work of God* (Boston, 1737). Major themes from these works made their way into Bellamy's notebook during the Northampton months, in which he exegeted New Testament passages on faith and grace, provided extended excurses on regeneration and spiritual rebirth, composed meditations on the happiness of heaven and the misery of worldly attachments, excerpted passages from English dissenters on the dangers of episcopacy, and wrote essays about the cross and Christ's role as Mediator.[13]

Bellamy and Edwards remained confidants and friends until Edwards's death in 1758. They visited each other's homes, shared each other's pulpits, and exchanged books. The Northampton pastor frequently acted as mentor to his younger colleague, counseling him on itinerant activities and professional decisions. Edwards recommended Bellamy to John Erskine (1721?–1803), the Scottish publisher of evangelical works, as "one of the most intimate friends I have in the world . . . one of very great experience in religion . . . of very good natural abilities, of closeness of thought, of extraordinary diligence in his studies, and earnest care exactly to know the truth." Such terms suggested the student's fidelity to the teacher's aims. Edwards expressed similar opinions in the preface to Bellamy's first major publication, *True Religion Delineated*. Unlike Hopkins and other leaders of the New Divinity movement, Bellamy shared with

Edwards the successes and optimism of the early revivals, and the ability to preach affecting and popular sermons. Not surprisingly, at virtually every point that Bellamy's early sermons demonstrated notable homiletical methods or theological positions, they corresponded to Edwards's methods and ideas in the same period.[14]

After the New Haven Association of ministers licensed Bellamy to preach in 1737, he gave some sermons in and near Cheshire, then took a temporarily vacant pulpit in Worcester, Massachusetts, from June to October 1738. In November he moved to Litchfield County in order to preach to the newly licensed meeting of the residents of the North Purchase of Woodbury. Settled in 1670, Woodbury had grown, prospered, and by 1730 encompassed most of the farmland around the town center. In the 1730s its younger farmers, as well as settlers from elsewhere, began to establish homes on the town's outlying lands. In 1731 Southbury was established on the southern perimeter of the town. In 1734 settlers moved onto lands to the north of Woodbury, purchased in 1710 from the Pomeraug Indians. Like most frontier communities, this North Purchase benefited from the economic climate of the 1730s. Land values there rose from their initial eighty pounds a share to five hundred pounds a share in 1742. Most of its early inhabitants built homes in the eastern section of the area, some eight miles from Woodbury's center.

In 1738 the Connecticut General Assembly granted North Purchase residents the right to hire their own minister for the winter months, and in November Bellamy came to North Purchase as the "winter preacher." His popularity and his unwillingness to stay there without a permanent call, and a growing desire for independence from Woodbury's taxes, led the settlers in the spring of 1739 to petition the General Assembly for status as a distinct ecclesiastical society, or parish. In the fall of 1739 the petition was granted and the new parish named Bethlehem, or, as it was often spelled in deference to local pronunciation, Bethlem. The following April, John Graham (1694–1774), a New Light pastor in nearby Southbury, preached the ordination sermon at the installation of the new minister. During the same year, Bethlehem became a distinct "society"—a legal category that made it responsible for its own school, church, and public works such as roads and bridges but left it an unincorporated part of Woodbury township for purposes of representation in the General Assembly, some matters of colonial taxation, legal affairs, and military organization.[15]

The establishment of outlying settlements often created tensions with parent towns, and Woodbury's case was no exception. Richard Bushman has analyzed how new patterns of activity in the second quarter of the eighteenth century divided Connecticut into several sets of competing interests: newer settlers and merchants against older inhabitants, debtors against creditors, aspiring farmers against land proprietors, and outlivers against inhabitants of the town center. Many local conflicts concerned taxation and support for public institutions.[16] With the autonomy of Southbury in 1731, Bethlehem in 1740, Judea (in the western half of the North Purchase) in 1741, and Roxbury (in the southeastern part of the North Purchase) in 1743, the town center saw its tax base depleted, its church rivaled, and its oligarchy contested. From 1734 to 1738 residents of Woodbury opposed the initiatives of the North Purchase settlers and successfully resisted Bethlehem's later efforts to incorporate until 1787. Townspeople in Woodbury, many of whom were proprietors of land around Bethlehem, began in 1740 to close down the sale of unsettled areas in order to impede emigration. The value of their property rose, yet they paid no taxes for the support of church, school, or roads in Bethlehem. Partly as a result, the new parish suffered. Although the church grew, it foundered economically in its early years; unable to afford a meetinghouse, the congregation met in a barn until 1744. The General Assembly, noting that the parish was "under a great disadvantage" in supporting its church, raised Bethlehem's tax values in 1741 and authorized a new tax collector in 1743. Throughout the 1740s Woodbury proprietors and Bethlehem settlers went to court in Hartford and New Haven to settle disputes over boundaries, taxes, public works, and other legal matters.[17]

In Bethlehem Bellamy found a people much like himself in social standing and equally receptive to the evangelical message. In the midst of resettlement and contention, outlivers in Bethlehem had little investment in Woodbury's social, political, and religious institutions. Founded on the principles of the Half-way Covenant, the Woodbury parish came to practice Stoddardeanism under the ministry of Solomon Stoddard's son, Anthony Stoddard (1678–1760), who led the church from 1702 to 1760. It accordingly evolved into the kind of territorial church characteristic of Old Light ministry; every resident in Woodbury more than fourteen years of age was a full member. Old Light practices there favored those who had established themselves in the community through long-term residence, family ties, and social position. Bellamy's parishioners, like their minister, had few of the social prerogatives of their Old Light adversaries in Woodbury. Often young and disenfranchised from the churches of their parents, they were attracted to a revival that appeared less circumscribed by the social precedents of family, moral and religious upbringing, age, and standing in the community. New Lights located the most important spiritual experience—and the prerequisite for church membership—in a direct, individual, and immediate encounter with grace. Evangelical conversion, as James Walsh has argued, provided Woodbury's outlivers with an accessible religious authority and social identity.[18]

In the winter of 1738–1739 Bellamy led the new congregation into the kind of awakening that had overtaken Northampton four years earlier. According to the pastor's account, "the first fruits of the gospel very soon appeared" after "the publick Worship of God was set up." Bellamy described his ministry in typical revivalistic terms. His "first sermons" in Bethlehem produced an immediate change of conviction and behavior, "a visible effect upon many of the people." Appealing "especially [to] the youth," his message provoked a renunciation of worldly preoccupations; "they soon became serious" about spiritual pursuits and "left off spending their leisure hours in vanity." He stressed an interior and emotional experience of evangelical humiliation and faith, and the new converts "gave themselves to reading, meditation and secret prayer—and not long after, some appeared to be under deep and thorough conviction of sin." Bellamy's people found purpose, security, and authority in his gospel: "altho' the people were so few, the place so small, yet almost every day, there were some going to their spiritual guide for direction and some time after were enlightened and comforted."[19]

Twenty months after this inaugural awakening, Bellamy gathered another spiritual harvest. He had written of the 1738 revival in a relatively modest way, mentioning the smallness of the place, the small number of people involved, and their dependence on a solitary "spiritual guide." During "some weeks" his sermons affected "some" people who came to Bellamy for advice. He described his congregation's second awakening in less qualified terms. He did not mention himself; Bethlehem seemed caught up in a religious current more powerful than his own efforts, one that affected almost everyone and involved every social class. Bellamy was now so bold as to write not merely of convictions but of conversions. His attitude paralleled that of Jonathan Edwards, who argued in *A Faithful Narrative* that the Northampton revival was part of a larger movement throughout New England. Many New Lights, influenced by Edwards and by the astonishing success of George Whitefield's first tour, adopted this perception of local revivals. Bellamy conceived of events in Bethlehem not as an isolated, provincial episode but as part of an intercolonial movement, symbolized by Whitefield's catalytic activity and later known as the Great Awakening:

> In the fall of 1740, a little after Mr Whitfield preacht through the country . . . religion was again greatly revived and flourisht wonderfully. Every man, woman, and child, about 5 or 6 years old and upwards were under religious concern. . . . Quarrels were ended, and frolicks flung up. Prayer meetings began and matters of religion were all the talk. The universal concern about religion in its height, many were seemingly converted.[20]

Bethlehem's settlers embraced Bellamy's preaching, became awakened, rejected Stoddardeanism, denied the Half-way Covenant, and undoubtedly approved of their pastor's lifelong protest against Old Light notions of covenant and ecclesiastical practice. Church membership in Bethlehem swelled, according to New Light ideals, with conversions; it did not follow merely from population increase. From 1739 to 1744 the number of household heads in the village rose from twenty-two to fifty, an increase of 127 percent; the number of adult church members rose from nineteen to seventy-three, an increase of 284 percent. At the height of revival, from 1741 to 1744, thirty-three adults were admitted to the church, far more than in any other four-year period.[21]

Bellamy's success in his own parish spread his name among other New Lights. John Graham, while lamenting his own revivalistic unproductivity, envied Bethlehem's pastor. "You," he wrote to Bellamy, "have so much of the presence of God with you in your work and are reaping such a harvest . . . Mr. Burr of Newark has heard of it." Samuel Finley (1715–1766) of New Jersey, Simon Backus (1701–1746) of Newington, Connecticut, Thomas Seymour (1705–1767) of Hartford, and Eleazar Wheelock of Lebanon, Connecticut, also noted Bellamy's popularity. Bellamy's later biographers gave some clues to his success; he had oratorical skills and a personal presence that outshone even those of Edwards and matched those of the great Whitefield. Bellamy was a large man, whose pulpit (still used in the Bethlehem church) befit someone more than six feet tall. "A Boanerges," according to one of his hearers, he had a booming voice. Emotionally intense in the pulpit, he combined colorful language with repetition and passionate oratory. His sermons display homespun eloquence and facility with common language. He also was noted for his acerbic wit and for his willingness to bring banter and anecdote into his preaching.[22]

Along with his talents, Bellamy began to exhibit what many of his colleagues deemed a lifelong combativeness and censoriousness. He was pugnacious, to be sure. He was also volatile. Throughout his career, he defiantly tended to extremes, however orthodox. In the early 1740s he pushed the evangelical cause with far less caution than did Edwards. Whereas Edwards repeatedly warned against New Light excesses and held onto much of the covenantal tradition, Bellamy at one time had preached with Davenport (later infamous for such revivalistic fanaticism that he was judged legally insane), supported some unapproved separatist meetings, and criticized covenant moralism with such insistence that he slighted the social application of doctrine. In the late 1740s and 1750s Bellamy defended Calvinism with far less nuance than did Edwards. While Edwards tempered Calvinist dogmatism with aesthetic and affective sensibilities, Bellamy forged a rigid and sometimes legalistic hyper-Calvinism. Bellamy, in fact, gained a measure of independence from his more sophisticated and patient mentor; where Edwards employed persuasion and logic, Bellamy relied on brute rhetorical force. As Ezra Stiles characterized him, Bellamy "was boisterous & vociferous in Preaching, of a dogmatical & overbearing Disposition, severe, rigid & uncharitable." A sometime target of Bellamy's, Stiles may have exaggerated. But he also may have been right when he observed that Bellamy never escaped the contentiousness of his background or the urge to assert his hard-won social and cultural prerogatives. It "was natural" for Bellamy to be "litigious & impatient in religious Matters," Stiles explained, since "his father was litigious in Law matters."[23]

Despite Bellamy's belligerence, his reputation recommended him to other evangelicals as an itinerant. In 1741 he accepted numerous invitations from Connecticut New Lights, preaching in such places as Kensington, North Preston, Branford, and Hartford and to a Baptist meeting in Wallingford. He traveled most of the year from the spring of 1742 to the spring of 1743, through western Connecticut to Boston, New Jersey, and Long Island. He received requests to preach from even further afield, from Pennsylvania and Virginia, although it appears unlikely that he took any revivalistic tours of great extent after his 1742–1743 journey. In the two most active years of his travels, Bellamy preached an astonishing amount: 458 times in 213 places in addition to Bethlehem and as frequently as on twenty-four consecutive days.[24]

Old Lights such as Stiles judged Bethlehem's pastor with a mixture of fear and distaste; revivalists admired him as a leader in their vast network. They knew of him through letters and publications such as Thomas Prince's (1687–1758) *Christian History*, a periodic account of awakenings to which Bellamy contributed. Bellamy frequently corresponded with Burr, Pomeroy, James Lockwood (1714–1772), Samuel Finley, William Tennent (1705–1777), and Samuel Davies (1723–1761).

As New Lights closed ranks over and against the established churches, they often stirred controversy. For instance, they positioned themselves against the college authorities in New Haven when the Awakening reached its height there. Incited by Tennent and Whitefield, New Light students in 1741 conducted unapproved meetings at which they vilified the standing order for its lifeless formalism and Arminianism. During commencement activities that September, Edwards delivered his important "Distinguishing Marks" sermon, a studied recommendation for the revival. At the same time, Bellamy, Jedidiah Mills (1697–1776), and Davenport spoke at informal evangelical gatherings that included day-long rounds of singing, praying, and extemporaneous preaching. The following year, a New Light faction, prompted especially by Davenport, separated from the First Church in New Haven. Thomas Clap, rector and president of the college from 1740 to 1766, forbade students to join the separates and subsequently expelled John Cleaveland (1722–1799) and Brainerd for doing so. On February 28, 1742, Bellamy, Graham, and Wheelock supported their brethren by preaching to the separates—an action for which they nearly were censured and fined. The next day Bellamy met with Cleaveland, Brainerd, and other evangelicals, advising them on how best to continue the New Haven revival. At the end of March, Clap and the pastor of the First Church, Joseph Noyes (1688–1761), asked Bellamy, Burr, and Jonathan Parsons (1705–1776) to preach at commencement. The Yale authorities hoped that these preachers would moderate their message, appeal to both evangelicals and conservatives, and thereby dispel separatist impulses among the students.[25]

No record of Bellamy's Yale performance survives, but he was prone to neither the reasonableness nor dispassion required for rapprochement between New Lights and the likes of Clap and Noyes. His itinerations implied that the established churches were complacent, did not produce true conversion, and hence required the ministrations of visiting preachers. As much as he remained faithful to orthodox Calvinist theology and rejected the full-blown separatism of radicals, he still demanded reform.

Bellamy and other evangelical Calvinists formed a loyal opposition to the standing order. They saw themselves as distinct not only from radical separatists but also from fellow congregationalists who spurned the Awakening and impugned its advocates as socially inferior. This self-understanding fostered an evangelical party spirit, evidenced in Bellamy's letters from the period. First, he encouraged a kind of spiritual fraternalism among New Lights. After Brainerd left Yale and began a troubled period of searching for a ministerial post, for instance, Bellamy assured the young man of his affections. "Dearest Brother," he wrote in March 1743, "I read yours of February" and "loved you. . . . It was not for want of love I did not come to see you [in Saybrook]; nor is it from want of love I do not now set for New York to meet you there." Although settled and secure in Bethlehem, Bellamy empathized with the wandering Brainerd and encouraged his itinerations. "We must travel," Bellamy told him, "through much the same wilderness. . . . All your sore conflicts do and will work for your good." Second, Bellamy urged other New Lights to publicize and defend the Awakening. He asked Wheelock to engage in such polemics, to "write and print on experimental" religion, "comfort the people of God," and "stop the mouths of the enemy." Third, Bellamy joined other New Lights who met together to develop a set of common goals and conventions for proper evangelistic activity. In December 1741 Wheelock suggested that Bellamy organize a meeting of evangelicals in the midst of an upcoming ministerial conference in Guilford (the annual meeting of the New Haven Association) in order to identify candidates for the Connecticut magistracy who sympathized with the revivals, since "the brethren, whom the world calls New Lights" ought to "be agreed among ourselves." In rhetoric that similarly stressed distinctions between evangelicals and outsiders, Bellamy informed Wheelock that he had indeed arranged this "meeting of our brethren, the favourers of itinerant preaching," to take place in February.[26]

From the evangelical perspective, those who impugned the Awakening as a threat to godliness and order were hypocrites twice over. They denied a work of the Spirit and were party to a socioreligious establishment that presided over an increasingly contentious and profligate commonwealth. For much of New England's early history, its leaders had envisioned a cohesive and godly society—what Kenneth Lockridge has labeled a "Christian, Utopian, Closed, Corporate Community." By the 1740s new settlements, a rise in population, and material prosperity nonetheless had created the conditions for factionalism, sectionalism, and secularism. The government, in fact, rarely succeeded in upholding the covenantal ideals so espoused by Old Lights. Many New Lights concluded that communal life no longer embodied godliness; the established order could not, therefore, claim to be a covenanted society. Bellamy witnessed Edwards's 1736 warning that "religion and contention do not consist together" go unheeded by authorities in Connecticut. As Bellamy complained, disputes over land, litigation, contests between Woodbury proprietors and Bethlehem farmers, and other worldly diversions of a growing settlement obviated the first successes of revival in his parish. "Some" of his people, he lamented, "fell away . . . by a Contention" and became so preoccupied with "society affairs" that "serious godliness was almost banished and hid in obscurity."[27]

Nowhere, however, was the failure of New England's public institutions more apparent to New Lights than in ecclesiastical affairs immediately before and during the Awakening. Evangelicals believed that town covenants and the colonial charters of Connecticut and Massachusetts obligated magistrates and pastors to support biblical polity in the churches and suppress practices inimical to religion. Clerical associations and colonial legislators perversely pursued the opposite course. Old Lights appealed to the constitution of Connecticut's churches—the 1708 Saybrook Platform—to reinforce the Half-way Covenant and impede revivalism. In the same year that the Platform was adopted, the Connecticut General Assembly succumbed to royal pressure and enacted the 1690 English Act of Toleration. The Assembly hardly could be blamed for compliance with a law that allowed Anglican and Quaker worship, but the growth of Anglicanism, which by 1742 included seven priests, thirteen congregations, and more than two thousand members, still chafed evangelicals, and the popularity of Quakerism, Rogerinism, and other heresies in New Milford (near Bethlehem) outraged Bellamy and Graham. While clerical authorities and magistrates in Connecticut resisted true revival, they were either unable or unwilling to stop priestcraft, Arminianism, and outright heresy.[28]

Adding insult to injury, antirevivalists dominated the General Assembly and the most powerful clerical associations in Connecticut during the early 1740s. For purposes of ordination, discipline, and ecclesiastical polity, the colony's clergy were organized into ministerial associations, sometimes called consociations if their boundaries were coterminous with counties. Disputes between pastor and parishioners, charges of heterodoxy or scandalous behavior within the ministry, and church separations came before associational or consociational courts, which often appealed to the Saybrook Platform as interpreted by the General Association of the colony's standing ministry.[29] Old Lights did not control every association, but they controlled most of them and wielded a colony-wide majority.

In Connecticut, Old Lights were ecclesiastical conservatives. Less inclined than their more liberal Massachusetts counterparts to reject evangelical theology wholesale, they nonetheless used institutional force against the Awakening. Opponents of the revivals successfully lobbied for the May 1742 "Act for Regulating Abuses and Correcting Disorders in Ecclesiastical Affairs," which prohibited itinerants from preaching in a parish without the permission of both the local Congregational minister and a majority of the local church members. The law also forbade any ministerial association from licensing ministers who were under the jurisdiction of another association. Local justices in Connecticut who refused to prosecute New Lights were removed from office, and many of Bellamy's itinerating friends subsequently suffered under the law; Pomeroy and Wheelock lost their ministerial salaries for several years, and Finley was forcibly ejected from the colony. The predominantly Old Light New Haven Association suspended Timothy Allen (1715–1806), Daniel Humphreys (1706–1787), and Mark Leavenworth (1712–1797), each of whom Bellamy knew from Yale. Philemon Robbins (1709–1781) was censured in 1742 for preaching at the Wallingford Baptist church, to which Bellamy had preached the previous year. Many Connecticut conservatives applauded New England's most emphatic condemnation of itineracy, *The Testimony of the Pastors of the Churches in the Province of Massachusetts-Bay, at their Annual Convention in Boston* (Boston, 1743).[30]

Bellamy used his position as leader of the New Light majority in the Fairfield Eastern District Association to promote evangelical resistance to official policy. The Bethlehem church, encouraged "by the pastor," promptly contradicted the intent of Connecticut's 1742 anti-itineracy act. In June 1742 it "unanimously voted" to issue a standing "general and universal invitation to all approved, orthodox preachers" who were "friends to the present religious concern in the land." Censured by ecclesiastical authorities, itinerant evangelicals were welcomed to Bethlehem "as they have opportunity," since they came "in to the help of the Lord among us." In July Bellamy illegally prepared Brainerd for ordination. When the Fairfield Eastern District Association licensed Brainerd to preach, it defied the judgment of the New Haven Association (which had expelled him) and exasperated Old Lights. Bellamy also helped organize his association's October 1742 petition, signed by twenty-three members, that protested the anti-itineracy act and requested its repeal. "It looks to us inconsistent with the Rules of common Equity," the petition read, since the law's prohibitions violated the "Natural and Lawfull Right" of individual pastors and their associations to chose whom they willed for the "Exercise of ministerial Communion." As in many other instances, the General Assembly denied the evangelicals' request. Bellamy also signed the Fairfield Eastern District's attestation to the pro-itinerant *Testimony and Advice of an Assembly of Pastors of Churches in New-England, At a Meeting in Boston July 7, 1743* (Boston, 1743), which was a rebuttal of the earlier *Testimony of Pastors.*[31]

As these protests fell on deaf ears, Bellamy became increasingly frustrated with the socioreligious establishment. In his revivalistic sermons, he repeatedly drew upon two images for his conception of the ministry: John the Baptist suffering persecution for his service to Christ and Jesus bringing the gospel into the midst of a hostile and unbelieving Israel. The Apostles also, he explained in a 1737 sermon, incurred official opposition, despite the popularity of their message:

> And multitudes were convinced and converted. But as to the body of the nation, and the leading men of it, it was sealed up under unbelief. . . . They were so prejudicial and enraged against the gospel and their seed that did embrace it that nothing less than a miracle of Divine glory like that which converted Paul would work upon them. And it could not be expected that such a miracle should be right, and so they were justly given up to judicial blindness and hardness.[32]

The parallels to events in New England were obvious. Massachusetts and Connecticut resembled the old Israel of Pharisaic hard-heartedness more than the New Israel of Christ's kingdom. The "body of the nation" had produced morally disastrous and religiously ruinous social policies. Congregationalism's vulnerability to apathy and apostasy derived as much from "the leading men" at Harvard, Yale, and the clerical associations as from outside influences. In their unbelief, they censured the revivalists, repudiated the Awakening, and rebuked their children for accepting it.

It was no wonder that Bellamy voiced such opposition to New England's social and religious hierarchy. He spoke on behalf of other New Lights who had little vested interest and less confidence in the standing order. He rejected New England's traditional blend of personal piety and public morality, fidelity to the church and loyalty to public institutions. Disillusioned with the customary formulations of federal theology—the covenantal system espoused by Old Lights—he emphasized an individual and inner spiritual experience that transcended worldly institutions. His early preaching deemphasized the corporate fortunes of New England and instead stressed salvation in the inner and private world of evangelical piety.

These concerns shaped the very structure and method of Bellamy's early theology. Controversy over revival led him (as had his Yale education) to occasional, polemical, and disputational writing, focused on selected evangelical themes. More concerned with denouncing social and religious abuses than with constructing a complete system of Calvinist teaching, he was not inclined to theology on the model of Samuel Willard's *A Compleat Body of Divinity* (Boston, 1726). Willard methodically treated the full scope of Reformed doctrine, included extensive discussions of the Old Testament covenant, and delineated the parameters of the social order by applying the covenant to civil law and to religious, economic, and political practices. Bellamy certainly relied on the dogmas of election, predestination, and original sin in his preaching. He did not ground them, however, on philosophical argument or construct from them a theologically coherent dogmatics. He and other evangelicals produced defenses of the

Awakening, critiques of established practice, sermons, short tracts, and narratives of revivals. Even Edwards's *Treatise on Religious Affections* (Boston, 1748), the longest work by the most thorough mind of the Awakening, dealt chiefly with psychological states, inner moral dispositions, conversion, and other revival issues. Only later in his career would Bellamy systematize and extend Calvinism along legalistic lines that linked doctrine to economic and political issues. In the 1730s and 1740s he associated legalism with Arminianism, systematic reflection with lifeless rationalism, and politics with rapacity.[33]

Of the established practices that Bellamy denounced, the most contested were Old Light models of church membership. His and Edwards's rejection of the Half-way Covenant in 1750 culminated a long-standing argument with New England's pattern of church membership. Bellamy was indignant at the Old Light proclivity toward identifying the responsibilities of the church with loyalty to corporate institutions. Civil and ecclesiastical organizations, from his vantage, could command conformity only to public, visible standards of behavior, that is, to ceremony and to law. In many sermons from the 1730s and early 1740s he charged that the resulting confusion of conversion (the true ends) with exterior religiosity (the presumed means) perverted religion into an illusory self-satisfaction. The prevalence of spiritual apathy, resistance to the revivals, contention, and greed made it apparent that covenant legalism was incapable of effecting either conversion or regenerate behavior. In a 1739 fast-day sermon, Bellamy accordingly omitted the usual demands for corporate acts of repentance and all but dismissed public observance of the fast by asserting that it was merely "the language of our action [instead of] the language of our hearts" and therefore tended to "prodigious hypocrisy." More properly, the event was a means for individuals to examine in private their sinfulness and need of Christ. In a Thanksgiving sermon from the same year, Bethlehem's minister made no mention of the political and ecclesiastical institutions that gave Old Light preachers cause for gratitude. He directed his congregation to perceive God's activity instead in tokens of grace to individuals—food, health, and family relations. Edwards drew similar distinctions between public religion and genuine piety. In *Some Thoughts Concerning the Present Revival* (Boston, 1742), he, like Bellamy, questioned "meeting in religious assemblies, attending sacraments and other outward institutions" as vain forms of speech, "of little use but as signs of something else," since they were "only a shewing [of] our religion by words, or an outward profession."[34]

Bellamy, then, aimed nearly all his revival sermons at the combination of formalism, legalism, and Arminianism that he thought had corrupted religious institutions in New England. According to him, customary exhortations to civic morality smacked of Arminian claims about the importance of human cooperation in the process of salvation, the wrongheaded "public spiritedness" of the rich young ruler who came to Jesus with claims of "moral fullness" and "law work" but who "would not yield" to the personal call of Christ. Whether or not many New Englanders self-consciously adopted Arminianism, Bellamy viewed it as a real threat, a "strange and dark" power seducing people away from Christ and the doctrines of irresistible grace. In his *Religious Affections*, Edwards likewise asserted that the "outward morality and external religion" of New England's churches had deceived people into professing Arminian doctrines.[35]

The doctrine of justification by faith alone became Bellamy's favorite weapon against religious externalism; he fastened on it to the exclusion of other motifs, especially those that legitimated social and public performance of moral duties. His sermons conspicuously lacked Old Testament covenantal ideas and spurned appeals for preparatory activity and public assent to Christianity. Focused on the conversion experience, they rarely addressed the social function of biblical commands. He argued in one sermon, for instance, that religious training, baptism, church membership, and standing in the community were vain pretenses, "self justifying" attempts to fulfill a legal covenant that had little to do with genuine faith. The whole Stoddardean system, he maintained, mirrored the religion of the Pharisees, who thought themselves righteous merely because they were born in Israel, had godly ancestors, and claimed to obey the law: "You who have enjoyed a happy education, and had pious parents to boast of, as the Jews boasted of Abraham; you who have many shining works of sobriety and righteousness . . . you must renounce all your pretended merit and accept of pardoning grace or you will never be saved."[36]

Moreover, Bellamy tended to dichotomize law and faith, moral obligation and regeneration. Prior to the exact moment of divinely initiated conversion, he maintained in a 1741 sermon, efforts to follow God's law only enhanced self-determined means and selfish ends. By legal obedience, the unregenerate avoided submission to Christ: with "his own endeavours and strivings he strives against [yielding himself up to God] and struggles to find relief some other way. The sinner is loath to yield." Such analyses paralleled Edwards's "Justification by Faith," which explained that "those that oppose the Solifidians," that is, Arminians and Old Lights, were wrong in thinking that "the meaning of [faith] is performing a course of obedience to his law. Believing on God as a justifier certainly is a different thing from submitting to God as a lawgiver." There were only two proper uses of law in evangelical preaching, according to Bellamy, and neither referred to the subjective experience of conversion. The first was to describe how Christ had procured salvation by fulfilling the law's demand for atonement for sin, and the second was to invoke the law as a means for self-examination, the prod to humiliation that led one away from law, to confession of sin and faith. Even this second use of the law, however, was subordinate to evangelical themes. As Edwards sarcastically put it in his

Yale commencement address, "the law is to be preached only to make way for the Gospel . . . for the main work of ministers of the Gospel is to preach the Gospel."[37]

Bellamy further attempted to undercut any use of covenant theology that would reintroduce legalism under a different name. English Calvinists had traditionally recognized three major covenantal modes of divine-human interaction. The covenant of works, made with Adam, required human obedience to the law in return for salvation. The covenant of grace, instituted with Abraham, promised redemption from the penalty for breaking the covenant of works, upon the volitional performance of faith. In the covenant of redemption, God gave faith to the elect as an instrument to be used for the reception of grace. Covenant theology represented the Puritan attempt to reconcile God's prerogatives and Christ's mediatorial work with norms of justice that required some sort of legal accountability. In general, each of the three covenants had a prominent place in New England's religious thought: the covenant of works framed the proper social and political order, the covenant of grace regulated ecclesiastical practice, and the covenant of redemption described the individual's relation to God.[38]

New Lights were persuaded that an overemphasis on the first covenant and a use of the second to mandate the implicit moralism of current religious practice eclipsed the gospel. Under Edwards's tutelage, Bellamy had observed that "obedience to the law which the covenant of works required" was "not consistent with the new Covenant, the Covenant of grace." By 1742 Bellamy replaced the traditional scheme with a simple division of the covenants into two opposing forms: Old Testament works and New Testament grace. The former was a terrifying dispensation of legal requirements and divine threats. The latter was pure mercy. "Out of Christ, God is a consuming fire," he wrote, since before regeneration

> we are under the first covenant, which requires perfect obedience and has made these [biblical laws] the conditions of our acceptance, which if we do not perform we have the curse pronounced against us. . . . Having lost our power and ability to keep God's laws, [we] must necessarily be miserable, and that forever, being exposed to the curse of the law and being liable to have all the threatenings thereof executed against us.

In contrast, if "we comply with the terms of the second covenant" and "have accepted of him for our Saviour and put our trust in him," then "there is mercy offered, and provision made for our restauration." Only by renouncing any claim to moral rights and trusting in Christ's redemptive activity could one experience the relief of justification and forgiveness.[39]

By using the phrase "unless we comply with the terms of the second covenant," Bellamy did not intend to affirm the covenantal principle that faith was a legal condition the performance of which obliged God to grant salvation. He asserted that "God is under no obligation," by legal or cov-

enantal standards, to save anyone. "Faith" described only a position vis-
à-vis Christ, effected by God's agency and not by human volition: "'tis to
believers that the Spirit of God is appointed to work that repentance and
faith." Bellamy argued at length that faith was the appropriate means of
justification (and therefore a "condition") not because of any moral or legal
merit in it but because God had so made the world that faith was simply a
"meet or fit" means of union with Christ. This union itself bestowed forgiveness; it was not an act of obedience done in order to receive forgiveness.[40]

Since faith was the existential posture of the self toward Christ, according to Bellamy, it was quite different from a notional understanding
of doctrine. As he saw them, New England's covenantal standards encouraged merely public assent to the creeds, intellectual belief often divorced
from the inner sensation or heartfelt conviction of a converting knowledge of grace. In a 1739 sermon, he emphasized this contrast. "By a firm
belief" he meant not "a weak and careless assent as makes no impression
on the mind and consequently has no influence on the life" but rather
"such a full persuasion of the mind of the truth of [the Gospel] as to fill
the soul with a lively sense thereof." This affective, sensible understanding of the gospel derived "from a sense of . . . the overflowing of divine
grace in the workings of redemption by the dearest blood of [God's] own
son." Notional knowledge, the intellect's assent to information, could effect
no true change of heart, while "such a sense" of Christ's work could "draw
his heart to believe and trust." As the convicted "thinks . . . that all his sins
have been counted against the lowly Jesus he now trusts in for salvation,
it breaks his heart and melts it down."[41]

Bellamy urged people, then, to "experience" the kinds of "lively im-
pressions" that "made [them] sensible" of their destitution and Christ's
ability to save them. Edwards's aesthetic and sensationalist formulation
of the principle of conversion, centered on the idea of religious affections,
combined a similar argument with the Calvinist doctrine of election. For
Edwards, faith in Christ and love to God signaled the heart's (or soul's)
inclination toward, and approbation of, God himself. This approbation
required an immediate experience of God in such a way that his excellencies, most clearly evident in Christ, were made sensible. Knowledge mediated by nature, law, or tradition could not elicit this sensation, nor could
human action. The Holy Spirit must, on God's initiative, enter the human
heart and stimulate gracious affections. The human passively depended
on God's self-presentation to the soul. This predestinarian rejection of
human cooperation informed Bellamy's explanation of conversion as a
sensation by which believers were "effectually called" and "made partak-
ers of that distinguishing grace." From the first "sense of sin and Danger
of it" to evangelical assurance, Bellamy wrote, the "grace of God" given as
"a divine decree" effected regeneration through the "introduction" of "new
operations or tendencies into the soul of man, new thoughts and appre-

hensions, new desires and inclinations, new appetites and dispositions, new passions and affections."[42]

Bethlehem's "Boanerges" defended revival oratory—weeping, imprecations, and blessings included—on the grounds that people needed emotional animation. He was, indeed, famous for such methods. Sermons alone could not stimulate gracious affections, but they could provoke a deeper apprehension of self and of the means by which God worked salvation. Doctrine most effectively illumined the understanding when expressed in vivid images and concrete illustrations. Bellamy hoped to elicit "fear" with warnings of "calamity" and "approaching fire" and to stimulate a desire for conversion by haranguing worldly New Englanders in terms such as "stupid and sottish"; most of his revival sermons paralleled, in form and content, Edwards's *Sinners in the Hands of an Angry God* (Boston, 1741).[43]

As early as 1737 Bellamy laid out a homiletical strategy that depended on vivid metaphors and common images for divine threats and promises. The Bible itself, he explained in one sermon, employed sensational and emotionally charged rhetoric to rouse the unregenerate from their apathy. He demonstrated the approach of the Scriptures; in them God "portends wilting flames without the least pity," while God also "speaks in the most winning manner and uses the most endearing expressions," setting "before them the glories of the heavenly world in darling brightness" with common images of riches and pleasure. In order to provoke feelings of spiritual destitution and desire, Bellamy then offered "some promises and motives to stir you up. . . . In what language shall I speak that may be effectual to quicken thoughtless and unconcerned sinners?" He took his cue from the Scriptures and contrasted the inner psychological state of the unconverted, who envisioned hell's torments, with that of believers, who confided in eschatological bliss:

> I say let [the unregenerate] speak out the secrets of his soul and he will tell you what cutting reflections pierce his heart . . . what sad and gloomy thoughts . . . sink down into his soul and fills him with horror and trembling. . . . Is there any such hell-hardened heart [that will not grasp] what terrors fright his soul? All he felt in the body [i.e., while living] was but . . . a foretaste of . . . a million of ages in the most extreme pain: weeping, wailing, sighing, groaning under the extremity of infernal plagues. [In contrast,] if we had a window through which we might look into that breast that fears and loves and trusts in the Lord . . . we should see such serenity and calmness, such peace and quietness, such contentment . . . [that] we should be filled with longing desires to taste of those sweet pleasures which are sweeter than honeycomb.[44]

Bellamy intended such preaching to cut through the superficial contentment and moralism of Old Light models of the covenant. The very notion of a federal covenant, with its implied obligations to a territorial church in league with the government, appeared to him as an impediment to salvation. The theological implications of his position were clear; Bellamy severed salvation history from the established ecclesiastical and social order. Traditional Puritan conceptions of the covenant presupposed that earthly collectivities, that is, nations and their churches, had a sacred mission and were therefore primary subjects of God's purposes in history. Many preachers legitimated this claim with reference to God's dealings with ancient Israel, which putatively revealed in types God's appointment of New England's public institutions. Cotton Mather's *Magnalia Christi Americana* (London, 1702), which identified America as the subject of biblical prophecy, most forcefully articulated this conviction. His *Malachi . . . and the Maxims of Piety* (Boston, 1717) was an extended exhortation for New Englanders to hasten the coming of the Millennium through corporate moral reformation. For Bellamy and other proponents of the Awakening, Mather's ideas represented a false legitimization of New England's institutional hypocrisy and legalism.[45]

Rather than maintain a theology of providential action through earthly institutions and national election, New Lights such as Bellamy adopted what Sacvan Bercovitch has described as an Augustinian perspective: pessimism about "providential history" and concentration on "redemptive history." Biblical history and prophecy, from this perspective, referred to a spiritual work of redemption, the significance of which lay outside earthly institutions. The Old Testament typified not New England's corporate destiny but Christ's incarnation; apocalyptic images signified the consummation of his activity at the end of history. Israel's religion (its covenants, ceremonies, and incorporation of the idea of a national "church") was but a temporary institution, nullified by the Mediator's appearance. Bellamy sustained such Christocentric exegeses in his evangelistic appeals. Jesus gave parables such as the wedding feast (Matthew 22:1–14), he argued, in order to impress individuals with the need for grace, not to predict the future of nations. Bellamy took passages that could have been turned to millennialist speculations and drew individual and spiritual applications instead. Jesus' words of caution, "ye know neither the day nor the hour in which the Son of man cometh" (Matthew 25:13), Bellamy emphasized, taught believers to avoid chiliastic predictions and to prepare for the judgment of God only in the afterlife.[46]

More important, Bellamy did not expand his interpretation of texts into a discussion of current collectivities. In a sermon on Luke 19, he interpreted "a time of visitation" only as an inner experience, "when the Spirit strives with us, and our consciences are startled and awakened." God's activity was concealed in the individual's spiritual transformation. As a result, he continued in this exposition, mundane affairs held no deep attraction for the believer. Bellamy counseled disengagement from temporal history and escape through the private experience of gracious affections into the transcendent realm of divine solace:

> Let us follow [the believer] through that vale of tears and troubles and
> sorrows and see him refreshing himself with the sense of God's favour,
> while he is alone, retired from the world. . . . See him humble at the feet
> of free grace in prayer. Oh, the unspeakable sense he tastes! Follow him
> into his field and see what serenity and calmness he carries along with
> him. And whilst he is about his worldly affairs how often does his soul
> look towards his heavenly home, hoping that after a few days he shall
> take his flight. . . . Nothing but God's favour and love can make us happy,
> and he that has this will be so—let Earth and Hell do their worst!

Riveted on the spiritual states of his individual listeners, Bellamy rarely
mentioned corporate destinies; when he did so, he did not use rhetorical
strategies that Mason Lowance refers to as the "language of Canaan."[47]

In contrast to Puritan proponents of millennialism, Bellamy held during the 1730s and early 1740s that temporal and institutional history, the
affairs of state, society, and ecclesiastical order, revealed little of God's
ultimate rule. There was no clear pattern of justice in worldly affairs, no
"law" of corporate rewards and punishments. As the law could not effect
conversion, so it could not determine earthly events. Antichrist would
prosper and the righteous suffer on this earth. As Bellamy put it, "the affairs of the world," with its "frequent disorders," its "hatred, anger, malice, envy," hid the ultimate purposes and triumph of providence; to "our
eyes" the victory of godlessness and the impotence of virtue often appeared
in mundane events. After all, Bellamy thought, there could be no justice
in a temporal judgment on corporate bodies, the individual members of
which stood in various moral and spiritual states. Misfortunes were not
the predictable outcomes of moral or religious misdeeds but often acci-
dental or natural events. "Think of the shortness and uncertainty of your
residence here," Bellamy averred, "what a troop of diseases infest mankind and help to thrust us out of the world. Innumerable casualties may
surprise us. Your breath may be stopped in a moment by any of them. Or
suppose you escape these and no strange and unexpected accidents be-
reave you," yet "your bodies are of that make that they will fall of themselves." He surmised that genuine Christians "enjoy much inward delight
. . . preferable to all outward things," since they trusted that in all conditions, prosperous or calamitous, God worked for their salvation.[48]

From Bellamy's perspective, then, temporal affairs of culture and politics demonstrated no clear improvement, while the inward and spiritual
life of believers assuredly advanced towards salvation. "A serious reflec-
tions on [God's] ways," he contended, would lead people to recognize that
"the most excellent and amiable of all beings, a God glorious and ador-
able," was "worthy of the highest love and esteem" because God was "before time creator" and at the end of history the "redeemer Christ"—the
judge who would rectify wrongs after "time flies away" and "all that is
good and valuable in this life" as well as "all that tends to the misery of

God's children" is gone. Edwards concurred. In *The History of Redemption* he attempted to render mundane events intelligible only by reference to the personal, however cosmic, battle between Christ and Satan—an evangelical theodicy that pointed beyond law and history to the eschatological judgment of individuals according to their relationship to Christ. To Edwards, the only obvious pattern in history was a cycle of spiritual decay and renewal beneath the convoluted and apparently capricious course of human affairs, a course that would be broken only by the posthistorical triumph of Christ. God effected these revivals outside of human agency, by the Holy Spirit, that is, "not by the authority of human princes nor [human] wisdom."[49]

Having thus severed public obligation from faith and the idea of national election from providential rule—in sum, having subordinated law to the immediate and transcendent experience of grace—Bellamy directed his people more to their individual spiritual and moral states than to their membership in New England's social and ecclesiastical order. His ethical recommendations reflected this agenda. The most immediate and notable effects of conversion, he explained, were interior sensations of peace, comfort, and joy, the "happiness in our souls" that came from a realization of one's justification by "the love and favour of God." To desire happiness as the outcome of regeneration, he argued, was only "natural," since "happiness is what all are seeking after. All mankind are in pursuit of this. They propose some good to themselves in whatever they do, either present or future, and they have been searching after that which is happifying, or, that which if we are possessed of will make us happy, and have found it to be the favour of God." Such joy, Bellamy believed, issued in truly virtuous affections or dispositions. Although he affirmed the traditional conviction that "divine knowledge must tend to and end in suitable practice," he described that knowledge as an inner sensation and the "acts" that issued from it as primarily "fervent and devout prayer" and secondarily as personal inclinations toward "justice, truth, and faithfulness." Vice, in contrast, was an "*internal disorder*," by which the "Reason is . . . governed by the basest passions—hatred, anger, malice, [and] envy." The essence of Christian gratitude was "not to crucify God [with] inordinate *affections*." When, in a 1739 fast-day sermon, he came to specific recommendations for moral improvement, Bellamy devoted only one sentence to "public duties," in which he paraphrased the golden rule. In contrast, he gave a lengthy exhortation to uphold "duties to God," explained as the individual's posture of trust, gratitude, worship, and prayer.[50]

As Bellamy focused on interior, affective standards of morality, so he refrained from casuistic delineations of social duties and deemphasized institutional and public contexts for moral behavior. The chief social duties of believers, he thought, concerned their private responsibilities to the family and to neighbors in economic need. Charity properly ruled one's social relationships; thus Christians were to refrain from slander and covetous actions, forgive their persecutors, and promote unity among believers through prayer.[51]

Bellamy's preaching during the revivals contained, then, few references to systemic questions of law, polity, and politics. When he addressed Christian behavior, he most commonly stressed the obligations of converts to escape worldly entanglements, particularly temptations to compete in the regnant social order. Materialism bothered him most. Sin, as he characterized it, prevailed in three forms, each of which was encouraged by the current prosperity: hedonism, the desire for social prestige, and greed. He chastised those who pursued "jollity," good food, loose women, and strong drink. The son of a tavern owner, he was acquainted enough with alcoholic overindulgence to describe its effects in detail: "Can any man think that he is a happy one and one that enjoys true peace and quietness in his mind that is every now and then intoxicating his brain with strong drink? Or will not every man say that such an one is a miserable slave, what a cruel master does he serve, and what a faithful servant is he. And what is his reward but anguish and pain, discontent and dissatisfaction, a wounded conscience . . . shame and blushing, disorder and confusion." He was so aware of the temptations to drink that when John Graham's ministerial assistant consulted Bellamy on the best means to get people to church on time, Bellamy supposedly told him to place a barrel of rum in the Southbury pulpit (to which the assistant replied, besting Bellamy, that the result would be a near-empty church in Bethlehem on the Sabbath). The wise man, Bellamy advised, perceived that pleasures produced illness, honors were treacherous, and riches caused only anxiety.[52]

Bellamy spent more effort in rebuking idle talk, tavern visiting, reveling, and Sabbath breaking and in applauding their unpopularity during revivals than in formulating social and political policy because he believed that genuine morality stemmed from a private, inner reorientation. His conclusions were understandable. He first arrived at Yale as an outsider to the centers of wealth and prestige, built his ministry on behalf of a new settlement in conflict with an established town, and struggled to promote revival against the policies of a recalcitrant Old Light order. All this taught him that reform, if it were to come to New England at all, would come outside of established institutions. New England, he decided, needed conversion, not catechesis; faith, not law; right affections, not proper polity.

In Bethlehem, among students at Yale, and in churches throughout New England, Bellamy's ideas, like those of Edwards and other moderate New Lights, were remarkably popular. Convinced that he competed for the salvation of his audience, Bellamy wrote and preached with such urgency and affection that he won many to the New Light message—not least his own parishioners. As the Awakening produced excesses and separations, however, the social and theological ethics of evangelicals attracted criticism. To many, Bellamy's preaching on conversion and escape from worldly temptation seemed a dangerous abandonment of the moral standards by which Christianity had exercised its social influence. The origins of the transformation of Bellamy's evangelical Calvinism into New Divinity theology lay in his response to these problems and criticisms.

Notes

1. Bellamy to Mrs. Charles Sheldon, Aug. 1, 1783, and Nov. 20, 1785, in Tryon Edwards, "Memoir," in Bellamy, *The Works of Joseph Bellamy, D.D., First Pastor of the Church in Bethlem, Connecticut, With a Memoir of his Life and Character, by Tryon Edwards*, 2 vols. (Boston, 1850), I:xlii, xlvi.

2. Many important discussions of the New Divinity contrast the ideas of Bellamy with those of Edwards through a static comparison of Bellamy's works in the 1750s and 1760s and Edwards's thought as a whole. See William Breitenbach, "The Consistent Calvinism of the New Divinity Movement," *WMQ*, 41 (1984): 241–64; Conforti, *Samuel Hopkins*, 23–124; and Haroutunian, *Piety Versus Moralism*, 3–176. Other interpretations link the two writers too tightly by viewing the New Divinity movement as a logical extension of Edwards's theology; see Michael P. Anderson, "The Pope of Litchfield County: An Intellectual Biography of Joseph Bellamy, 1719–1790" (Ph.D. diss., Claremont Graduate School, 1980); Frank Hugh Foster, *A Genetic History of the New England Theology* (Chicago, 1907; rep. New York, 1963), 47–223; Edwin Scott Gaustad, *The Great Awakening in New England* (New York, 1957), 126–40; and Alan Heimert and Perry Miller, "Introduction," in Heimert and Miller, eds., *The Great Awakening: Documents Illustrating the Crisis and Its Consequences* (New York, 1967), xii–lxi. Bellamy's nineteenth-century biographers described his piety in typical New Light terminology: see, e.g., Noah Benedict, "Funeral Sermon with Appendix," in Bellamy, *Works*, I:22.

3. None of Bellamy's writings before 1736 are extant. Biographical data for him may be found in Benedict, "Funeral Sermon," in Bellamy, *Works*, I:11–40; *HW*, 239–53; Tryon Edwards, "Memoir," vii–xlv; Percy Coe Eggleston, *A Man of Bethlehem, Joseph Bellamy, D.D., and His Divinity School* (New London, Conn., 1908); Franklin Bowditch Dexter, *Biographical Sketches of the Graduates of Yale College, with Annals of the College History*, 9 vols. (New York, 1885–1912), I:522–29 (this volume hereafter cited as Dexter, *Sketches*); and William B. Sprague, *Annals of the American Pulpit; or Commemorative Notices of Distinguished American Clergymen of Various Denominations*, 9 vols. (New York, 1857–1869), I:404–12 (this volume hereafter cited as Sprague, *Annals*). Anderson's "Joseph Bellamy" provides little analysis, but it documents most of what we know about Bellamy's life.

4. Ralph D. Smyth, "Matthew Bellamy of New Haven, Conn., and His Descendants," *The New England Historical and Geneological Register* 61 (1907): 338–40; and Anderson, 114–22.

5. Anderson, 122–27.

6. See Chapter 3 for evidence of Bellamy's social and economic sensibilites during his long career in Bethlehem. Bellamy's probate and land records from

Woodbury township, of which Bethlehem was a part, show no evidence of any inheritance from Matthew: WPR, 9:113–14; WLR 6:155, 161; 7:16, 17, 21; 9:12, 137. There is no record of the will of Joseph's father, Matthew Bellamy, at the most complete repository of Connecticut probate records, the Connecticut State Library, Hartford.

7. For the best recent survey of the type of Puritanism that achieved a broad consensus by the beginning of the eighteenth century, see Harry S. Stout, *The New England Soul: Preaching and Religious Culture in Colonial New England* (New York, 1986), 12–181; for one reading of how New England's covenantal religion played out in daily life, see David D. Hall, *Worlds of Wonder, Days of Judgment: Popular Religious Belief in Early New England* (New York, 1989). Detailed discussions of the Half-way Covenant and Stoddardeanism are contained in Edmund S. Morgan, *Visible Saints: The History of a Puritan Idea* (Ithaca, N.Y., 1963), 139–52; Norman Pettit, *The Heart Prepared: Grace and Conversion in Puritan Spiritual Life* (New Haven, Conn., 1966), 158–211; Robert G. Pope, *The Half-way Covenant: Church Membership in Puritan New England* (Princeton, N.J., 1969); and David Laurence, "Jonathan Edwards, Soloman Stoddard, and the Preparationist Model of Conversion," *Harvard Theological Review* 72 (1979): 267–83. Bushman, *Puritan to Yankee*, 147–63, surveys the adoption of Stoddardeanism in Connecticut. For Bellamy's Old Light classmates, see Dexter, *Sketches*, 421, 437, 470–73, 521–22.

8. Richard Warch, *School of the Prophets: Yale College, 1701–1740*, (New Haven, Conn., 1973), 118–85; Edmund Morgan, *The Gentle Puritan: A Life of Ezra Stiles, 1727–1795* (New Haven, Conn., 1962), 42–63; Norman Fiering, *Jonathan Edwards's Moral Thought and Its British Context* (Chapel Hill, N.C., 1981), 132 n. 60; Henry F. May, *The Enlightenment in America* (New York, 1976), 42–87. For the rise of liberal Protestantism in Boston, see John Corrigan, *The Prism of Piety: Catholick Congregational Clergy at the Beginning of the Enlightenment* (New York, 1991). Pedagogical and curricular changes are discussed in Mary Latimer Gambrell, *Ministerial Training in Eighteenth-Century New England* (New York, 1937), 29–83.

9. Warch, *School of Prophets*, 169–85; Samuel Hopkins, *Sketches of the Life of the Late, Rev. Samuel Hopkins, D.D.*, ed. Stephen West (Hartford, 1805), 30–38; Chauncey A. Goodrich, "Narrative of Revivals of Religion in Yale College," *The American Quarterly Register* 10 (1858): 289–310; and Stephen Nissenbaum, ed., *The Great Awakening at Yale College* (Belmont, Calif., 1972).

10. Conforti, *Samuel Hopkins*, 9–22; Harry S. Stout, "The Great Awakening in New England Reconsidered: The New England Clergy," *Journal of Social History* 8 (Spring 1974): 21–48; and James W. Schmotter, "Ministerial Careers in Eighteenth-Century New England," *Journal of Social History* 9 (Winter 1975): 249–67. Of the top eight students in Bellamy's class, seven were the sons of pastors, and seven came from cities (i.e., commercial towns) in the east, on the coast, or on the Connecticut River. Of the middle eight, no professional background is listed, but all eight came from eastern, coastal, or river towns. Of the last eight, none were the sons of professionals, and only three were from eastern, coastal, or river towns. See Dexter, *Sketches*, 438–620. On social ranking at Yale, see Warch, *School of Prophets*, 255–57. On the political status of frontier settlers, see Charles S. Grant, *Democracy in the Connecticut Frontier Town of Kent* (New York, 1961); John J. Waters, "Patrimony, Succession, and Social Stability in Guilford, Connecticut," *Perspectives in American History* 10 (1976): 131–60; Bruce C. Daniels, "Large Town Officeholding in Eighteenth-Century Connecticut," *Journal of American Studies* 9

(1975): 1–12; and William F. Willingham, "Deference, Democracy, and Town Government in Windham, 1758-1786," *WMQ* 30 (1973): 401–22.

11. "The Resolves of the General Association," Nov. 24, 1741, quoted in Oscar Zeichner, *Connecticut's Years of Controversy: 1750–1770* (Chapel Hill, N.C., 1949), 22. If we divide the Yale classes from 1732 to 1738 into upper and lower social groups and count those whose religious orientation is clear, we see that nine of the top group became Old Lights, three Episcopalians, and four New Lights. In the lower group, four became Old Lights, four Episcopalians, and twenty-one New Lights. See Dexter, *Sketches*, 438–620. For a helpful overview of the literature on the demographic and social background to New Light adherence, which supports my generalization here, see Michael J. Crawford, *Seasons of Grace: Colonial New England's Revival Tradition in Its British Context* (New York, 1991), 6–15.

12. For Bellamy's friendships, see Anderson, 274–92, 337–38. On ecclesiastical differences between moderates and radicals, see Gaustad, *Great Awakening*, 102–25, and C. C. Goen, *Revivalism and Separatism in New England, 1740–1800: Strict Congregationalists and Separate Baptists in the Great Awakening* (New Haven, Conn., 1962), 36–67. On theological distinctions, see J. M. Bumsted and John E. Van de Wetering, *What Must I Do to Be Saved?: The Great Awakening in Colonial America* (Hinsdale, Ill., 1976), 96–115, and Heimert and Miller, "Introduction," xiii–lxx. Bellamy and Edwards accepted the Westminster Confession of Faith (1647) and admired the doctrinal formulations of Peter van Mastricht (1630– 1706) and Francis Turretin (1623–1687); see Edwards to Bellamy, Jan. 15, 1747, in "Six Letters of Jonathan Edwards to Joseph Bellamy," ed. Stanley T. Williams, *New England Quarterly* 1 (1928): 229–32. Conrad Cherry, *The Theology of Jonathan Edwards: A Reappraisal* (New York, 1966), 12–88, discusses Reformed orthodoxy as background to Edwards. Bellamy often referred to Reformed creeds and dogmaticians; see, e.g., *A Careful and Strict Examination of the External Covenant* (New Haven, Conn., 1770), in *Works*, III:355–57, and *The Half-way Covenant: A Dialogue Between a Minister and His Parishioner* (New Haven, Conn., 1769), in *Works*, III:445 (hereafter cited as *HWC*, with reference to this volume). One indication of the moderates' loyalty to Reformed orthodoxy, which distinguished them from radicals and Old Lights, was their tendency, unlike later revivalists such as Charles Finney, to remove the faculty of volition from the act of faith; see Norman S. Fiering, "Will and Intellect in the New England Mind," *WMQ* 29 (1972): 515–58.

13. Bellamy, Student Notebook, 1736, Joseph Bellamy Papers, Miscellaneous Personal Papers, Ms. Group 30, Box 179, Yale Divinity School Library, New Haven, Conn. (hereafter cited as Student Notebook). Edwards's "Justification by Faith Alone" was published as part of *Discourses on Various Important Subjects Nearly Concerning the Great Affair of the Soul's Eternal Salvation* (Boston, 1738) in the first year of Bellamy's ministry. The confusing chronology of events from 1735 to 1738 is sorted out in Anderson, 132–39. On Samuel Hall, see Dexter, *Sketches*, 154–56.

14. Edwards to Bellamy, Jan. 9, 1748, HS document number 81175 (documents from this collection hereafter cited in the following manner: HS 81175); Edwards to Bellamy, Feb. 28, 1754, quoted in Anderson, 473; Edwards to Erskine, July 5, 1750, quoted in Sereno E. Dwight, *The Life of President Edwards* (New York, 1830), 406; and Williams, ed., "Six Letters," 226–42. For evaluations of Bellamy's preaching, see Sidney Earl Mead, *Nathaniel William Taylor, 1786–1858: A Connecticut Liberal* (Chicago, 1942), 17, and Anderson, 195–202.

15. *CR*, VIII:265–66; James Walsh, "The Great Awakening in the First Con-

gregational Church of Woodbury, Connecticut," *WMQ* 28 (1971): 543–62; *HW*, I:239–42; and Anderson, 176–83. With adjustments to the inflation rate for this period, the real increase in property value amounted to 389 percent; see John J. McCusker, *Money and Exchange in Europe and America, 1600–1775: A Handbook* (Chapel Hill, N.C., 1977), 141, 153. Bellamy, his contemporaries, and some nineteenth-century writers used "Bethlem"; I will use the more recent standardized spelling.

16. Bushman, *Puritan to Yankee*, 41–134; see also Albert Laverne Olson, *Agricultural Economy and the Population in Eighteenth Century Connecticut* (New Haven, Conn., 1935).

17. The key legal documents in Bethlehem's ecclesiastical settlement are contained in CA, VI:309–29a; see also *CR*, VIII:539, 265–66, 310, 409, and 425. For background, see Walsh, "Woodbury"; *HW*, I:239–42; and Anderson, 172–78.

18. Anderson, 172–73; Walsh, "Woodbury." Bellamy's personal account of the revival in Bethlehem dwelt on the attraction of young people to his preaching. This document is part of Bellamy's handwritten entries into the official statistics and covenants of the Bethlehem church, bound as "Bethlehem, Connecticut, Congregational Church Records, 1738–1850," Connecticut State Library, Hartford. Bellamy's narrative in the church records covers only the first few years of Bethlehem and are entered on the back of the final three pages, upside down. (Hereafter, Bellamy's personal account will be cited as Personal Account; other material in the church records will be cited as Church Records.) For the economic and social status of New England's youth, and the popularity of the Awakening with them, see John M. Bumsted, "Religion, Finance, and Democracy in Massachusetts," *Journal of Social History* 57 (1971): 817–31; Jackson Turner Main, "The Distribution of Property in Colonial Connecticut," in James Kirby Martin, ed., *The Human Dimensions of Nation Making: Essays on Colonial and Revolutionary America* (Madison, Wis., 1976), 54–104, and especially Patricia J. Tracy, *Jonathan Edwards, Pastor: Religion and Society in Eighteenth-Century Northampton* (New York, 1980), 86–108. For a provocative analysis of the social appeal of New Light individualism, see Patricia U. Bonomi, *Under the Cope of Heaven: Religion, Society, and Politics in Colonial America* (New York, 1986), 131–60. Reference to social appeal should not obscure the fact that Bellamy and his parishioners believed the truth claims of evangelical theology—a point that I take for granted in this and subsequent discussions of the social appeal of Bellamy's message.

19. Bellamy, Personal Account.

20. Bellamy, Personal Account. Bellamy's view thus contrasts sharply with that of recent historians who argue that the Awakening was a modest series of revivals reinterpreted as a great event by nineteenth-century evangelicals. See Jon Butler, "Enthusiasm Described and Decried: The Great Awakening as Interpretive Fiction," *The Journal of American History* 69 (1982): 305–25, and Joseph Conforti, "The Invention of the Great Awakening," *Early American Literature* 26 (1991): 99–118. For Whitefield's influence, see Harry S. Stout, *The Divine Dramatist: George Whitefield and the Rise of Modern Evangelicalism* (Grand Rapids, Mich., 1991).

21. Membership numbers are taken from Church Records; for comparative figures, see Howard Frederic Vos, "The Great Awakening in Connecticut" (Ph.D. diss., Northwestern University, 1967), 171. Total population figures for Bethlehem in this period are unavailable. Until 1787 Bethlehem was part of Woodbury, legally

a separate parish but not incorporated as a town. Figures for household heads are taken from the Woodbury town tax records (WTR), which list taxpayers by subdivision of the town (Woodbury proper, Southbury, Bethlehem, Judea, and Roxbury). Church Records notes the end of the Half-way Covenant in Bellamy's church; for further detail on Bellamy's sacramental theories see Chapters 2 and 5.

22. Graham to Bellamy, Feb. 17, 1742, PHS; Backus to Bellamy, June 22, 1741, PHS; Seymour to Bellamy, June 20, 1741, PHS; and Wheelock to Bellamy, Dec. 27, 1741, PHS. The apellation of Boanerges, from one Timothy Stone, is quoted in Anderson, 199; further details and evidence of Bellamy's preaching manner are given in Anderson, 195–202, 257–73. The best available examples of Bellamy's pulpit rhetoric are given in this chapter and in Chapters 3 and 5.

23. Ezra Stiles, *Literary Diary of Ezra Stiles, D.D., LL.D., President of Yale College*, ed. Franklin Bowditch Dexter (New York, 1901), III:385; Anderson, 260–73, compiles further testimony to Bellamy's character. Edwards's warnings may be seen in his *Some Thoughts Concerning the Present Revival* (Boston, 1742). For Edwards on the covenant, see Harry S. Stout, "The Puritans and Edwards," in Nathan O. Hatch and Stout, eds., *Jonathan Edwards and the American Experience* (New York, 1988), 142–59.

24. See, for example, Hezekiah Lord to Bellamy, June 2, 1742, PHS; Samuel Blair to Bellamy, Sept. 20, 1744, PHS; Edwards to Bellamy, Jan. 9 , 1749, HS 81175; Tryon Edwards, "Memoir," x, xiii–xiv; and Anderson, 331–41. The 213 places noted for Bellamy's itinerations includes separate visits to towns in which he preached more than once.

25. Such correspondence may be found throughout the PHS and HS collections and in Tryon Edwards, "Memoir." For Graham, see Sprague, *Annals*, 314–16. For Bellamy's visits to Yale, see Christopher M. Jedrey, *The World of John Cleaveland: Family and Community in Eighteenth-Century New England* (New York, 1979), 17–42. Only a special plea from the separatists to the New Haven magistrates apparently kept Bellamy and Wheelock from punishment; see the open letter of Oct. 20, 1742, CA, VII:264a.

26. Bellamy to Brainerd, Mar. 7, 1743, quoted in Tryon Edwards, "Memoir," xii–xiii; Bellamy to Wheelock, Dec. 21, 1742, in Tryon Edwards, "Memoir," xi–xii; Wheelock to Bellamy, Dec. 27, 1741, PHS; and Bellamy to Wheelock, Jan. 1742, HS 81158. In *Seasons of Grace*, 167–79, Crawford demonstrates that this evangelical network was transatlantic as well as intercolonial.

27. Kenneth A. Lockridge, *A New England Town, The First Hundred Years: Dedham, Massachusetts, 1636–1736* (New York, 1970), 16; Edwards, "Charity and its Fruits," in *Ethical Writings*, Vol. 8 of *The Works of Jonathan Edwards*, ed. Paul Ramsey (New Haven, Conn., 1989), 146; Bellamy, Personal Account. Bellamy transcribed the first three of Edwards's Charity sermons: HS 81466–81468. Edwards made similiar observations on the correspondence between economic development, social contention, and religious apathy in "The State of Religion in Northampton in the County of Hampshire," in *The Great Awakening*, Vol. 4 of *The Works of Jonathan Edwards*, ed. C. C. Goen (New Haven, Conn., 1972), 544–57, and in Edwards to Thomas Gillespie, July 1, 1751, in Dwight, *Life of Edwards*, 464. Bellamy's preaching about New England's economic development is discussed in Chapter Three. For New England's covenantal ideals and their fate in the midst of economic change, see also Sacvan Bercovitch, *The American Jeremiad* (Madison, Wis., 1978); Stephen Foster, *Their Solitary Way: The Puritan Social Ethic in the*

First Century of Settlement in New England (New Haven, Conn., 1971); Michael Zuckerman, *Peaceable Kingdoms: New England Towns in the Eighteenth Century* (New York, 1970); Zeichner, *Connecticut's Years of Controversy*, 3–19; and Bushman, *Puritan to Yankee*, 41–81.

28. Bushman, *Puritan to Yankee*, 164–82; M. Louise Green, *The Development of Religious Liberty in Connecticut* (Boston, 1905), 186–219; John Graham, *The Christian's Duty of Watchfullness Against Error* (New London, Conn., 1733); and *CR* 8: 521. For a description of the Rogerine movement and similiar heresies, see Chapter 5.

29. Congregational Churches in Connecticut, Saybrook Synod, 1708, *A Confession of Faith* (New London, Conn., 1710).

30. Colony of Connecticut, "An Act for Regulating Abuses and Correcting Disorders in Ecclesiastical Affairs," in *Acts and Laws passed by the General Court* (New London, Conn., 1742); Philemon Robbins, *A Plain Narrative* (Boston, 1747); Gaustad, *The Great Awakening*, 32–34, 61–79; Goen, *Revivalism and Separatism*, 58–67; and Bushman, *Puritan to Yankee*, 237.

31. Church Records; "Petition of the Fairfield Eastern Association," Oct. 1742, CA, VII:262b. See Goen, *Revivalism and Separatism*, 60–61, and Anderson, 348–50, 445. The Fairfield Eastern attestation was not initially published with the *Testimony and Advice*.

32. I have transcribed Bellamy's sermons from the original manuscripts, transposing his shorthand, adding punctuation, and expanding abbreviations. Citations will be given according to the biblical text on which Bellamy based each sermon. For the above quotation: Bellamy, Luke 19:41–42, Oct. 12, 1737, HS 81430. A further example is Bellamy's sermon on John 3:19, Sept. 25, 1740, HS 81454.

33. The sheer number of evangelical tracts during the Awakening denoted a polemical temper; New Lights published far more than either contemporary Old Lights or seventeenth-century ministers. See Stout, "The Great Awakening," 28–29.

34. Bellamy, Lev. 23:27, Apr. 1739, HS 81443; Ps. 107:31, Nov. 8, 1739, HS 81447. Edwards, "Some Thoughts," in *The Great Awakening*, ed. Goen, 522–23.

35. Bellamy, Luke 18:18–19, Mar. 14, 1741, HS 81455; and *True Religion Delineated*, in *Works*, I:49 (herefter cited as *TRD*, with reference to this volume); Edwards, *Religious Affections*, Vol. 2 of *The Works of Jonathan Edwards*, ed. John E. Smith (New Haven, Conn., 1959), 173. In *A History of the Work of Redemption*, Edwards ranked Arminianism among the most horrendous deviations, including superstition, Socinianism, Arianism, Quakerism, and Deism; see Edwards, *A History of the Work of Redemption*, Vol. 9 of *The Works of Jonathan Edwards*, trans. and ed. John F. Wilson (New Haven, Conn., 1989), 430–32. On Arminianism, see Goen, "Editor's Introduction" to Edwards, *The Great Awakening*, 4–18, and Cherry, *Jonathan Edwards*, 186–96. The antagonism of the Williams family toward Edwards, according to Perry Miller, stemmed from their recognition that evangelical denunciations of Arminianism, and subsequent emphases on pristine Calvinist soteriology, implied a deprecation of the clerical establishment and social elite; see Miller, *Jonathan Edwards* (New York, 1949; rep. Cleveland, Ohio, 1959), 101–26.

36. Bellamy, Matt. 25:13, Feb. 21, 1738, HS 81435. Crawford maintains that New Lights often spoke of communal revival and a recovery of a proper reading of the covenant. True enough, but Bellamy thought that the means to such cor-

porate revival lay outside the existing institutions and practices of the covenant. In *An Humble Inquiry Into the Rules of the Word of God* (Boston, 1749), Edwards argued that the prevailing use of the Half-way Covenant falsely assumed a correspondence between ancient Israel, with its covenantal prerogatives of a socioreligious order, and contemporary New England. Israel, according to Edwards, typified only the spiritual kingdom of Christ, not an earthly society mixed of sinners and saints. Baptism and church membership, in this context, could be merely "exterior badges of Christianity," the abuse of which had led to an "over-valuing of *common* Grace and *moral Sincerity*"; see Edwards, *An Humble Inquiry*, 87–99, 129.

37. Bellamy, Luke 15:18–19, Mar. 14, 1741, HS 81455; Edwards, "Justification by Faith Alone," in *Discourses*, 10–11; Bellamy, Isa. 43:25, Oct. 5, 1737, HS 81429; and Edwards, "The Distinguishing Marks of the Work of the Spirit of God," in *The Great Awakening*, ed. Goen, 248. Throughout his evangelical sermons, Bellamy drew upon the standard Calvinist *ordo salutis* in such a way as to denigrate law work and moral preparation in favor of the moment of faith. Examples include Bellamy's Lev. 23:27; Luke 15:18–19, Mar. 14, 1741, HS 81455; Hab. 5:31, July 20, 1739, HS 81445; and John 3:19.

38. Cherry, *Jonathan Edwards*, 107–23, and Perry Miller, *The New England Mind: The Seventeenth Century* (New York, 1939; rep. Boston, 1963), 365–462.

39. Bellamy, Student Notebook, and Matt. 11:28, ca. 1742, HS 81461.

40. Bellamy, Isa. 43:25 and Matt. 22:9, Dec. 8, 1737, HS 81434.

41. Bellamy, Lev. 23:27.

42. Bellamy, Ps. 119:59–60, Mar. 1739, HS 81441; Matt. 25:13; Student Notebook. Edwards's key texts are *Religious Affections*, ed. Smith, 100–102, 272 ff., and *A Divine and Supernatural Light* (Boston, 1734). The most relevant of the many commentaries on Edwards's aesthetic and sensationalist ideas are Roland Andre Delattre, *Beauty and Sensibility in the Thought of Jonathan Edwards: An Essay in Aesthetics and Theological Ethics* (New Haven, Conn., 1968), and Terrence Erdt, *Jonathan Edwards and the Sense of the Heart* (Amherst, Mass., 1980).

43. Bellamy, Luke 16:31, Dec. 19, 1741, CHS (most of Bellamy's sermons from this collection are uncatalogued).

44. Bellamy, Matt. 22:9.

45. See John F. Wilson, *Pulpit in Parliament: Puritanism During the English Civil Wars, 1640–1648* (Princeton, N.J., 1969), 166–96; Bercovitch, *The Puritan Origins of the American Self* (New Haven, Conn., 1975), 41–50; and Robert Middlekauff, *The Mathers: Three Generations of Puritan Intellectuals, 1596–1728* (New York, 1971), 320–49.

46. Bellamy, Matt. 22:9; Matt. 25:13, Feb. 21, 1738, HS 81435; Bercovitch, *Puritan Origins*, 41–50.

47. Bellamy, Luke 19:41–42; Ps. 119:59–60, HS 81441; Mason I. Lowance, Jr., *The Language of Canaan: Metaphor and Symbol in New England from the Puritans to the Transcendentalists* (Cambridge, Mass., 1980).

48. Bellamy, Ps. 119:59–60; Luke 13:24.

49. Bellamy, Ps. 119:59–60; Edwards, *History of Redemption*, 460. See also Edwards, "An Humble Attempt," in *Apocalyptic Writings*, Vol. 5 of *The Works of Jonathan Edwards*, ed. Stephen J. Stein (New Haven, Conn., 1977), 326, 364–65. For overall perspectives on Edwards's view of history, see the following essays by John F. Wilson: "Jonathan Edwards as Historian," *Church History* 46 (1977): 5–18; "History, Redemption, and the Millennium," in Hatch and Stout, eds., *Jonathan*

Edwards and the American Experience, 131–41; and "Editor's Introduction" to Edwards, *History of Redemption,* 13–100. See also David Ernest Lawrence, "Religious Experience in the Biblical World of Jonathan Edwards" (Ph.D. diss., Yale University, 1976); Peter Gay, *A Loss of Mastery: Puritan Historians in Colonial America* (Berkeley, Calif., 1966), 88–117; Ruth H. Bloch, *Visionary Republic: Millennial Themes in American Thought, 1756–1800* (New York, 1985); and James West Davidson, *The Logic of Millennial Thought: Eighteenth-Century New England* (New Haven, Conn., 1977), 37–80. Contrary to some interpretations, Edwards did not regard the Millennium as the gradual consummation of human progress in America. Reluctant to locate the time or place of Christ's earthly reign, he did not have enough confidence in millennial speculations to give them formal or public attention. More important, he was assertive in culminating the Redemption sermons with an extensive, almost hymnic, description of Christ's postmillennial victory over the forces of sin and Satan. See Edwards to William McCulloch, Mar. 5, 1744, quoted in Stein, "Editor's Introduction" to Edwards, *Apocalyptic Writings,* 29; Edwards, *History of Redemption,* ed. Wilson, 332–34, 358–92; Edwards, "Apocalypse Series," in *Apocalyptic Writings,* ed. Stein, 135; and Stein, "Editor's Introduction" to Edwards, *Apocalyptic Writings,* 8–54. For a fuller study of Edwards that confirms my reading here, see Gerald R. McDermott, *One Holy and Happy Society: The Public Theology of Jonathan Edwards* (University Park, Pa., 1992).

50. Bellamy, Luke 19:41–42; Josh. 24:15, ca. 1740, HS 81460; Ps. 119:59–60; John 5:40, Sept. 1737, HS 81427; and Lev. 23:27. The emphases are mine. For similar perspectives in Edwards, see Edwards, "Charity and Its Fruits," in *Ethical Writings,* ed. Ramsey, 226–40, and Clyde A. Holbrook, *The Ethics of Jonathan Edwards: Morality and Aesthetics* (Ann Arbor, Mich., 1973), 54–65.

51. Many of Bellamy's sermons illustrate such emphases. Examples are Josh. 24:15; Matt. 5:44, Feb. 24, 1740, HS 81449; and Eccles. 12:1, ca. 1738, HS 81459.

52. Bellamy, Luke 19:41–42; the rummy anecdote is related in Sprague, *Annals,* 315.

2

Law

Among the wares that Boston dockworkers unloaded from a ship on a summer day in 1755, we might imagine, was a large package, damp and heavy after its long voyage from Scotland. It was addressed from "J. Erskine, Edinburgh" to "S. Kneeland, bookseller, Boston, New England." The parcel lay for a few hours on the wharf before a messenger came, signed for it, and lugged it up to Queenstreet. At the shop, Samuel Kneeland cut open the cover and quickly thumbed through the books. He set aside and bundled nine of them and the next day sent them along with a rider to Hartford. During the next ten days several travelers carried the parcel to the inland trading town of Litchfield, where a militia captain on his way to Danbury agreed to take the books to a small village some fifteen miles away. After a morning's ride, the captain knocked at the door of the village's parsonage and handed the somewhat worn package to the large, deep-voiced man who shared courtesies and a draught of cider. The pastor then took the parcel upstairs to the study, sat at his desk, and read the address: "To the Rev. Joseph Bellamy, Bethlem." Inside the wrapper was a short note—a bill, Bellamy presumed. He put aside the note and opened the books: Johan Friedrich Staupfer's five-volume *Institutiones Theologae Polemicae*, David Hume's *Enquiry Concerning the Principles of Morals*, the third earl of Shaftesbury's *Characteristics of Men, Manners, Opinions, Times*, and Francis Hutcheson's two-volume *A System of Moral Philosophy*. Before looking more carefully at these publications from Zurich, London, and Glasgow, the Calvinist parson put them on his shelves. They sat incongruously next to older copies of William Ames's *Medulla Theologicae,* Samuel Willard's *Compendium Divinitas,* David Brainerd's *Journal,* Jonathan Edwards's *Religious Affections,* the hymns of Isaac Watts, and several biblical commentaries. The New Light preacher, trained in the traditions of strict Calvinism and nurtured in the power of evangelical piety, smiled to himself, briefly. Then he set about to read—not Samuel Willard nor Jonathan Edwards, but David Hume.[1]

How did Joseph Bellamy, the archdefender of Calvinism in western Connecticut, come to collect rational theologies and scandalously seditious books? The contents of his library puzzled some neighboring pastors who upon his death found what one nineteenth-century commentator denigrated as "the publications of infidels and heretics."[2] Bellamy had not turned heretic, despite the conclusions of later historians who have placed him within a New Divinity movement that supposedly capitulated to the moral agendas of rationalists such as Hutcheson and Hume.[3] He remained firmly committed to the doctrines of evangelical Calvinism. Yet his reading of rationalist moral philosophies did reflect changes in his theological perspective after the revivals. As he settled into his ministry in the stable community of Bethlehem, Bellamy strove to articulate the social and institutional implications of Calvinism and establish an evangelical leadership over the standing order. To defend the public place of Calvinism— indeed, to assert its superiority to all other parties—Bellamy turned from a critique of institutionalized moralism to a construction of a system of doctrine that was philosophically and ethically defensible. He became an apologist. As such, he searched for a theological paradigm that would answer the liberal critique of Calvinism without deference to the covenantalism of the old standing order. He found that paradigm in a most unlikely place: the moral discourse of the Enlightenment. "Infidels," whose treatises were brought from Britain and Europe to Bethlehem, provided Bellamy with the concept of a universal, absolute, and reasonable standard for religious and moral judgment—the moral law—that he used to vindicate profoundly Calvinist convictions. The antecedents of the New Divinity appeared from 1745 to 1760, when Bellamy expressed the doctrines of grace in the language of law.[4]

Initially, however, it was James Davenport rather than David Hume who instigated Bellamy's apologetic turn. As the Awakening reached its height in 1742, enthusiasm appeared in New England in the form of frenzied religious meetings, visions and prophecies, late-night singing in the streets, and a rash of church separations. A pietistic strain within Puritanism had long nurtured the ideal of the saint who challenged creed and custom with scripture. Enthusiasts went further. They subordinated circumscribed and rational interpretations of the Bible to individual and immediate perceptions of the divine will. Claiming such revelation, Davenport and other enthusiasts accused many ministers and church members of spiritual hy-

pocrisy, advocated lay exhortation, and encouraged public displays of rap-
ture. In practical terms, enthusiasts made what Leigh Eric Schmidt calls
"a theology out of disorder." They subordinated public morality to religious ecstasy and thus infuriated Old Lights, violated the Saybrook Platform, and jeopardized the moderates' attempts to reinvigorate established
churches from within.[5]

New Light enthusiasm was obviously troublesome, if not illegal; more
dangerous for its subtlety and apparent affinity with Calvinist preaching
was evangelical antinomianism, popularized especially through the min-
istries of Ebenezer Frothingham (1717?–1785) and Andrew Croswell
(1709–1785). Moderates and radicals alike favored justification by faith
alone, but Croswell gave such precedence to inner faith that he denied
any value to moral obedience. Opposed to both Arminian ethics and Calvinist dogmatics, eighteenth-century antinomians reduced the meaning
of faith to assurance, or confidence, in being forgiven. True faith, Croswell
asserted, was a subjective persuasion that Christ removed sin from the
sinner. He urged the unconverted to assure themselves of God's love and
relinquish disaffecting notions of legal obligation and culpability. He and
other antinomians rejected preparatory activities such as repentance and
humiliation and denied the usefulness of moral works as evidence of sanctification. Since Bellamy, a favorite object of Croswell's denunciations, and
other moderates maintained the Calvinist position that faith followed
repentance and led to sanctification, Croswell assailed them as crypto-
Pelagians and Romanists, purveyors of "*abominable* good Works."[6]

Led by Edwards, New Light moderates positioned themselves against
the radicals by declaring unconventional ecclesiastical practices, commu-
nally disruptive behavior, and false doctrines of assurance the perversions
of an otherwise godly movement.[7] Old Lights such as Isaac Stiles
(1696–1760) and Charles Chauncy (1705–1787) disagreed. Convinced that
antinomianism and enthusiasm were necessary corollaries to evangelical
Calvinism, they depicted the entire Awakening as spurious—a declension
from reason, the Bible, and morality. Stiles argued that the revivals broke
the harmony established on natural, moral, religious, and civil law and
thereby threatened the prosperity of both church and commonwealth; he
encouraged Connecticut's magistrates to suppress New Lights. Of Massachusetts Old Lights, Chauncy was the most influential and the most per-
sistent in asserting that the moderates had a defective corporate ethic. In
his *Seasonable Thoughts on the State of Religion in New-England* (Boston, 1743),
he impugned the preaching of terror as enthusiasm and attributed offen-
sive forms of public behavior—church schisms, censoriousness, and the
ordination of unqualified itinerants—not to the misconceptions of New
Light exhorters but to the conduct and character of the most distinguished
evangelicals. Connecticut readers might well have concluded that these
charges applied to the parson from Bethlehem, who was famous for im-

precatory preaching, known as a friend to separates, slow to condemn Davenport, and implicated in the illegal licensure of Brainerd. Chauncy asserted that Edwards, Bellamy, and their followers had so elevated religious affections over legal convention that they had unleashed a carnal spirit in violation of every sentiment of decency and goodness.[8]

Fearing that the Awakening had gone too far, many of Bellamy's colleagues prompted him to moderate his revivalism. In 1742 Burr relayed to Bellamy Edwards's opinion that New Light extremists had given ammunition to the opponents of the Awakening. Burr furthermore urged Bellamy to distance himself from Davenport, whose preaching was not "well calculated to do good to mankind in general." According to Edwards, much of the disrespect with which evangelical Calvinism was held in New England could be traced to "the extravagant notions . . . strange practices" and "vice and immorality" that accompanied enthusiasm. Brainerd admitted to Bellamy that they both needed to take more caution in their preaching, lest they appear to condone censorious judgments of other ministers. The radicals' abandonment of the established churches and their threat to social order seemed increasingly to justify the liberals. Connecticut and Massachusetts magistrates, from this perspective, could hardly be blamed for censuring a movement that so destroyed incentives to reform and threatened law and authority.[9]

Bellamy concluded too that enthusiasts and antinomians threatened to disgrace the revival movement. He began to sever relations with them. Once friendly to Moravians whom he had encountered in New York and in Litchfield County, he disowned them in 1743, claiming that their antinomianism—their "talk as if a *law-work* was not very needful, but that all sinners have to do is *believe*"—had caused him to doubt their Christian profession. Later in the same month, he sat on a ministerial council that fined Davenport for book burning in New London and heard Edwards deliver a diatribe against disorderliness. Bellamy then sought Wheelock's advice in 1744 on the best means to withdraw support from New Haven and Wallingford separatists, to whom he had become an unwilling patron. Admitting to Brainerd that the "usefulness [of itineration] was clouded," he began to refuse invitations to visit parishes outside of those controlled by his closest associates. He even repudiated his previous method of preaching, convinced that it relied more on a manipulation of emotions than on divine instruction and so tended toward enthusiasm. It was misguided, even dangerous:

> Is it possible, that the Holy Ghost so regards me, as in connection with my words and voice, to bring up a crowded congregation to their feet, or prostrate them on the floor, with wailing or joy inexpressible? I have seemed able, at such moments of overwhelming excitement and agitation, to do any thing I pleased with an audience. . . . Can it be pleasing to Christ? . . . No, I fear not . . . it must be mere *animal* excitement, and not the work of the Holy One. . . . I will go out thus no more.[10]

Bellamy also lashed back at Croswell. In 1745 he complained to Samuel Finley about the misdeeds and the attacks of the "Eastern Exhorters" on the established ministry. Bellamy branded "the separatists" as "lurid" proponents of a "false religion," ready to swoop down on innocents such as his people in Bethlehem. Finley agreed with Bellamy that preachers such as Croswell, Davenport, and Allen represented "the declension of religion" and promulgated "horrendous principles" that were "Antinomian and Enthusiastic"; the radicals, who "pervert the Scripture," resembled no one so much as those sixteenth-century miscreants, "the unhappy Munsterian Anabaptists in Germany and the highflying Millenists at once." In his first publication, a short sermon entitled *Early Piety Recommended* (Boston, 1748), Bellamy charged antinomians with a host of socially deviant behaviors, including "debauchery and corruption . . . pride and vanity" and "lasciviousness."[11]

Old Lights and Arminians continued nonetheless to insist that evangelical Calvinists, for all their remonstrances, were responsible for New England's descent into cultural and social chaos. Indeed, the more Edwards and Bellamy defended themselves, the more antirevivalists left Croswell and his cohorts to their ecstasies and attacked moderate New Lights instead. After 1745, Old Lights such as Samuel Hall and Samuel Moody (1676–1747) intensified their protest against evangelical ecclesiology. At the same time, more liberal Congregationalist preachers—chiefly Chauncy, Jonathan Mayhew (1720–1766), Lemuel Briant (1722–1754), and Ebenezer Gay (1696–1786)—broached the fundamental propositions of Bellamy's and Edwards's theology. They proposed various alternatives to the Calvinist conceptions of divine rule, humankind, and society. Described by historians as liberals, social elites, rational supernaturalists, or American proponents of natural religion and Latitudinarianism, these critics of New Light Calvinism formed no distinct party or monolithic theology. Some, such as Mayhew and Gay, initially welcomed the revival, only to be repulsed by its excesses. Others found nothing of value in the Awakening. In common, they came to affirm Arminianism as informed by rationalist and humanocentric ethics.[12]

Liberals argued that genuine religion, unlike revivalism and its Calvinist underpinnings, upheld the dictates of reason and obligations to the corporate order. These were the standards of social responsibility as defined by the moral theories of the British Enlightenment. During the middle third of the eighteenth century the ascendant moral school was the Moral Sense, chiefly associated with Francis Hutcheson (1694–1746). A Presbyterian of deistic bent and holder of the chair of moral philosophy at the University of Glasgow, Hutcheson was immensely popular among British ethicists and their American counterparts. Colonial colleges in the 1750s used Hutcheson's texts; Chauncy, Mayhew, and Edwards referred to his theories. Bellamy owned several of his most influential books, drafted a lengthy discourse explicitly aimed at his ideas, and most frequently associated the theological position of the liberals with the ideas of the Scottish moralist.[13]

Methodologically, Hutcheson represented Enlightenment claims that morality should be established on a reasoned observation of human experience. The authority of ethics, so conceived, surpassed that once claimed by confessional orthodoxy. Substantively, Hutcheson argued that proper moral choices could be derived neither from abstract rationalizations of the intellect (Lockean ethics) nor from passions of self-interest (Hobbesean ethics). Drawing on the writings of Anthony Ashley Cooper, the third earl of Shaftesbury, Hutcheson grounded moral choices on an innate faculty for, or sense of, benevolence (thus Moral Sense ethics). Moral agents could sense pleasure when they acted in the interest of the greatest good for the most people and so judge benevolence the prime virtue; they could sense pain when they rejected the greatest good in favor of self and so judge self-interestedness the root vice.

Hutcheson's moral universe, then, embodied a law of reward and punishment: virtue yielded pleasure, vice yielded pain. British ethicists and their American counterparts disagreed over the extent to which this law in the end justified self-interest (since Hutcheson proposed pleasure as a motive for virtue). They nonetheless agreed with the Glasgow moralist that social benevolence, or regard for human happiness in aggregate, was the summum bonum; that people were innately capable of, even predisposed to, benevolent choice and behavior; and that the social welfare depended on the willingness of rational agents to conform to this virtue.

By such criteria, Arminians insisted, evangelical Calvinism was an ethical embarrassment. Chauncy, Mayhew, and Briant viewed themselves as heirs to Puritanism and protectors of New England's churches. They were not enemies to piety per se. They did conclude, however, that evangelical emphases on election by sovereign decree to either salvation or damnation and the passive reception of grace imputed a moral arbitrariness to divine action. This vilified the fundamental truth and appeal of Christianity—God's goodness—offended people of reason, and gave cause for the popularity of Anglicanism and religious skepticism. In his *Seven Sermons* (Boston, 1749), Mayhew complained that "those people [i.e., New Lights] who are offended with moral discourses, under the notion that they are not *evangelical*, are grossly ignorant of the spirit and design of Christianity." He exhorted people to think of God as a Moral Governor, who "with a steady, uniform principle of justice and goodness . . . governs the world with a view at promoting the moral rectitude, and so of advancing the happiness of his creatures." Arminians guarded New England's social order also against the evangelical assault on religious training and covenantal obligations. Those who spoke of moral depravity and rejected the public performance of good works—who, in effect, denied what Hutcheson described as an instinctual capability for virtue—encouraged moral apathy at best, vice at worst. The subordination of legal obedience to faith,

Chauncy argued, was "repugnant to all the conceptions we have of God" as "just and holy"; it encouraged people to assume that *"Virtue* was of no Account in the Eye of Heaven." In *The Absurdity and Blasphemy of Depretiating [sic] Moral Virtue* (Boston, 1749), Briant characterized Calvinist objections to the moral efforts of the unregenerate as a vain but dangerous mischief, "a groundless Recumbency."[14]

Arminians' accommodation to rationalist ethics and natural religion thus eventuated in an assault on what Mayhew called the "capricious, humoursome, and tyrannical" dogmas of Calvinism. Edwards warned his friends that Chauncy and Mayhew portrayed Reformed doctrine as an uncharitable bigotry; the God of irresistible grace and sovereign decrees seemed a tyrant in comparison with the predictable, reasonable, and benevolent Author of Nature's law. To Edwards's dismay, liberals asserted that Arminianism held more promise for the commonweal than did Calvinism, which they believed to "enervate all principles of morality, and in effect annul all differences between virtue and vice."[15]

Bellamy and Edwards advised each other on their responses to the outburst of Arminian tracts in the mid-1740s. Bellamy, for instance, sent to Northampton *A Vindication of God's Sovereign Free Grace* (Boston, 1746), a rebuttal by Jonathan Dickinson (1688–1747) to the Arminianism of Briant and of Experience Mayhew (1673–1758). Edwards encouraged Bellamy in 1747 to read seventeenth-century Reformed scholastics such as Peter van Mastricht and Francis Turretin for disputational purposes, informed him of the importance of the anti-Calvinist writings of the Englishman Daniel Whitby (1638–1726), and implored Bellamy to visit Northampton in order to discuss the current debates. Bellamy asked Edwards to help him answer some of the Arminians' most perplexing questions about the confrontation between grace and virtue. How was it not unreasonable "to blame" sinners for that which was "not voluntary?" Was it "not Inconsistent" for evangelical Calvinists to argue that only a regenerate heart or "good Temper" could truly "sense . . . divine Beauty" when they also argued that this "Temper" itself derived "from a sense of the divine Beauty"? Which, indeed, came first: love for, or knowledge of, God? When the American Samuel Johnson (1696–1772), an Anglican who combined George Berkeley's philosophical theories and Hutcheson's ethics, produced the first American textbook of moral philosophy and published it with a sermon that appeared more traditionally pious, Bellamy sent an edition to Edwards. Bellamy also wrote to Johnson, posing several problems in theological ethics. He wanted to know, for example, how Johnson possibly could reconcile the sermon, which posited a theocentric origin of moral obligations, with the moral text, which recommended human happiness as the source of moral duties.[16]

Bellamy was in no position, however, to arrive at quick solutions. In fact, he suffered a nearly debilitating confusion in the aftermath of the revivals. His confidence was so shaken that "sometimes," he confessed to

Brainerd, he was "ready to turn sceptic, atheist, deist, and every thing that is bad." Bellamy realized that Old Lights and liberals, even if dreadfully wrong to reject the doctrines of Calvinism, were right about the revival in this respect: it did not produce a godly society. It was bad enough that radicals pushed the Awakening beyond orthodoxy, threatened towns such as Bethlehem with disorder, and slandered moderates for not doing likewise. Now it appeared that in their haste to critique covenant legalism, moderates themselves failed to offer an alternative conception of moral and social obligation. Evangelical preaching thus ironically endangered Calvinism's public appeal. In this crisis of conscience, Bellamy was "almost ready to conclude that" he would "never more put pen to paper." His "ideas" were "gone or confused," and he thought himself "quite good for nothing."[17]

Bellamy had not lost his faith. He had begun to believe that evangelical Calvinism would flourish only if reshaped to rebuff antinomianism and answer Arminianism. This conviction motivated him to seek a connection between regeneration and moral virtue, the doctrines of Calvinism and duties to social order. In 1745 he had not yet located that connection. It was time, he wrote Wheelock, "to remain in my study" in Bethlehem in order to reconsider fundamental doctrines. "The delusions which I saw take place in New Light times," he recalled sometime in the 1760s, "have engaged me, as well [has] the divided state of the Christian world in general, to devote my whole time for above twenty years to enquire into the nature of Christianity. I have conversed with all men of genius" and "have read all the books I could come at."[18]

Bellamy did what most scholars do when they cannot write: read books. Those that he "came at" were the very ones used by liberals, delivered to him via Scotland, the home of the new British ethics. From 1747 to 1755 Bethlehem's minister was engaged in widespread and frequent correspondence, through which he gained access to treatises of the British Enlightenment and writings of European rationalists. He repeatedly requested information from Erskine about the latest philosophies and received in response both a running commentary on and books by Anglican apologists, rationalist critics of Calvinism, natural theologians, English dissenters, and deists—the common theme of which was the association between ethics and religious belief.

"As to the subjects you mentioned," Erskine wrote in 1753, "the following Books partly occur'd to me. . . . On the nature of and obligations to moral virtue . . . Hutchison on beauty and virtue," along with essays by Shaftesbury and rationalist opponents of the Moral Sense such as John Balguy. For "the nature of God's moral government" and "reward and punishment," Erskine counseled Bellamy to purchase several publications "on the origin of evil" and Joseph Butler's *The Analogy of Religion, Natural and Revealed* (London, 1736). He also gave references for a "reconciliation of the Calvinist scheme with moral government" and recommended Isaac Watts on original sin and the Trinity. Bellamy took advantage of Erskine's offer to provide books. From 1753 to 1755 Erskine sent to Bethlehem what amounted to a library of the preponderant British moralists, most of whom (such as Butler, Lord Kames, and Hume) were decidedly anti-Calvinist. Other works also suggested Bellamy's growing interest in ethical and legal theory and in the Enlightenment's attack on orthodoxy; in addition to several volumes by Hutcheson and numerous tracts and essays by obscure French and British disputants (on issues such as free will, depravity, and the Trinity), he also owned treatises by John Locke and George Berkeley, Samuel Clarke and Ralph Cudworth (rational moralists), Thomas Chubb and William Sherlock (Latitudinarians and protodeists), Daniel Whitby and Arthur Ashley Sykes (both Arians), and John Taylor (a critic of Calvinist doctrines of human nature).[19]

Bellamy gradually emerged from his study committed more firmly than ever to Calvinism. Indeed, he realized a new and more robust formulation of experimental religion. The first fruits of these discoveries comprised some of Bellamy's most notable publications: his systematic theology, *True Religion Delineated*, and two lengthy sermons, *The Great Evil of Sin, as it is Committed Against God* (Boston, 1753) and *The Law, Our School-master* (New Haven, 1756).[20] These treatises were to refurbish the public image of evangelical Calvinism—to show that it was superior to both Arminianism and antinomianism as doctrine and, moreover, as social authority. Edwards indicated in the preface to *True Religion Delineated* that the work originated with the author's "conversing freely and friendly with gentlemen in the Arminian scheme, having also had much acquaintance, and frequent and long conversation with many of the people called Separatists." Bellamy focused especially on the "gentlemen." Hutchesonian ethics, rationalist morality, and natural religion turn up at every corner of Bellamy's arguments, characterized as "Pelagianism, Arminianism and Neonomianism, an epicurean and atheistical temper, *the modern scheme of divinity*, and *public spirit*." The very title of Bellamy's major work marked it as a reaction to liberal religion; *True Religion Delineated* stood in contrast to William Wollaston's *The Religion of Nature Delineated* (London, 1725) and to what Bellamy, in reference to Hutcheson, parodied as "The Religion of (deprav'd) Nature Delineated." The full title page of *True Religion Delineated* reiterated Bellamy's purpose of establishing the rational integrity and religious fidelity of Calvinism. He offered the work as a defense of "Experimental Religion, as distinguished from Formality on the one hand, and Enthusiasm on the other."[21]

True Religion Delineated, The Evil of Sin, and *The Law* did not respond to Calvinism's critics with mere polemic. Bellamy's reading had taught him instead to utilize the moral discourse of Enlightenment ethics. He finally had found a grammar with which to unite doctrinal fidelity and ethical responsibility—without concession to Arminian notions of the covenant.

The rhetoric of law could be made to chasten radicals, disprove liberalism, and vindicate Calvinism.

His works from the 1750s, then, were remarkably different in tone and method from evangelical preaching, which depended chiefly on an affective rendition of biblical texts. First, he began with generic, philosophical definitions of religion that transcended particular religious experiences and subjective interpretations of the Bible. Second, he made, as he put it in *True Religion Delineated*, an "appeal to reason and common sense," an effort to show Calvinism to be "a scheme perfectly rational" as well as "divine." According to the regnant moral discourse, doctrine was subject to a test of moral verification, so Bellamy was compelled to demonstrate how Calvinism satisfied the canons of natural law—observable, uniform, and universal principles that, in Hutchesonian terms, upheld the virtue of benevolence. Bellamy assumed that by deducing evangelical doctrine from this moral law, he could meet the objections of his detractors without capitulating to Arminian soteriology and anthropology.[22] Third, he subsequently developed the doctrinal and practical emphases of his Calvinism in terms of moral and legal obligation. He thought that he could affirm the superiority of Calvinist theology without following the antinomian path away from social and moral obligations.

This apologetic method led Bellamy to a new theological paradigm. In the early revivals, he had focused on conversion, described in sensationalist language as a series of internal experiences, or affections, that ensued from the work of God in the soul. Now, he embraced the rubric of law. *True Religion Delineated* began with the declaration that "[r]eligion consists in a conformity to the *law* of God" as well as "in a compliance with the *gospel* of Christ." To "set many of the important doctrines of religion in a clear and easy, in a scriptural and rational light," he continued, it should "be clearly determined what the nature of the moral law is, and there will be a final end put to a hundred controversies." In *The Evil of Sin* and *The Law*, Bellamy reiterated his claim that "a right understanding of the law" would clarify all confusion about virtue and grace; by a proper appreciation for the law "every thing appears in a different light. The controversy is now at an end."[23]

Thus, while he maintained the evangelical insistence on conversion, Bellamy reoriented his theology around the interplay of divine rule and moral law—how God's conduct both conformed to the natural law and enforced its obligations. His major work included an extended commentary on this "first, and fundamental principle of all religion, natural, and revealed . . . that there is a God, an absolutely perfect" and morally "amiable BEING." Bellamy's burden was to elucidate this axiom in a way that rendered experimental Calvinism ethically compelling. He wished to show the likes of Mayhew a Calvinist God who was neither mysterious, capricious, nor tyrannical but intelligible in common moral discourse. We should allow that "virtue in God" was not "specifically different from virtue in man," Bellamy later advised one of his students, lest we come to the sad conclusion that "God's moral character cannot be ascertained."[24]

Moral amiability implied an objective standard for virtue, so Bellamy devoted the first ninety pages (over one fifth) of *True Religion Delineated* to foundational moral definitions. He argued that his opponents on the left (antinomians) and on the right (Arminians) had failed to locate anything close to the essence of moral goodness. In their theological voluntarism, he argued, antinomians defined goodness as God's will to save them. Believing that whatever challenged their claim to salvation was morally bad, they rejected moral and social obligations in favor of the subjective benefits of faith. On the other side, Arminians defined goodness as that which produced the happiness of God's creatures. This emphasis on human happiness, technically known as humanocentric eudaemonism, was just as subjective as antinomian voluntarism, and it equally confused moral reasoning. Antinomians and liberals alike denied the divine prerogative to judge and condemn people according to transcendent and objective principles of justice.

Regardless of their consequences for particular agents, moral laws, according to Bellamy, were infinitely and eternally binding. While even Edwards and Samuel Hopkins held "benevolence to being" as the definitive moral standard, Bellamy eschewed this formulation as a possible justification for eudaemonism. In contrast to such putatively subjective standards, Bellamy proposed "an intrinsic moral fitness and unfitness, absolutely in things in themselves." An action was virtuous, or good, right, and just, only to the extent that it "fit" the system of nature. Here Bellamy's analysis stopped short, or rather became tautological. He proposed that conformity to natural law defined such "fitness," but he could describe the content of that law only in moral terms—goodness, rightness, and justice —whose meanings were in dispute. The meaning of virtue, in sum, was conformity to the law of virtue.[25]

If not necessarily logical, Bellamy's subsequent argument about the relationship of moral goodness and the moral law to the nature of God was nonetheless uncanny. According to Bellamy, God was, as Creator, naturally perfect: independently existent, omnipotent, and omniscient. These ontological perfections implied moral deserts such as obedience and love from created agents. Bellamy's only demonstration of this inference was, again, that it appeared fit, as though creation gave God something akin to property rights. Natural law therefore dictated that God enforce his "proprietorship" over creation by legislating commands that prohibited disobedience and commanded obedience to himself. This, God had done. Revealed law (the Bible) commanded love for God, not out of any selfishness on God's part but out of an objective moral judgment. That law also displayed God's benevolence, since it demanded that people love one another. As a moral legislator, then, God was impartial, just, benevolent, and therefore good. His law duplicated natural law, so that "the law given at Mount Sinai, as to its moral precepts, was nothing more than a new and plainer edition and republication of the law of nature . . . equally binding to all nations in all ages." To further display his moral goodness, God was "infinitely engaged to maintain the rights of the Godhead" and "to secure all his subjects their own proper rights" by enforcement of the divine law in history. Evil people and societies were destroyed or threatened with punishment, while good people and divine societies (Israel and the church) prospered or were promised salvation. As if that were not enough, Bellamy continued, God revealed the divine goodness through his "work" (nature), "word" (human history as recounted in Scripture), and "Spirit" (in the human conscience). In sum, God was morally perfect four times over—as creator, legislator, judge, and revealer—and accordingly due unmitigated love and glory.[26]

Bellamy then doubled back to the authority of God's law. He maintained that revealed commands were as perfect as God. Since the law both came from and commended love for God, it was "holy, just and good," a reflection of "the infinite glory of the divine nature." In the argument just described, Bellamy assumed the divine authorship of the Bible in order to prove God's goodness. Here he assumed God's goodness in order to prove the divine authorship of the Bible. Even if Bellamy's circular logic proved neither assumption on its own merits, it did convey the central principle of his system: genuine religion originated with the conviction that the law was objectively and universally valid, whatever its effects. Individuals or collectivities could not claim to love God if they in any way doubted the justice of the law or wished to be excluded from its demands. All motivations except for reverence for God and his law were merely self-love, the subordination of transcendent moral values to subjective interests. "The great Governor of the world," Bellamy wrote, "made this law *not arbitrarily*, but because, in the nature of things, *justice called for it*. . . . For any, therefore, to desire to have it repealed, is to turn enemy to the holiness, and justice, and honour of the Supreme Ruler of the world, as well as to his law and government; and argues that they have no regard to the rectitude and fitness of things, but only to *self-interest*."[27]

Within this legal paradigm, Bellamy characterized regeneration (the effect of divine activity on the soul) as recovery from a damning self-love to a saving love for God and his law. In his description of the nature of that love, Bellamy returned to the affective rhetoric that reinforced evangelical Calvinism. Preachers were to teach the glories of the divine law and especially to lead the unregenerate to understand the doctrines of divine election and judgment, "the reasonableness of God's having mercy only on whom he will have mercy." He differed here, according to Allen Guelzo, from those Calvinists who held that sin had so damaged the understanding that the unregenerate could not grasp such truths. Bellamy believed that "the law set home upon the conscience" led naturally to a recognition of the glories of God's impartial justice. From this noetic "foundation" all people could realize that they were fallen and deserved condemnation. Sinners "must see wherein" they "have been to blame," Bellamy explained, before they could "see the law reasonable, fit and beautiful" and accordingly consent to it.[28]

After sinners were thus prone and helpless before a sentence they knew to be righteous, God could choose justly, out of his sovereign, free, and self-glorifying will, to capacitate them to embrace affectively the law, love its Author, and receive justification. In such consent to God's governance and legislation, the saint acquiesced "in all the high prerogatives God assumes to himself." This regeneration preceded conversion, the initial exercise of this new disposition as an individual began actively to obey God because of the dignity, excellence, holiness, or beauty of the divine character.[29]

Such sensationalist language did not deflect Bellamy from an insistence on the universal obligations of moral law. In contrast to Hopkins, whose uncompromising critique of Mayhew stressed the criminality of unregenerate doings, Bellamy argued that knowledge of and attempted obedience to religious and ethical duties enhanced the unregenerate's moral status. Where he had once rejected the usefulness of legal obedience, he now emphasized its value for each stage of salvation. The "Second Discourse" of *True Religion Delineated* thus countered antinomian claims to spiritual superiority with reference to the importance of moral obedience; the Bible revealed the "necessary duties of religion" to be individual and corporate acts of "repentance, love, and holiness." Efforts to "reform, read, watch, pray, run, fight, strive" constrained people to "less sin" than did moral passivity. They were social obligations and, Bellamy conceded to Old Lights, aids to conversion. "The precepts of the law," he clarified in a later sermon, were "in fact binding on Sinners as well as Saints, on the unregenerate as well as the regenerate."[30]

As Bellamy pressed this point against antinomians, he argued that true repentance was not a mercenary retreat from the threat of hell but a heartfelt recognition of the glory of the law and the evil of sin. Sinners repented out of shame and guilt, not out of fear. Even faith, which followed repentance, required an appreciation for, and thus was a fulfillment of, the law. It embodied the knowledge that in Christ God had satisfied the law's demands for retribution and had provided the legal basis for offering grace to those who, properly repentant, depended on Christ for salvation. As Bellamy put it, "faith" implied a sense of "the honour of the law," of oneself as "worthy only of destruction, according to law and justice," and "of Christ as a Mediator appointed to be a propitiation for sin, to declare God's righteousness and secure the divine honour, and so open a way wherein God might be just, and yet justify the sinner that believes in Jesus." In their subsequent conversion, believers consented to their moral obligations and began to exercise their regenerated dispositions in acts of moral goodness. According to Bellamy, the sum of such constant, daily "exercise of all

Christian graces" in "external conduct in the world" was sanctification. True assurance, Bellamy fired back at the radicals, was neither the subjective sense of being forgiven nor the experience of immediate revelation, but conformity to God's law in belief and action.[31]

For Bellamy, then, Calvinism provided the most effective incentives to moral reformation. Arminianism protested God's judgments, rejected the need for grace, disparaged divine law, and tempted sinners to delay repentance through merely preparatory means. Antinomianism taught an equally bad self-contentment. In contrast, the message of God's sovereignty, humanity's depravity, and the glories of law gave sinners a certain knowledge: they owed God an urgent, wholehearted, and active repentance. This teaching became known as consistent Calvinism because it yielded none of the doctrines of divine omnipotence to Arminian notions of human freedom. Bellamy claimed that Calvinism offered, rather than moral offense, the only remedy for spiritual and moral apathy—regeneration from hate to love of divine things. Thirty years after the publication of *True Religion Delineated*, one of his antagonists understandably lamented Bellamy's success in providing consistent Calvinists a claim that they preached "up law and duty, and the character of God, as King and Lawgiver."[32]

Bellamy's striking shift from otherworldly piety to the worldly demands of moral law was not merely a strategy for theological controversy but also a response to changes in the social context of his ministry. He had once been alienated from established powers and authorities. Now he settled into a position of prominence within local and colonial institutions, in which he gained a vested interest. Increasingly engaged in public affairs, he began to take responsibility for the shape of New England society. His law-based theology addressed a corporate need for social order.

What little we know of his external biography from the mid-1740s through the early 1760s suggests that Bellamy's new social concerns were in no small part domestic. In 1744 he married the pious and respectable Frances Sherman (1723–1785) of New Haven, with whom he had eight children: Lucy (b. 1745), Rebecca (b. 1747), David (b. 1750), Jonathan (b. 1752), Samuel (b. 1756), Elizabeth (b. 1759), William (b. 1770), and Joseph (b. 1773). Leaving off his itinerations and attending to domestic duties, he became known as an astute financial manager, which enabled him to build a conspicuously elegant house in 1754. Obligations to run home, farm, school, and church at once drove Bellamy to at least one quite personal application of the moral law: the maintainence of household order, or family governance. In *Early Piety Recommended* he observed that divine command offered "a most effectual method to make [children] obedient." A previous skeptic about religious "means," Bellamy now stressed training in piety "to the intent our child may be preserved from the ways of vanity and sin" and made more dutiful. Parents, from his scholarly perspective, were to warn children against disorderly frivolities such as parties and dances and "improve their minds" with "valuable books." When it came to keeping children at home—in the study or tending livestock rather than in social diversions—Bellamy clearly favored the message of moral obligation over gracious affections. He even suggested that the church "encourage and promote good family government."[33]

Bellamy's responsibilities had grown far beyond his household. The most celebrated minister in what was to become Litchfield County, he eventually controlled ecclesiastical affairs in the region. Beyond Bethlehem, his theological reputation, already established through his preaching, grew with the publication of *True Religion Delineated* and successive works and with an expanding correspondence. Despite the view of some historians, who have seen him as part of a reactionary Calvinism born of cultural and social isolation, Bellamy in fact developed his moral system as he was exposed to widespread intellectual currents and increasingly exercised power in religious and political institutions. He matured into leadership also over one small society (Bethlehem) within a larger commonwealth (New England) that now recognized him as a public figure. Indeed, since Bellamy now had much at stake in the moral circumstances of worldly institutions, from family and parish to the churches of Connecticut, he intended to recover the public voice of Calvinism and so assert its authority over those institutions. He accordingly refashioned evangelical Calvinism into popular moral idiom.[34]

Other Calvinists joined Bellamy. During the decade following the Awakening, he and Samuel Hopkins formed the younger two thirds of a triumvirate over which presided Jonathan Edwards, who produced two of his most remarkable essays in this period: *Freedom of the Will*, a philosophical defense of the Calvinist doctrine of human nature, and *The Nature of True Virtue*, an analysis of the relationship between common and theological virtues. Hopkins, like Bellamy, had gone to Yale, studied under Edwards, and settled in western New England. He began his ministry in 1743 in Housatonic (Great Barrington), Massachusetts. After prolonged financial hardships, extended quarrels with the townspeople, and dismissal in 1769, he moved to Newport, Rhode Island. Although he did not reach prominence until the 1770s, he was active in theological dispute during the 1750s. In conversation with leading intellectuals of Calvinist and liberal persuasion on both sides of the Atlantic, Hopkins also turned his interests toward theological ethics and apologetics.[35]

To advance evangelical piety within New England's religious and social order, Bellamy and Hopkins began to train a younger generation of ministers in the methods and doctrines of what they thought of as consistent Calvinism, their enemies impugned as New Divinity, and subsequent historians have labeled Edwardseanism. Bellamy was the more successful in gathering a cadre of aspiring Calvinists. An expert on moral philosophy, he received frequent requests for his opinion on the relation of Christian apologetics to rationalist ethics. Typical was a rural Massachusetts parson who thanked Bellamy for *True Religion Delineated*, which gave him a "reason" and "system," that is, a method for defending evangelical Calvinism. Bellamy advised Calvinists throughout New England about Hutcheson, Tillotson, and other proponents of natural religion. With the death of Edwards in 1758, he became the Calvinists' intellectual authority, to whom Hopkins frequently deferred in theological dispute. After hearing Bellamy preach in 1755, Hopkins declared that "there is not a better Preacher in America—on all Accounts." This was high praise from someone who had studied with Jonathan Edwards.[36]

Bellamy was also the first New England clergyman to institute a private school of theological instruction. It had been customary since New England's founding for college graduates to spend from three to twelve months with a licensed minister to prepare for ordination. During the revivals, evangelical students dissatisfied with Harvard and Yale particularly depended on further study with New Light pastors. Bellamy turned this sporadic practice into a system, initiating a "school of the prophets" that lasted until the establishment of collegiate theological faculties and seminaries in the nineteenth century. Between 1750 and 1780 he housed and trained more than sixty students, most of whom came to Bethlehem in the late 1750s and 1760s. Bellamy's institute produced many future leaders and teachers of New England's Calvinists: Gideon Hawley (1727–1807), later an assistant to Edwards in Stockbridge, Massachusetts; John Smalley, who later tutored dozens of ministerial students; Levi Hart (1738–1808), a popular preacher who married Bellamy's daughter Rebecca; Ammi Ruhamah Robbins (1740–1813), reputed "to have prepared more students for college than any other man" in post-Revolutionary Connecticut; Ephraim Judson (1737–1813); Jonathan Edwards, Jr., the namesake of Bellamy's teacher, a student also of Hopkins's and a celebrated divine in New Haven; and Samuel Spring (1746–1819), one of the founders of Andover Theological Seminary. Not all of Bellamy's students became ministers; Aaron Burr, Jr. (1756–1836), turned skeptic and became a lawyer, a New York politician, Thomas Jefferson's vice president, and an infamous dualist.[37]

Infidel or not, Bellamy's pupils received instruction in the importance of moral law for a proper understanding of theology. He exhorted them to expand their mental universe beyond interior experience: to "contemplate," more than "ourselves," the "natural world" and "the heavens," which directed them to "the Moral law" and, even higher, to "the most noble object" of inquiry, "God, the greatest being—the head of the moral system." Bellamy's students accordingly read, from his vast library, Hutcheson on ethics, Turnbull on natural religion, Hume on skepticism, and assorted apologetic works. They wrote essays on the nature of divine government, the moral law, and the ethics of civil government. They also practiced sermons on the rational foundations and moral implications of the Bible. Among several anecdotes from his nineteenth-century biographer, one, at least, illustrated Bellamy's insistence that evangelical students learn to preach a morally reasoned Calvinism. To an overly emotional novice Bellamy related his own repudiation of homiletical excess: "When I was young, I thought it was the *thunder* that killed people; but when I grew older and wiser, I found it was *lightning*. So I determined to do what I advise you to—thunder less and lighten more!"[38]

Bellamy meant to "lighten" the next generation of New England Calvinists particularly in the correspondence between natural, moral, and biblical law. In 1756 he suggested to Hopkins that they compose a curricular outline for young divinity students. This proposed "Philosophems," which the two discussed for several years but never published, amounted to little more than a fragmentary series of questions. Yet if Bellamy's notes reveal his teaching method, then he followed perfectly the apologetic agenda that he set out in *True Religion Delineated*. The first subject, "Natural Religion," included proofs for God's existence, the "moral character" of God, "the foundation of moral obligation," the nature of moral agency, and moral reward and punishment. The second, "On Revealed Religion," surveyed the authority of God's law, the veracity of the Scriptures, the work of Christ, regeneration, and sanctification. The third subject, "Of a Christian Church," concerned ecclesiastical issues such as the covenant and constitution of churches, membership and sacramental qualifications, and the authority of creeds.[39]

Hopkins and Bellamy led this new party of consistent Calvinists, but it was Bellamy who took command of the campaign for social and ecclesiastical power in the 1750s. Ousted from Northampton in 1750, Edwards labored in the obscurity of an Indian mission at Stockbridge, on the Massachusetts frontier, until shortly before his death in 1758. Hopkins suffered from an unsuccessful, even unpopular ministry. Meanwhile, Bellamy directed a resurgence of Calvinism in Connecticut's institutions.[40]

It was not surprising that Bellamy should find success in Connecticut, since other evangelicals had achieved at least temporary political power there. After 1749 "New Light" became somewhat of a political label for those who favored not only the ecclesiastical aims of Calvinists but also the economic interests of new traders and farmers. Opposed to the conservative fiscal policies and predominantly Old Light sympathies of the upper house of the colonial legislature and of the governorship, New Lights gained the majority in the lower house, succeeded in reinstating several New Light justices whom Old Lights had ousted, blocked many of the proposals of Governors Roger Wolcott (in office 1750–1754) and Thomas Fitch (in office 1754–1766), and had enough power in 1755 to win the support of Yale's president, Thomas Clap (1703–1767). Once persona non grata in New Haven, Bellamy returned in 1749, at Clap's invitation, to address Yale's undergraduates.[41]

Bellamy did not agree with many of the economic aims of political New

Lights, but he certainly endorsed their attempts to force Calvinist ortho-doxy on the ministry. In 1749 Wheelock advised Bellamy that the time was ripe for Connecticut Calvinists to seize power. Churches were in dis-array. Antinomian intrusions into the ministry brought their "usual moral concomitants," a "distemper" of "growing *Immorality*, justified by" their "*wildness* and *errors*." Yale produced mostly Arminians, "unfit" ministerial candidates. To Wheelock, "the want of a good *Discipline*" suggested that Calvinists should form a "presbytery" to oversee the ministry. Bellamy needed nothing so controversial. He could use the existing consociational structure, in which he was a leading player in the 1750s and 1760s. The Saybrook Platform had not clarified the relative powers of magistrates, consociations (or associations), and congregations. It mandated that the magistracy establish orthodox Calvinist churches by civil law and support them by taxation. It instituted clerical associations to discipline (and, of necessity, define) heterodoxy. Yet it also embodied the principle of con-gregational autonomy, the right of each church to judge its pastor. It lodged ecclesiastical authority variously with the state, the consociation, and the congregation and so threw open the door to dispute.[42]

Once hostile to a hierarchical reading of the Platform, Bellamy now favored governmental and consociational intervention in local affairs. The creation of Litchfield County in 1751 gave him, the most powerful mem-ber of the newly established Litchfield Consociation, opportunity to wield these institutions against his opponents. Fifteen churches constituted the Consociation in 1751; by 1769 eight more had joined. Its first meeting took place in Bellamy's church, where he immediately threatened to bring charges of civil disobedience against uncooperative congregations. Elected to several ecclesiastical councils, a frequent moderator over disciplinary courts in Litchfield County and elsewhere in the colony, and delegate to the clergy's General Association, Bellamy used his authority particularly to discipline Arminian congregations and pastors. His "slaying and turning out Ministers in Litchfield County," Old Light Ezra Stiles complained, resulted in the ouster of at least ten ministers (many of whom were Stiles's protégés). In one of his most publicized decisions, Bellamy voted in favor of the Gen-eral Association's 1759 ruling that the New Haven Consociation (largely New Light at that time) had properly vetoed the Southern Hartford Consociation's ordination of James Dana (1735–1812), a quasi-Arminian, to the pastorate in Wallingford. Regarded by friend and foe alike as politically influential, Bellamy gained undisputed control over clerical politics in western Connecti-cut. Old Lights took to calling him "the Pope of Litchfield County" and "our Sovereign Lord Bellamy."[43]

In this highly politicized context, Bellamy expanded his use of "law" beyond theology and ethics to notions of civil prerogative. The more he campaigned for the public authority of orthodoxy, the more his rhetoric mirrored legal conceptions of right, that is, consent to public contract, civil statute, and juridical procedure. While the implications of a legal hermeneutic for transatlantic and national politics became apparent in the late 1760s and 1770s, its effect on Bellamy's work in the 1750s and early 1760s concerned the political status of orthodoxy in Connecticut—specifically, the rights of Calvinists to impose creedal standards on Congregational pastors.

Bellamy's first publication on this subject came in support of Yale's President Clap, who had stirred debate with proposals that the General Assembly raise more taxes for the college and require a confession of orthodoxy from its professors. Liberals claimed that such a provision would force them to pay taxes for an institution that excluded them, a violation of their consciences. Clap responded with *The Religious Constitution of Colleges* (New London, 1754), a legal defense of confessional requirements. Civil statutes from the time of James I to a 1753 Connecticut act, Clap argued, defined the purpose of state-supported colleges as education of an "Orthodox Ministry." It might have irked liberals to pay for an orthodox Yale, but it was a civic duty nonetheless. The state did not violate "Liberty of Conscience" by the enforcement of creeds; people still had the freedom to participate in or withdraw from a Calvinist order as taught at the college and practiced in the churches.[44]

Bellamy endorsed these juridical arguments and provided some of his own. In response to protests against Clap, Bellamy wrote a short essay for the *Connecticut Gazette* in which he maintained that "particular Christian communities" had "a right" to establish confessional standards, which summarized "the true sense of Scripture." Denial of that right presented churches with two unpalatable options: accept the doctrines of anyone, from Socinian to antinomian, who could cite a Bible verse, or "go back to the pope to be set right." The debate turned vicious when the Old Light William Hart replied that creeds could not account for new and better interpretations of the Bible and merely masked the authoritarianism of Bellamy and others who "love to be distinguished as heads of powerful parties." Bellamy then brought out a legal argument strengthened by equally acerbic rhetoric. Out of "their own consciences," he claimed, people established New England's churches on confessional principles that remained in effect. The government rightly protected these voluntary organizations. Since Yale trained pastors for those churches, the state ought to ensure that the college adhered to the creed. By law, Calvinism had its political prerogatives.[45]

It was furthermore, Bellamy continued, a deception, almost a crime, for all but Calvinists to minister to Connecticut's standing churches. Those churches, he reasoned, were established on the Saybrook Platform, which embodied the Reformed Savoy Confession. A case in point was the recent affair in Wallingford. Its congregation, Bellamy indicated, was "formed a Calvinistic church. The *doctrines of faith* which they drew up, to be used in the admission of members, were strictly Calvinistic." Its history and charter, then, constitutionally obligated its ministers to Calvinism. Yet Dana was "bold to settle" there, "although opposed as a heretic by near half the town." This "young gentleman" proposed lax admission requirements, "suited to the *latitudinarian* scheme" and "subversive of the very foundations on which all our churches in New England were originally settled." If anyone hid behind masks, it was Arminians such as Dana. "So that it is plain," Bellamy wrote, "that all the great zeal, loud out-cries, and hot disputes over creeds and confessions" arose from a "misunderstanding" of Connecticut's legal history or from the dishonesty of liberals who wanted positions in what ought to have been Calvinist churches and so came "to hate and want to get rid of the established creed of their country." Which, Bellamy asked William Hart, was the present case? "Do you hate Calvinism? Do you dispute against creeds, because you disbelieve our confession of faith?" Even if Hart were a sincere Calvinist, which Bellamy doubted, he still had to admit that Arminians, Arians, and Socinians were "*pious frauds*" who had taken many pulpits in New England. Bellamy, who had previously deemphasized the role of institutional duties, now demanded that the churches erect a "PUBLIC STANDARD OF ORTHODOXY" for the common good, institute stricter, more visible requirements for communion, and corporately discipline individuals' misbehavior.[46]

Old Lights had their own version of law with which to resist the Calvinist ascendancy. They proposed that the chief end of civil government was the promotion of temporal prosperity and social concord. The commonweal depended on enforcement of corporate virtue. As Connecticut Old Lights such as Samuel Hall, Nathanael Hunn (1707–1749), Jonathan Todd (1713–1791), and Ebenezer Devotion argued in their election sermons from 1746 to 1753, magistrates ought to support Protestant Christianity because it was a superior form of natural religion, that is, morality, that provided motives for obedience to the laws of nature and society, laws that patently were *not* contained in the Savoy Confession or in any other Calvinist creed.

According to Hall, Hunn, and Devotion, Calvinists such as Bellamy fought jealously for their doctrines while they neglected the most important public function of Christianity—the inculcation of virtue. Indeed, Bellamy taught that the unregenerate could not even aspire to virtue. This did not make good citizens out of non-Calvinists. In contrast to such pernicious doctrines, Old Lights and Arminians recommended the volitional performance of social virtues such as benevolence. However unfair to Bellamy and Hopkins, who never denied the civil benefits of common morality, these arguments gained some credence in Hartford and elsewhere. Even Noah Hobart (1706–1773), a New Light in political causes, urged Connecticut's clergy to adopt a version of Christianity that appealed to common moral sentiments and thus included unbelievers: "Explain and enforce Relative Duties, or the virtues which are peculiarly necessary and conducive to Social Happiness. Religion never appears in a more amiable Light than when it disposes men to a ready and cheerful Performance of relative and social Duties." The Old Light message was clear. Magistrates ought not interfere with dogmatic quarrels, which were schismatic, or defend specific doctrines—particularly those of Bellamy and his co-religionists.[47]

By the mid-1750s, many liberals had grown impatient with Old Light attempts to bury Arminianism in the rhetoric of civic duty and religious precedence. In some quarters, Bellamy's opponents denied the very premise of his position, that Calvinism defined orthodoxy. Hints and vague protests soon yielded to thorough and explicit critiques of fundamental Calvinist doctrines. Using scriptural exegesis and ethical logic, many self-proclaimed Arminians confidently asserted the ideals of natural and rational religion as the only proper form of Christianity. Mayhew's *Sermons on the Following Subjects* (Boston, 1755) took an optimistic view of human nature, a Pelagian position on soteriology, and an Arian stance on the Trinity, all in an effort to present Christianity as consonant with the most reasonable standards of benevolence and justice. In *Two Sermons on the Nature, Extent, and Perfection of the Divine Goodness* (Boston, 1763), Mayhew affirmed that God would eventually resolve all moral actions into universal salvation, a doctrine so radical that Chauncy, who had written similar speculations by 1760, did not publish his own version of it until 1784.[48]

Bellamy thought that Chauncy and Mayhew simply had unveiled the logical end of Arminianism. Objections to the Calvinist doctrines of God's sovereignty and humanity's sinfulness, he warned in *True Religion Delineated*, derived from a distaste for God's law and implied a denial of Christ's divinity. Arminians defined moral qualities by the moral axiom of Hutcheson's eudaemonism, which, according to Bellamy, "estimated the measure of criminality" in any vice only by its effect on other people. In so limited a sense, no sin was "an infinite evil or deserved infinite Punishment." Therefore, Bellamy reasoned, liberals saw no "need for an atonement of infinite value and so no need of a Savior of infinite dignity." Without total depravity and the necessity of vindictive justice, there was no requirement for a mediatorial sacrifice; the incarnation was both inexplicable and unnecessary. As Bellamy complained to Chauncy, "an incarnate God dying on the Cross" was to Arminians "an incredible story."[49]

Events in New England in the late 1750s confirmed Bellamy's long-held suspicion that Arminian theological ethics led to Arianism and Socinianism. He derided the members of a New Hampshire congregation who, "to adjust" their confession of faith to Calvinism's critics, omitted the Trinity, original sin, election by grace, the atonement, and saintly perseverance. They foolishly came "from New-Hampshire along to Boston" and there fell under the spell of Mayhew, "a celebrated D.D." who "boldly ridicules the doctrine of the trinity, and denies the doctrine of *justification by faith alone*." In his 1758 essay *The Divinity of Christ*, Bellamy observed "that those among professed christians, who have denied the divinity of Christ, have been wont generally also to deny our natural depravity" and "the necessity of any proper satisfaction for sin. . . . To be a little more consistent with themselves, they ought to deny the inspiration of the *Old* and *New Testaments.*" There appeared to Bellamy no alternative to strict Calvinism but sheer unbelief.[50]

Bethlehem's folk, if Bellamy had his way, would wander neither into the streets of Boston's unbelief nor into the wilderness of antinomianism. In 1754 he led his church to adopt its first formal confession of faith, the public terms for admission to the sacraments. Saints in Bethlehem assented "particularly" to the very doctrines in dispute: the Trinity, original sin ("out of which state" man "cannot recover himself"), the "Mediation" of Christ and his "Sacrifice of atonement," the "everlasting Punishment" of all the unregenerate, and the utmost necessity of "the special influences of divine grace" for conversion. As no Dana could hide in Bellamy's church, so too no Croswell. The confession quite pointedly affirmed "that altho' we are Justified by faith and saved by Grace, yet the Law as a rule of life remains in full force to believers: So that perfect Holiness of heart and life is their Duty, nor does the Gospel of free grace in any Sort Countenance or Encourage them to live in the least degree of Sin." In the covenantal oath that attended this confession, people vouched themselves above all else to the "performance of Christian duties." To enforce its rhetoric, the church developed strict disciplinary policies. Rarely mentioned before 1745, censures against members who violated the Sabbath, contravened the civil authority, frolicked in public, or otherwise scandalized the community filled the pages of Bethlehem's church records from 1745 to 1760.[51]

Since Bethlehem was to display Calvinism's power to shape the public order, its pastor shifted the focus of his preaching from the joys of escape into the realm of the spirit to the social demands of the law. Richard Bushman has suggested that evangelical religion was so focused on the private aspirations of individuals that it deflected New Lights from loyalty to community and authority. Bellamy's version of Calvinism did not imply this sort of individualism. He rejected the covenant communalism of Puritan tradition, but his application of the moral law advanced the sense of Bethlehem, the public community or gemeinschaft, as the outlet and context for Christian virtue. In a 1754 sermon, for instance, he argued that a congregation resembled the heavenly Church to the extent that earthly "discipline" was "carefully maintained according to the rule of law, with all love and tenderness, for edification" of the individual *and* the community. His preaching fused imprecations on self-serving sinners, encouragements to evangelical humiliation, careful expositions of the moral and biblical law, and Moral Sense appeals to benevolence. Hutcheson and his Arminian admirers may have been wrong about God, Christ, sin, and salvation, but they were right to stress love to neighbor as a moral good and rule by which societies prospered or withered. During the 1750s and 1760s Bellamy pleaded fervently and frequently for corporate acts of benevolence—to "end all division, contention" and "vice" for the love of church, town, and country.[52]

However eclectic his exhortations, Bellamy's homiletical method recapitulated his systematic. He introduced his sermons with reference to the nature and wisdom of the divine government. He then discussed the primacy of law for understanding religion and ethical obligations, the moral perfection of God, and imitation of divine benevolence. His closing application addressed specific moral duties. This heightened sense of communal activism, of the importance of admonishing every member of society to do and act in behalf of the corporate welfare, led Bellamy to warn his people not simply to flee to Christ for consolation but to imitate Christ's moral goodness "in our daily conduct." Christ was more than Redeemer; he was an "example" of "the obligation we are under to imitate" God's "law" and "to persevere in duties."[53]

To instruct the community in moral law, Bellamy also instituted what some commentators have described as one of New England's first systematized Sabbath schools. He led children through catechetical exercises and Bible verses on Sundays and weekdays. He also organized classes for adults, who gathered at his house in between Sunday services to discuss the Bible and the creeds. More remarkably, he often called church meetings to debate questions that he prepared on current theological and ecclesiastical controversies such as the authority of creeds and covenants, requirements for membership, the relation between moral benevolence and church discipline, the nature of heresy, and grounds for excommunication. Bellamy also opened his personal library to the townspeople. In a dedicatory sermon he articulated "motives to study" and "directions to a profitable reading" in this "town library." It may be difficult to imagine how rural parishioners warmed to such exercises, but some of them had enough enthusiasm to purchase their pastor's publications. Other Calvinist ministers, at least, regarded Bellamy as a popular teacher and successful disciplinarian. Clap asked him to tutor, or rusticate, a few particularly rebellious undergraduates until they came to their senses. In 1756 and 1757 Edwards sent some of Stockbridge's more unruly Indian boys to Bethlehem, where Bellamy tried to teach them arithmetic, writing, and the Bible. (Bellamy's letters to Edwards about the Indian boys indicate that he had little success and explain why he thought the better part of valor was to return them and raise money in support of Indian missions instead.)[54]

With all his efforts to assert the public, moral implications of evangelical theology, Bellamy was galled when Old Lights regained control of Yale and once again campaigned to discredit consistent Calvinism. Moreover, in the 1760s they implicated the Edwardseans in the rise of a new and virulent strain of antinomianism. Croswell and other extreme New Lights had entered the controversies of this period with appeals to English opponents of Latitudinarianism and Wesleyanism, particularly James Hervey

(1714–1758) and William Cudworth (1717–1763), who were known for their extreme solifidianism.

In *Theron and Aspasio* (London, 1755), Hervey gave popular expression to the idea that genuine faith was a subjective persuasion, an inner assurance, of forgiveness. Claiming to be a Calvinist, he argued that the doctrine of the imputation of Christ's righteousness signified the utter worthlessness of any human acts prior to justifying belief—including repentance, moral reformation, and prayer—and of any external evidences for conversion. Sinners, Hervey insisted, were to trust that they had been made literally righteous apart from "works" such as humiliation or repentance. Since true faith grasped the beneficent posture of God in Christ toward the self, any attention to divine, vindictive justice was unwarranted and malicious; individuals could not trust a deity who threatened to destroy their happiness. Hervey even denigrated calls to love and honor God, asserting that they demand the impossible, which "diminishes our Comfort" and "subjects Us to that Fear, which hath Torment."[55]

Theron and Aspasio, frequently reprinted along with the work of an earlier Nonconformist of similar views, Walter Marshall (1628–1680), provoked a heated and extended debate in New England on the nature of faith and assurance. Bellamy thought the opinions of Hervey and Marshall painfully reminiscent of the radicalism of the 1740s. They were particularly dangerous since they approximated a Calvinist view of regeneration while they denied the crucial tenet upon which Bellamy had defended Calvinism—the moral law. Once again, he faced assaults on two fronts: from Arminians who attacked his doctrine of regeneration as antinomian and from antinomians who assailed his use of law as Arminian.

Bellamy responded with *Theron, Paulinas, and Aspasio, or, Letters and Dialogues upon the Nature of Love to God, Faith in Christ, Assurance of Title to Eternal Life* (Boston, 1759). He distinguished his views (represented by Paulinas) from those of the Arminians (Theron) and the antinomians (Aspasio). In a stinging polemic against Hervey, Bellamy maintained that Aspasio, as much as Theron, deprecated moral law in favor of a narrow, subjective concern for human happiness. Both denied the law's mandate of divine retribution and thereby implied amoral universalism: by assuming that human virtue could merit felicity (Theron), and by refusing to acknowledge the repentance and humiliation required by law (Aspasio). The antinomians' succinct creed—"the thing I believe, was not true before I believed it"—conveyed their conviction that an individual should presume to be pardoned at an instant of faith. Bellamy ridiculed this formula as naive self-justification; it removed all foundation for a reasoned self-examination according to external standards of righteousness. Visible acts of sanctification were the only reliable means of testing an individual's spiritual state. Mindful of the recent excesses of preachers such as Davenport, Bellamy warned that reliance on the immediate witness of the Spirit for self-assurance inevitably led to the horrors of enthusiasm. "My dear

Theron," Paulinas asked, "how will you know whether your immediate revelation comes from God, or from the devil? . . . Will you know without any respect to the fruits? But how? Leave holiness out of the account, and what is there of this kind, but what the devil can do?" Indeed, the devil already had done too much. Those tempted to deny the moral law should "go to the Anabaptists in Germany, in Luther's time; go to the enthusiasts in England, in Cromwell's time, and see what the devil has done in former ages. Yea, I could name towns and persons in New-England, where and in whom satan's mighty works have been to be seen, within less than twenty years ago." The Scriptures, Bellamy concluded, revealed the salvation of no particular person; they provided universal and legal criteria for justification. To reduce those standards to an inner persuasion deluded people into thinking that the law and divine election were either inapplicable or tyrannical.[56]

Theron, Paulinas, and Aspasio entangled Bellamy in further polemics. Hervey countered with a 1762 letter to the *New York Gazette or Weekly Post-Boy*, while two of his English supporters, William Cudworth and David Wilson, attacked Bellamy in essays circulated widely in New England. Cudworth's *A Defence of Mr. Hervey's Dialogues against Mr. Bellamy's Theron, Paulinas, and Aspasio* (Boston, 1762) described Bellamy's vindictive God as an ungracious tyrant in whom no one could trust. Bellamy would do better to urge faith in God's love rather than repentance out of a fear of divine punishment. In *An Essay on the Nature and Glory of the Gospel* (Boston, 1762), Bellamy insisted that Hervey's and Cudworth's protests amounted to little more than the same carnal selfishness promoted by rational humanitarianism. Denial of God's right to condemn people, who were sinners, implied that "we are not so much to blame as [the] law supposes." If that were the case, then God's law was a lie, its Author the criminal, and "repentance, restitution, and reformation" all vicious. "Arminians and Pelagians are professed enemies to the law" and "so," Bellamy drove home his point, "are Antinomians." In both cases, "a self-justifying is a God-condemning disposition."[57]

Wilson's *Palaemon's Creed Revised and Examined* (Boston, 1762), another statement of the antinomian doctrine of assurance, appeared in short order. Somewhat weary of the debate but dutiful to his role as spokesman for Calvinists, Bellamy retaliated with a sardonic tract, *A Blow at the Root of the Refined Antinomianism of the Present Age* (Boston, 1763). He was more reasonable, if nonetheless polemical, when Croswell entered the fray. The American antinomian charged that Bellamy and Alexander Cumming (1726–1763) had brought people to despair by maintaining the popish doctrine that repentance preceded faith. Bellamy's *Remarks on the Revd. Mr. Croswell's Letter to the Rev. Mr. Cumming* (Boston, 1763) continued his moral defense of Calvinism. "Faith [is] *a holy Act*," he maintained; it necessitated active repentance, since without repentance there was no consent to the moral and legal requirements of justification.[58]

In the midst of this controversy, which occupied much of his correspondence from 1759 to 1763, Bellamy went to great lengths to explain how consistent Calvinism differed from both Arminianism and antinomianism. Ezra Stiles and several professors at Yale resented his equation of Arminian with antinomian ethics. Provoked enough by his intransigence on the issues of total depravity and divine sovereignty, they returned the compliment: Bellamy was the true antinomian. Forced to exonerate himself, Bellamy explained that he thoroughly objected to Hervey's disregard for moral activity. He protested to Old Light critics that he never intended to assert that repentance was unnecessary but only to affirm the doctrine that legal repentance was legally (i.e., "in order of nature") distinct from the granting of grace. Bellamy exhibited his orthodox credentials by referring to Croswell's antagonism towards him. "*All Calvinists understand*" repentance "*as I do,*" to wit "Mr. Croswell has printed against me for holding that *repentance is implied in faith, and is before forgiveness.*" Bellamy's "controversy" was "not with" orthodox Calvinists "but with the Antinomians." To those who asked him his opinion of the antinomian view he repeatedly affirmed the doctrine that repentance and humiliation preceded justifying faith. In 1763 he warned Lambert De Ronde, a recently settled Huguenot minister in New York, that Hervey and Marshall, distressingly popular in America, were as antinomian as the Moravians. Bellamy advised De Ronde that the only true means to assurance were "lively fruits shining forth in holiness and obedience" and an apprehension of "God's moral excellencies."[59]

Bellamy's castigations of Hervey and Croswell reflected his determination to assert Calvinism's moral and social integrity. The theological and social climate had radically altered since the early 1740s, when he had disparaged legalism and institutional loyalty. Bellamy found himself in a position not unlike that of John Calvin, who two centuries earlier, as William Bouwsma tells us, struggled to find a way between the labyrinth of nomianism and the abyss of antinomianism.[60] During the late 1740s and 1750s, Bellamy thought that he had found the way. It was marked by a moral discourse that allowed him to articulate a consistent Calvinism and distinguish it from both Arminianism and antinomianism.

If Bellamy was overconfident, as some contemporaries maintained, then he feared the labryinth not nearly enough. In his penchant for social order, Bellamy produced a system that lost something of the theocentric focus—and with it the vibrancy—of Edwards's piety. Because law could not unite all the doctrines of Calvinism, Bellamy's logic sometimes failed; he never fully or successfully accomodated a sovereign God and redeemer Christ to the moral law.[61] Such was the judgment of Robert Riccaultoun, an evangelical-Calvinist contemporary of Bellamy's from Scotland. Riccaultoun warned Erskine (rather ironically, given Erskine's advice to Bellamy) that "modern philosphical divines," with their concepts of "the nature of things" and "moral sense," had so captivated Bellamy that he founded *True Religion Delineated* on "a sort of idea of God and his essential . . . moral perfections" rather than on God's revelation of "himself in Christ." Even Hopkins began to wonder if his colleague might not attend a bit more to the inadequacy of human reason, a bit less to the reasonableness of divine doctrine. Hopkins perhaps came to perceive some of the inherent incompatabilities between Calvinism and eighteenth-century moral discourse.[62]

In Bellamy's heyday, however, the promise of a socially engaged Calvinism overshadowed these contradictions. Bellamy and other New Divinity adherents believed that evangelical Calvinism could conform to common moral assumptions and still retain its integrity. He did not jettison his evangelical commitments to the individual experience of grace and the necessity of divine regeneration. Bellamy intended to disprove the critics of Calvinism and so extend evangelical piety into public and institutional affairs. By organizing his theology around the concept of law, he claimed, in effect, that Calvinism rationally, morally, and politically superseded other forms of doctrines. This claim drew quite near to people's concerns. More than ministerial techniques—witty sermons, Sabbath schools, and his general amiability—the message accounted for Bellamy's popularity. It was, as he might have put it, "fit" for Bethlehem's settlers as they secured a social order, for students who sought an intellectually pursuasive evangelicalism, and for colleagues who valued morally sound doctrine as a counter to religious subjectivism.

It was one thing, however, to construct creeds, theologies, and tracts: quite another to demonstrate how the specific doctrines of Calvinism effected a virtuous and happy commonwealth. If Bellamy were to link theology to practice, then he had to address the mundane temptations and struggles of New Englanders. That task required him to bring the speech of Calvinism to bear more directly on his people's communal affairs—their economic aspirations and their fear of powers much more daunting than antinomianism or liberalism. To understand the appeal of Bellamy's Calvinism, we should know how his ideas about sin and salvation were embedded in social realities.

Notes

1. Each of the titles in this imaginary account appear either in Bellamy's correspondence or in his will, filed in Connecticut Probate Records, Woodbury District, Connecticut State Library, Hartford, Connecticut. As the following letters from Erskine to Bellamy show, Erskine sent such books to Bellamy through agents in New York and through Kneeland in Boston, and they most likely came to

Bethlehem through Litchfield: Mar. 2, 1754, HS 81212; Mar. 24, 1755, HS 81234; June 8, 1759, PHS; and Aug. 8, 1760, PHS. Kneeland published Bellamy's works and supplied him with various books; see Kneeland to Bellamy, Aug. 28, 1758, HS 81252. Stapfer was published orginally in Zurich (1743–1747); Hume in London (1751); Shaftesbury in London (1711); Hutcheson in Glasgow (1755); Ames in Amsterdam (1634); Willard in Boston (1726); Brainerd in Boston (1749); and Edwards in Boston (1746). Of the several editions of Watts's *Hymns and Spiritual Songs* published in New England, the first to appear during Bellamy's ministry was in Boston (1742).

2. North and South Consociations of Litchfield County, Connecticut, *Proceedings in Convention at Litchfield, July 7 and 8, 1852* (Hartford, 1852), 86.

3. Some historians assert that Bellamy and Hopkins vitiated genuine Calvinism by complying with the moralistic demands of what was known as natural religion. Their argument, which concentrates on the differences between the hyper-Calvinism that arose after the death of Edwards and the evangelical piety of Edwards's earlier theology, tends to neglect Bellamy's earlier commitment to the Awakening. See especially Haroutunian, *Piety Versus Moralism*, 14–71, and Charles Joseph Constantin, Jr., "The New Divinity Men" (Ph.D. diss., University of California at Berkeley, 1972).

4. Scholars who characterize the New Divinity as a polemic against rationalist religion or as a critique of the individualism of liberal society so emphasize contrasts between Calvinists and their opponents during the final third of the eighteenth century that they underestimate the importance of Bellamy's apologetic shift—his appropriation of rational moral discourse. In their interpretation, Hopkins, the most outspoken and intransigent critic of liberalism, appears as the typical post-Awakening Calvinist. See Foster, *Genetic History*, 106–61, and Conforti, *Samuel Hopkins*, 109–24, which analyzes the social reformism and stringent moral standards of Hopkins's activities. Richard D. Birdsall views the New Divinity as an eighteenth-century version of Neo-Orthodoxy, a theology of radical transcendence in opposition to liberal optimism; see Birdsall, "Ezra Stiles versus the New Divinity Men," *American Quarterly* 17 (Summer 1965): 248–58. My view comes closer to that of William Breitenbach, who understands the New Divinity in the context of its struggle against Arminians and antinomians; see Breitenbach, "Consistent Calvinism," and "Piety *and* Moralism: Edwards and the New Divinity" in Hatch and Stout, eds., *Jonathan Edwards*, 177–204.

5. Leigh Eric Schmidt, "'A Second and Glorious Reformation': The New Light Extremism of Andrew Croswell," *WMQ* 43 (1986): 214–44, quotation from 222. On enthusiasm and separatism, see Bushman, *From Puritan to Yankee*, 205–8; Goen, *Revivalism and Separatism*, 8–90; and William G. McLoughlin, *New England Dissent, 1630–1833: The Baptists and the Separation of Church and State*, 2 vols. (Cambridge, Mass., 1971), I:329–59. Throughout this chapter, "enthusiasm" and "antinomianism" will refer to positions that Bellamy and other Calvinists labeled as such. Self-respecting eighteenth-century theologians, of course, did not identify themselves as enthusiasts or antinomians, since the terms were pejorative.

6. Croswell, *Boston Weekly Post-Boy*, April 12, 1742, quoted in Schmidt, "'Second and Glorious Reformation,'" 222. Croswell's most noted work was *What Is Christ to Me if He is Not Mine?* (Boston, 1745); the best commentary on Croswell is Schmidt's. Brief descriptions of antinomianism are in Goen, *Revivalism and Separatism*, 46–48, and in Heimert and Miller, "Introduction," li. A full discussion of

the origins of antinomianism in New England is William K. B. Stoever, *"A Faire and Easie Way to Heaven": Covenant Theology and Antinomianism in Early Massachusetts* (Middletown, Conn., 1978). Bellamy's ideas on faith and repentance are discussed below in this chapter.

7. See Edwards, *Some Thoughts Concerning the Present Revival* (Boston, 1742), in *The Great Awakening*, ed. Goen, 414–95.

8. See Stiles, *A Prospect of the City of Jerusalem In Its Spiritual Building* (New London, Conn., 1742), 4, 22–23, 26, 48–49; and Chauncy, *Seasonable Thoughts on the State of Religion in New England* (Boston, 1743), 33, 68, 96–109, 171–72, 322. For more explicit charges of New Light immorality, see Windham Churches, *The Result of a Council of Churches of the County of Windham* (Boston, 1747), 11–13, 17. Some critics charged revivalists with outright fraud. Whitefield and Croswell, for example, were accused of bilking people with spurious charitable schemes; see, for example, *Boston Evening Post*, Sept. 30, 1742.

9. Burr to Bellamy, Jan. 13 and June 28, 1742, PHS; Edwards, "An Humble Attempt," in *Apocalyptic Writings*, ed. Stein, 357–58; Brainerd to Bellamy, Feb. 14 and Mar. 26, 1743, PHS. On the opposition of Connecticut magistrates to the Awakening, see Chauncy, *Seasonable Thoughts*, 294–97; Zeichner, *Connecticut's Years of Controversy*, 24; McLoughlin, *New England Dissent*, I:335, n.5; Goen, *Revivalism and Separatism*, 59–62; and Bushman, *From Puritan to Yankee*, 193–95, 200–204.

10. Bellamy to Brainerd, Mar. 3 and 7, 1743, PHS; Bellamy to Wheelock, Feb. 4, 1744, cited in Anderson, 352; Bellamy, unaddressed letter, c. 1744, quoted in Tryon Edwards, "Memoir," lxiii. For Bellamy's attendance and vote at Davenport's trial, see Goen, *Revivalism and Separatism*, 70. Under Count Zinzendorf's direction, Moravian missionaries worked among the Pomeraug Indians in Woodbury in 1742 and 1743; see Benjamin Trumbull, *A Complete History of Connecticut, Civil and Ecclesiastical*, 2 vols. (New London, Conn., 1898), II:58–59.

11. Bellamy to Brainerd, Mar. 7, 1743; Finley to Bellamy, Sept. 20, 1745, PHS; Bellamy, Personal Account; Bellamy, *Early Piety Recommended* (Boston, 1748), in *Works*, III:478–79. Edwards's shift from a preoccupation with Arminianism to a fear of enthusiasm, his attempts to moderate between these extremes, and subsequent New Divinity efforts against antinomianism are lucidly discussed in Breitenbach, "Piety *and* Moralism." For further illustrations of Edwards's fear of radicalism, see Goen, "Editor's Introduction" to Edwards, *The Great Awakening*, 56–89, and William Costello Spohn, "Religion and Morality in the Thought of Jonathan Edwards" (Ph.D. diss., University of Chicago, 1978), 43–53.

12. See Heimert, *Religion and the American Mind*, 42–53; Miller, *Jonathan Edwards*, 256–61, 269–70; Norman Fiering, "The First American Enlightenment: Tillotson, Leverett, and Philosophical Anglicanism," *New England Quarterly* 54 (1981): 307–44; May, *The Enlightenment*, 42–149; Herbert M. Morais, *Deism in Eighteenth Century America* (New York, 1934), 54–84; H. Sheldon Smith, *Changing Conceptions of Original Sin* (New York, 1955), 1–59; Conrad Wright, *The Beginnings of Unitarianism in America* (Boston, 1955), 9–222; David Harlan, *The Clergy and the Great Awakening in New England* (Ann Arbor, Mich., 1980), 49–96; Edward M. Griffin, *Old Brick: Charles Chauncy of Boston, 1705–1787* (Minneapolis, Minn., 1980); Charles W. Akers, *Called Unto Liberty: A Life of Jonathan Mayhew, 1720–1766* (Cambridge, Mass., 1964); and Robert J. Wilson, *The Benevolent Deity: Ebenezer Gay and the Rise of Rational Religion in New England, 1696–1787* (Philadelphia, 1984).

13. For the importance of moral philosophy, see Norman Fiering, "President

Samuel Johnson and the Circle of Knowledge," *WMQ* 28 (1971): 199–236, and *Jonathan Edwards's Moral Thought, passim.* Bellamy's most thorough discussion of Hutcheson is his unpublished manuscript, "The Religion of (deprav'd) Nature Delineated," HS 81480. On Hutcheson, see David Daiches Raphael, *The Moral Sense* (London, 1947). For extended commentary on Hutcheson's currency in America, see Garry Wills, *Inventing America: Jefferson's Declaration of Independence* (Garden City, N.Y., 1978), 149–255; Caroline Robbins, "'When It Is That Colonies May Turn Independent': An Analysis of the Ethics and Politics of Frances Hutcheson (1694-1746)," *WMQ* 11 (1954): 214–51; and Wright, *Unitarianism,* 144–45.

14. Mayhew, *Seven Sermons upon the Following Subjects* (Boston, 1749), 109, 159 (see also 38–39); Chauncy, *Seasonable Thoughts,* 282–83 (see also 274–78); and Briant, *The Absurdity,* quoted in May, *The Enlightenment,* 56. See also Chauncy's *Cornelius' Character* (Boston, 1745), which associated true religion with moral education.

15. Mayhew, *Seven Sermons,* 106; Edwards, "An Humble Attempt," in *Apocalyptic Writings,* ed. Stein, 359.

16. The following letters from Edwards to Bellamy: Jan. 15, 1747, in Williams, "Six Letters," 228–32; Jan. 9, 1749, HS 81175; and Jan. 15, 1750, quoted in *Jonathan Edwards: Representative Selections, with Introduction, Bibliography, and Notes,* ed. Clarence A. Faust and Thomas H. Johnson (New York, 1935), 390; Bellamy to Johnson, Apr. 7, 1747, PHS. Edwards's answers to Bellamy ("yes," sinners were still culpable; "no," it was not inconsistent) became treatises: Edwards, *A Careful and Strict Inquiry into Freedom of the Will* (Boston, 1754), published as *Freedom of the Will,* Vol. 1 of *The Works of Jonathan Edwards,* ed. Paul Ramsey (New Haven, Conn., 1957), in which Edwards explicitly argued that Calvinism could sustain a more virtuous moral life than could Arminian theological ethics (see 304); and *Two Dissertations, I. Concerning the End for Which God Created the World. II. The Nature of True Virtue* (Boston, 1765 [posth.]). Johnson's publications were *Ethices Elementa. Or the First Principles of Moral Philosophy* [under the pseudonym of Aristocles] (Boston, 1746) and *A Sermon Concerning the Obligations We are under to Love and Delight in the Public Worship of God* (Boston, 1746).

17. Bellamy to Brainerd, Mar. 7, 1743, PHS.

18. Bellamy to Wheelock, ca. 1745, quoted in Tryon Edwards, "Memoir," xiii, n.; Bellamy to Noah Hobart, n. d., PHS.

19. The following from Erskine to Bellamy: Jan. 26, 1753, HS 81199; Mar. 2, 1754, HS 81212; and Mar. 24, 1755, HS 81234. Bellamy also acquired works by standard Puritan divines and Reformed thinkers such as Calvin and van Mastricht. His books are listed in his probate records at the Connecticut Historical Society; for further identification of their authors, see Gambrell, "Ministerial Training," 108–11; and Anderson, 375–86. Edwards too was busy collecting and commenting on authors such as Locke, Shaftesbury, Clarke, and Hutcheson; see Jonathan Edwards, "Catalogue of Books," Jonathan Edwards Papers, Beinecke Library, Yale University, New Haven, Connecticut. For a splendid discussion of the extensive importation of British and European books to America, see Edwin Wolf II, *The Book Culture of a Colonial American City: Philadelphia Books, Bookmen, and Booksellers* (New York, 1988).

20. *The Great Evil of Sin* will be cited as *The Evil of Sin* with page references to *Works,* Vol. III. *The Law, Our School-master* will be cited as *The Law,* with page references to *Works,* Vol. III.

21. Edwards, "Preface," in Bellamy, *TRD*, 45; Bellamy, *TRD*, 241; *The Law*, 54; and *The Evil of Sin*, 499. For examples of explicit references to enthusiasm and antinomianism, see *TRD*, 250, and *The Law*, 63–69. In *The Law*, 35, Bellamy provided brief descriptions of the views of Hutcheson, Turnbull, Taylor, and Tindal. In *Edwards on the Will*, 1–59, Guelzo demonstrates how this Calvinist agenda played out in the technicalities of one dogmatic issue: the nature of human volition. According to Guelzo, Edwards sought a middle way between the amorality of Hobbesean determinism (a secular version of antinomianism) and Arminianism.

22. Bellamy, *TRD*, 50–51. Bellamy's apology, then, rarely broached epistemological or aesthetic issues, the chief concerns of apologists during the late eighteenth and nineteenth centuries. The clearest evidence of Bellamy's method is his "Religion of (deprav'd) Nature Delineated," in which he commented on Hutcheson point by point—in agreement with many of the philosopher's moral premises and in disagreement with most of his theological conclusions. Edwards adopted a similiarly apologetic method in this period. In *Jonathan Edwards's Moral Thought*, 9, Fiering thus contends that Shaftesbury and Hutcheson forced Edwards to "construct a new philosophical anthropology that would meet naturalism on its own grounds."

23. Bellamy, *TRD*, 52, 254–56; *The Law*, 72.

24. Bellamy, *Essay on the Nature and Glory of the Gospel* (Boston, 1762), in *Works*, II:337 (hereafter cited as *Essay*, with page references to this volume); Bellamy to Punderson Austin, Apr. 6, 1766, in Tryon Edwards, "Memoir," xxix. See *TRD*, 54–67.

25. Bellamy, *TRD*, 78–79, 83. Bellamy's attitude toward Edwards's position is best illustrated in a letter to Hopkins in which he intimated that he could not distinguish between "the Moral Taste of Mr. Edwards" and that of the deist Turnbull: Bellamy to Hopkins, Dec. 22, 1755, HSP. In his arguments on behalf of an "objective" ethical standard, Bellamy followed the method of Hutcheson's *An Inquiry into the Original of our Ideas of Beauty and Virtue* (4th ed., London, 1738), 105–31, even if he thought that Hutcheson's chosen standard—the social welfare—fell far short of true objectivity. In his later writings, Bellamy did refer to "love to being in general" as "the sum of all virtue," but he qualified its meaning. Such love was virtuous only if directed primarily to God and "in due proportion" to people, and if willing to approve of God's "excommunication" of unrepentant sinners. See Bellamy, unaddressed letter, Oct. 20, 1764, in Tryon Edwards, "Memoir," xxix.

26. Bellamy, *The Law*, 29; *TRD*, 82; see 69–97. In his *Two Dissertations*, Edwards also argued that God's moral goodness was evident in the fact that God honored himself in all that he did.

27. Bellamy, *TRD*, 121; see 116–27.

28. Bellamy, *TRD*, 227; *The Law*, 58; see *TRD*, 54–67, 226–29. Guelzo, *Edwards on the Will*, 102–11.

29. Bellamy, *TRD*, 59; see 69–97. Like most Reformed thinkers, Bellamy understood repentance, faith, and conversion as logically sequential yet, sometimes, temporally concurrent actions of the soul undergoing regeneration. For similar ideas in Edwards's theology, see Fiering, *Jonathan Edwards's Moral Thought*, 47–82, 105–49. Hopkins followed the same line of analysis in his *Inquiry into the Promises of the Gospel* (Boston, 1765), 74–81.

30. Bellamy, *TRD*, 226; John 8:48, ca. 1760, HS 81465.

31. Bellamy, *TRD*, 437; *Theron, Paulinus, and Aspasio, or, Letters and Dialogues upon the Nature of Love to God* (Boston, 1759), in *Works*, II:275 (hereafter cited as *TPA*, with page references to this volume). For extended discussions of these points, see *TRD*, 431–61; *The Law*, 58–60; *Essay*, 438–85; and *TPA*, 293–303.

32. Holly, *Old Divinity*, 62.

33. Bellamy, *Early Piety Recommended*, in *Works*, III:468–69, 486. Bellamy's correspondence from the 1750s and 1760s contains frequent reference to his financial affairs; his domestic relations are documented in Anderson, 140–69.

34. In *Nathaniel William Taylor*, 97, Mead caricatured Calvinists as culturally isolated cranks who "had an irritating [and impractical] tendency born of long hours of quiet meditation to spin out a point until the fine line of reasoning became all but invisible." Conforti, *Samuel Hopkins*, 41–58, 125–41, gives a nuanced analysis of the social position of New Divinity ministers, an uncareful reading of which might seem to reinforce Mead's position. In "The American Revolution Considered as an Intellectual Movement," in *Paths of American Thought*, eds. Morton White and Arthur M. Schlesinger, Jr. (Boston, 1963), 11–33, Edmund S. Morgan misleadingly describes the New Divinity as composed almost solely of unpopular, isolated, introspective, and speculative metaphysicians. Although Bellamy gained a reputation for censoriousness (at least among the likes of Ezra Stiles), he was rarely seen by his contemporaries as either isolated or aloof. More likely, his enemies lamented his popularity; to describe his theology as metaphysical and aloof is to misunderstand how contemporaries heard it. See Stiles, *Literary Diary*, III:419.

35. Hopkins's first major publication was *Sin, thro' Divine Interposition, an Advantage to the Universe* (Boston, 1759). His reputation was not solidified until the appearance of his *An Inquiry into the Nature of True Holiness* (Newport, R.I., 1773) and his systematic theology, *The System of Doctrines Contained in Divine Revelation*, 3 vols. (Boston, 1793). Hopkins's early career is examined in Conforti, *Samuel Hopkins*, 41–121.

36. Nehemiah Greenman to Bellamy, Jan. 16, 1751, CHS; Hopkins, manuscript diary, Aug. 28, 1755, Samuel Hopkins Papers, Trask Memorial Library, Andover-Newton Theological School, South Andover, Massachusetts (this library hereafter cited as ANTS). For Bellamy as a philosophical authority, see Samuel Davies to Bellamy, May 15, 1750, PHS, and James Davenport to Bellamy, May 29, 1753, HS 81201. For Bellamy's advice on rationalist writers, see his letter to Graham et al., Oct. 1, 1761, PHS, in which Bellamy warned a group of New England pastors against assisting in the Presbyterian ordination of a candidate in Albany who had expressed admiration for Tillotson despite Bellamy's efforts to convince him of "the inconsistency of the Hutchesonian scheme with the truth of divine revelation." Other examples abound from Bellamy's correspondence from these years. Hopkins's letters to Bellamy during the 1750s, e.g., Oct. 8, 1758, HS 81268, exhibit Hopkins's eagerness to let Bellamy speak publicly for the Calvinists.

37. See Anderson, 356–450, for information on Bellamy's school and students. The statement about Robbins's teaching comes from Adele Green, "Norfolk, and that Neighborhood," *The Connecticut Quarterly* 1 (1895): 109–22, 115, quoted in Anderson, 432.

38. Bellamy, Prov. 24: 13–14, May 1, 1749, YS; Tryon Edwards, "Memoir," lviii. Evidence of Bellamy's teaching method is contained in several letters and in

the diaries of his students. Illustrative is Levi Hart, Diary, HSP, which includes 1760–1761 notes on "The Ends of God's Moral Government" and mentions, among other books prescribed by Bellamy, those of Shaftesbury, Hutcheson, and Hume. Hart's dependence on Bellamy's theology, including a duplication of Bellamy's apologetics, is also evident in his "Papers on Religious and Other Subjects," 1763, Levi Hart Papers, Connecticut Historical Society, Hartford, written a year after Hart left Bethlehem.

39. Bellamy, Questions in Theology, appended to Stephen West's 1774 syllabus of questions for theological students and catalogued under Bellamy's name in the American Antiquarian Society, Worcester, Mass. For Hopkins's and Bellamy's correspondence concerning these "Philosophems," see Anderson, 651.

40. For Edwards's circumstances in Stockbridge, see Ola Elizabeth Winslow, *Jonathan Edwards: 1703–1758* (New York, 1940), 268–312. Excerpts from Hopkins's journal in Edwards A. Park, "Memoir," in Samuel Hopkins, *The Works of Samuel Hopkins, D.D.*, 3 vols. (Boston, 1854), I:33–39, exhibit his troubles in Housatonic.

41. For overviews of New Light politics, see Bushman, *From Puritan to Yankee*, 211–18, 229, 236–66; Louis Leonard Tucker, *Puritan Protagonist: President Thomas Clap of Yale College* (Chapel Hill, N.C., 1962), 175–231; and Zeichner, *Connecticut's Years of Controversy*, 29–35. Bellamy's sermon at Yale was his Prov. 24:13–14, May 1, 1749, YS.

42. Wheelock to Bellamy, Jan. 9, 1749, PHS.

43. Stiles, *Literary Diary*, III:419, 464; John Devotion to Ezra Stiles, Dec. 4, 1766, in Stiles, *Extracts*, 460. One anxious correspondent pleaded for Bellamy's support in the midst of such a controversy, illustrating Bellamy's power: Philemon Robbins to Bellamy, Feb. 8, 1757, PHS. Governor Fitch also admitted Bellamy's popular influence in a letter to Bellamy, Feb. 1, 1762, CHS. Anderson, 511–49, 567–68, and 580–81, cites numerous letters concerning Bellamy's involvement in clerical politics. Membership in the Litchfield Consociation is described in North and South Consociations of Litchfield County, *Proceedings*, 11.

44. Thomas Clap, *The Religious Constitution of Colleges, Especially of Yale College in New Haven* (New London, Conn., 1754), 9, 15. A helpful discussion of legal rhetoric, ecclesiastical factions, and political discourse during the late eighteenth century, which informs my analysis, is Christopher Grasso, "Between Awakenings: Learned Men and the Transformation of Public Discourse in Connecticut, 1740–1800" (Ph.D. diss., Yale University, 1992).

45. Bellamy, *A Letter to Scripturista . . . Wherein the Nature of a Test of Orthodoxy is Exactly Stated* (New Haven, Conn., 1760), printed in *Works* III:371, 379, 382 (hereafter cited as *Scripturista*, with page references to this volume). Bellamy's piece originally appeared under the pseudonym Paulinus, in the *Connecticut Gazette*, Feb. 11, 1758; William Hart (under the pseudonym Scripturista), *A Letter to Paulinas* (New Haven, Conn., 1760), 26. Bellamy wrote the 1758 newspaper piece in response to a feisty tract by Benjamin Gale, a liberal physician from Killingworth: [Gale], *The Present State of the Colony of Connecticut Considered* (n. p., 1755).

46. Bellamy, *Scripturista*, 377–78, 381, 387–90.

47. Hobart, *Civil Government the Foundation of Social Happiness* (New London, Conn., 1751), 46–47. For similar arguments, see the following election sermons: Samuel Hall, *The Legislature's Right, Charge, and Duty in Respect to Religion* (New London, Conn., 1746); Nathanael Hunn, *The Welfare of a Government Considered* (New London, Conn., 1747); Jonathan Todd, *Civil Rulers the Ministers of God, for*

Good to Men (New London, Conn., 1749); and Ebenezer Devotion, *The Civil Ruler, a Dignified Servant of the Lord* (New Haven, Conn., 1753).

48. Wright, *Unitarianism*, 91–114; Smith, *Original Sin*, 13–59; Clyde A. Holbrook, "Original Sin and the Enlightenment," in *The Heritage of Christian Thought: Essays in Honor of Robert Lowry Calhoun*, ed. Robert E. Cushman and Egil Grislis (New York, 1965), 142–65; May, *The Enlightenment*, 51–59; Holbrook, "Editor's Introduction" to *Original Sin*, Vol. 3 of *The Works of Jonathan Edwards* (New Haven, Conn., 1970), 1–26, 67–85; and Griffin, *Old Brick*, 111–12, 172–75.

49. Bellamy to Chauncy, ca. 1760, cited in Wright, *Unitarianism*, 200; Bellamy, "The Religion of (deprav'd) Nature Delineated." See *TRD*, 294–320.

50. Bellamy, *Scripturista*, 387; *The Divinity of Jesus Christ* [published as part of *Sermons Upon the Following Subjects*] (Boston, 1758), printed separately in *Works*, I:488 (hereafter cited as *Divinity of Christ*, with page references to this volume). Hopkins, among many others, urged Bellamy to refute Mayhew and Chauncy; see the numerous letters cited in Anderson, 758–64. On Arminian Arianism, see Wright, *Unitarianism*, 201–09, and Akers, *Jonathan Mayhew*, 115–22.

51. Bethlehem Congregational Church, Bethlehem, Connecticut, "A Confession of Faith" and "A Covenant," HS 81668; also in Church Records, 57–59. Records of disciplinary cases are contained in Bethlehem's Church Records, *passim*.

52. Bellamy, Eph. 5:25–27, Apr. 14, 1754, CHS. Other sermons on discipline include Bellamy's Matt. 13:23, Oct. 17, 1754, CHS, and Eph. 6:10, May 12, 1754, CHS. The English dissenter Philip Doddridge (1701–1751), whose posthumous *A Course of Lectures on the Principal Subjects in Pneumatology, Ethics, and Divinity* (London, 1763) was well liked among New England Calvinists, provided one model for the moral and theological eclecticism of Bellamy's preaching. Doddridge quoted Hutcheson, Tillotson, Clark, Shaftesbury, et al. at length, yet excerpted them to substantiate evangelical themes. He laid moral-philosophical, biblical, and confessional quotations side by side. The contrast between my perspective here and Bushman's in *Puritan to Yankee* is further illustrated in Chapter Three.

53. Bellamy, 1 Pet. 2:21, Mar. 25, 1769, CHS. Some of the many illustrations of Bellamy's method are his sermons on Matt. 22: 36–40, July 8, 1764, CHS; Matt. 11:20, Mar. 5, 1768, CHS; John 8:48, ca. 1760, HS 81465; Acts 2:37, Oct. 29, 1764, CHS; and John 3:18, Dec. 13, 1767, CHS. Chapter 3 discusses in detail other sermons that addressed social problems in the 1750s.

54. Bellamy, John 5:39, Jan. 26, 1757, YS. One list of questions that Bellamy brought before his parishioners is in Church Records, 61–62. WPR indicates that townsmen Hezekiah Hooker and Daniel Everitt owned several of Bellamy's publications. Anderson, 226–32, 641–46, documents Bellamy's sabbath school, work with the Indians, and rustication of Yale students.

55. James Hervey, *Theron and Aspasio*, 3 vols. (London, 1755), III:365–66. Croswell's fondness for Hervey is exhibited in his letter to Hervey, June 7, 1758, Croswell Letterbook, Massachusetts Historical Society, Boston.

56. Bellamy, *TPA*, 235, 294–95; see 205, 230–337, 311–21.

57. Bellamy, *Essay*, 375. Hervey's letter to the public was printed along with advertisements for his *Theron and Aspasio* and his biography; see *New York Gazette or Weekly Post-Boy*, Jan. 14, 1762.

58. Bellamy, *Remarks on Croswell*, 25. Croswell's essay was entitled *A Letter to the Reverend Alexander Cumming* (Boston, 1762).

59. Bellamy to Jedidiah Mills, May 24, 1759, PHS; Bellamy to Cumming, May 15, 1763, PHS; Stiles, *Literary Diary*, I:278–80; Punderson Austin to Bellamy, Feb. 25, 1763, HS 81294; Finley to Bellamy, Oct. 1761, PHS; Bellamy, letters to several objectors, Feb. 15, 1763, quoted in Tryon Edwards, "Memoir," xxv; Bellamy to Pitkin, Mar. 27, 1763, HS 81601; and De Ronde to Bellamy, Oct. 1763, PHS. See also Anderson, 677–79, 682–84, 781–805.

60. William J. Bouwsma, *John Calvin: A Sixteenth-Century Portrait* (New York, 1988).

61. I refer here not only to the logical flaws outlined earlier in this chapter but also to Bellamy's legalistic rendition of the doctrines of Original Sin (see Chapter Three) and Providence (see Chapter Four).

62. To this extent, Haroutunian was right: Bellamy veered into legalism. Haroutunian was mistaken, however, to describe this movement without reference to the social and cultural context of Bellamy's innovations. This context helps to explain (as Haroutunian did not) Bellamy's popularity and his claim to have defended rather than abrogated central Calvinist tenets. Haroutunian also fails to elucidate how differences among New Divinity men belied a single, sustained decline into rationalist moralism. Bellamy took an apologetic approach based on law; Hopkins produced a dogmatic defense of Calvinism: Hopkins, *System of Doctrine*, esp. the "First Part." For Hopkins's objection to Bellamy's use of a rationalist discourse of virtue, see Park, "Memoir," 50–51; Conforti, *Samuel Hopkins*, 62–75; and McLoughlin, *New England Dissent*, II:735. The letter quoted is Riccaultoun to Erskine, n. d., in Richard Webster, *A History of the Presbyterian Church in America, from its Origin until the Year 1760* (Philadelphia, 1857), 630.

3

Original Sin

In the spring of 1758 Bellamy traveled to Boston to hear Thomas Frink (1705–1777) deliver the annual election day sermon for Massachusetts. Bellamy had been to New England's largest town and most active port before, and he knew of its reputation as a commercial center rife with riches and commodities, poverty and indebtedness. Accustomed to life in a small village, Bethlehem's pastor must have viewed the culture of the city and its market economy as twin vexations. Less than a week after Frink gave a millenarian depiction of the war between England and France, Bellamy preached at a Boston church on different concerns. He spoke of the need to give alms to the poor. Pursuit of profits, he argued, diverted Bostonians from their duties to an increasing number of "poor people that need our help." He called for charity and, more tellingly, for "a new benevolent principle" of "disinterested benevolence" that rightly "ordered our loves" and produced "an inward free propensity to do good, prompting us . . . where there is no desert—yea, where there is ill desert." Only this change of heart, he insisted, would motivate people to sacrifice their interest in money for the good of the poor. He thought that New England was beset not only by the French but also by depraved self-love.[1]

In the fall Bellamy returned to Boston to visit his publisher. A delay in the printing of his *A Letter to the Reverend Author of the Winter-Evening Conversation on Original Sin* (Boston, 1758) frustrated Bellamy, since he wanted the work to appear in time for Yale's commencement that autumn. Boston publishers were profiting from a furious "paper war" over the doctrine of original sin; they brought out eight treatises on the subject in seven months. Samuel Webster's *A Winter Evening's Conversation Upon the Doctrine of Original Sin* (New Haven, 1757), which declared the dogma unscriptural and perverse, provoked much of the argument. One Old Light, Peter Clark (1694–1768), attempted to salvage the doctrine by jettisoning one of its most distressing corollaries, the damnation of infants. The Arminian Charles Chauncy declared that Clark had given up the ghost of Calvinism and called on him to admit that the whole system was an obnoxious compilation of irrational and dark dogmas. Into this fray entered New England's troika of hard-line Calvinists: Bellamy, Hopkins, and Edwards. Edwards's last treatise, taken by Calvinists as a magisterial utterance, was *The Great Christian Doctrine of Original Sin Defended* (Boston, 1758). Determined to be heard as well, Bellamy told the publisher Samuel Kneeland to advertise *A Letter to the Reverend Author* prominently in Boston and New York newspapers.[2]

It was no mere coincidence that Bellamy preached about poverty and generosity during the same period that he attacked Webster. According to his law-based theology, the moral law demanded almsgiving and condemned the self-interestedness of sinners bent on pursuing wealth to the detriment of neighborly love. Likewise, the prevalence of self-love proved at least one tenet of Calvinism: the depravity of human nature. Since depraved, people required evangelical conversion. Bellamy concluded that New England needed both virtue and grace, social reformation and spiritual regeneration, the urgent call to self-sacrifice and the message of original sin.

This convergence of doctrine and practice further pushed Bellamy's theology into the realm of public issues. He joined commentators on both sides of the Atlantic for whom the language of moral philosophy linked fundamental ideas about God and human nature to questions of polity and rules for common life. Thus united to social issues, theological argument implied differences in cultural ideals, and by mid-century public discourse focused on what Alan MacFarlane has described as the emergent culture of capitalism.[3] Contrasting theories of human nature revealed profound disagreements about the growth of commerce and its chief premise: the autonomous pursuit of wealth in an open market. Bellamy wrote of self-denial and the subjugation of self-interest when proponents of the market lauded self-interest as the proper means to prosperity. The debate about original sin was furious because it referred to that most mundane of matters—the economy.

Puritans had long reproved greed, covetousness, and contention, but such admonitions took on new meaning in the context of the transformation of the Anglo-American economy in the eighteenth century. During that period new cultural sensibilities and material conditions coalesced in the emergence of mercantile capitalism. In the social theory of classical republicanism, a land-based economy protected the commonweal. Private citizens pursued wealth by enhancing the productivity and protecting the value of the nation's lands. Britain's financial revolution, as described by P. G. M. Dickson, allowed modes of economic activity that defied republican ideals. The creation of a national debt and the growth of banking nurtured a new economic type, the entrepreneur who used credit to speculate in annuities, stocks, or other promissory notes. The market determined the worth of these notes, and did so capriciously. The new entrepreneur borrowed heavily and risked misfortune to invest not in the public trust, land, but in private notes that had no intrinsic or absolute value. It appeared to many that the new money economy would destroy the commonweal. It enriched investors and stock jobbers who made money and flaunted their luxuries but produced nothing. It wasted wealth on consumption and speculation, reducing the capital available for investment in land. Rather than encourage the virtue of public spiritedness, the market nurtured the vice of self-interested, private ambition. According to pamphleteers such as Erasmus Jones (d. 1740), the market threatened the very worth of the nation, casting Britain's fortunes—along with its economic values—into the unpredictable waters of credit, speculation, and fluctuating prices. English opponents of the new economy heaped pejorative upon complaint, describing economic man as voluptuous, selfish, indolent, avaricious, and fraudulent and the market as a bane to England.[4]

Nothing in New England matched the specter of the stock market in London, but Bellamy and his colleagues did encounter economic forces that marked New England's transition, in the formulation of Allan Kulikoff, from yeoman society to agrarian capitalism.[5] Throughout the 1730s and 1740s Connecticut and Massachusetts experienced unprecedented growth and prosperity, much of which depended on trade. Signs of this turn to commerce appeared most clearly in Boston. The only New England port to deal directly with Europe, it developed a genuine mercantile elite. Connecticut had no city to compete with Boston, but its urban centers—New Haven, New London, Hartford, and Norwich—had a large class of merchants and artisans who, supported by the government in Hartford, dealt with Boston, New York, and other American ports. Secondary market towns on the Connecticut River and the Long Island Sound, or inland trading centers such as Litchfield, funneled goods between the frontier and the urban centers. Agriculture still predominated in New England, but even remote country towns traded. By the time people from Woodbury founded Bethlehem, most of New England's prime farmland had been settled. As population pressure forced newer farmers onto rocky and hilly terrain, they turned to cash crops marketed through a growing network of roads and commercial contacts. In turn, farmers patronized local entrepreneurs who provided a small stock of manufactured goods such as farm tools, furniture and cloth, some consumer items such as tea and paper, and even a few luxury products such as glass or silver. Aspiring merchants in the countryside often began as tavernkeepers, whose liquor provided ready profits for investing in merchandise.[6]

New England's commercialization confounded at least one aspect of government, fiscal policy. Neither Connecticut nor Massachusetts mastered the instrument of commerce; efforts to provide a stable medium of exchange ranged from futile to calamitous. The northern colonies never had enough silver to back their paper currency or bills of credit. Shortages of money tempted governments to print more bills, and each new issue, as London banks warned, depreciated the value of the currency relative to silver.

During the 1720s and early 1730s Connecticut's currency fared better than did that of Massachusetts, which plummeted in value. Even in the "land of steady habits," however, fiscal matters came to a crisis. Newer settlers and merchants, debt-ridden farmers in the inland, and would-be speculators in land schemes such as the Susquehannah Company wanted bills of credit to repay loans or invest in merchandise or western lands. Merchants in eastern Connecticut joined the cry for money, eager to make a profit from the burgeoning trade with Massachusetts. At the same time, creditors, long-time landowners, and merchants from Hartford and New Haven advocated restraint. The Connecticut General Assembly initially took a conservative position, shutting down several private banks that offered their own paper money and a proposed land bank that would have given loans in return for mortgages. In the late 1730s and early 1740s, however, the government yielded to popular pressure and began to issue bills of credit in large amounts. The resulting inflation injured creditors and more established settlers, whose loans, lands, and investments were valued at older rates. By royal standards, Connecticut's Old Tenor notes issued in 1735 were worth less than one half their original value in 1740, one fourth in 1744, and one eighth in 1749. Humiliated by criticism from the Lords of Trade, the Assembly attempted to reassert its control over money, clamping down on counterfeiting, banning "bad" money such as Rhode Island bills, and prohibiting new banking schemes. It reformed the currency in 1740, issuing New Tenor notes to replace the Old Tenor of 1709. The result was nonetheless disastrous. Without the backing of real coin, the new notes quickly lost value. Debtors could not amass enough of the depreciating notes to repay creditors. New Tenor bills issued in 1740 fell to one half of their original value by 1749. At the height of the crisis, in 1746–1747, inflation reached 60 percent in Connecticut. It was no consolation that it reached nearly 300 percent in Massachusetts in those same years.[7]

Connecticut's military obligations and increasing reliance on credit made for further complications. Campaigns from the War of Jenkin's Ear (1739) and King George's War (1744) through the Seven Years' War (1755–1763) compelled the colonial government to print even more bills of credit, while waiting for reimbursement from London. In the late 1740s and 1750s, prices soared, fueled by wartime spending and profiteering by merchants who provided supplies for the troops. Indebtedness and disparities between rich and poor increased. Parliament forced currency reform on the colonies in 1751, resulting in a scarcity of money. Wealthy proprietors bought the estates of cash-poor debtors, many of whom were reduced to tenancy, unemployment, or debtors prison. Litigation over indebtedness rose markedly in this period, as Yankees went to civil courts to adjudicate disputes that involved the complications of different currencies, absentee landowners, distant creditors, obligations to and from London, and varying rates of credit. In the early 1760s the end of wartime spending and a series of severe droughts throughout New England eventually depressed the economy, pushing the colonies toward social crisis and political protest against the empire.[8]

Other transformations in social and cultural values accompanied the new economy. Where the market prevailed—that is, in highly commercialized settings—what Bruce C. Mann has characterized as "impersonal commercial behavior" often supplanted the more flexible and intimate relations of commodity exchange within a community.[9] As credit replaced local trading and bartering, individuals were thrust out of the confines of the town into an impersonal network of legal and political complexities. Although most rural communities did not overthrow older ideals of covenant and consensus, even country farmers brought financial disputes to Hartford, borrowed money from New Haven, and sought English products marketed through Boston. Indeed, one important sign of commercialization was the growing appetite for consumer goods. Between 1750 and 1773 an enormous increase of English imports to America signified, according to T. H. Breen, the birth of a consumer society. China, silver utensils, linen, silks, and fashionable furniture distinguished the well-to-do from the commoner in urban centers; in trading towns, possession of several types of tables or a looking glass might have set the prosperous apart from struggling citizen. Money and goods gradually replaced traditional marks of social distinction such as age, leadership in the church, or length of residency in the community.[10]

To many, the price of economic expansion—inflation, abuse of credit, competition, confusion in public policy, social schism—appeared exorbitant. Such unwholesome economic practices prevailed that in 1750 the General Assembly outlawed excessive wage demands, unreasonable prices, and oppressive interest rates. Several commentators argued that a new class of rich oppressed a new class of poor; expressions of popular discontent fastened on the story of Lazarus and Dives. Furthermore, wartime business created the image of the mercenary merchant who prospered at home while troops died in Canada, bribed British officers for lucrative contracts, and traded with the French. Such "divers evil-minded Persons," according to the General Court, were mere traitors.[11]

Proponents and detractors in New England viewed the new economy with equal awe, if not dread. Even clergymen recognized that its moral challenge was systemic. One rural Massachusetts preacher marveled at the "new power of money" to control "all the Necessaries and Conveniences of Life," as though money were a new sort of god—a "universal and transcendental . . . Desire." Some twenty years after the heyday of Connecticut's economic expansion, Ezra Stiles recalled the confusion: "How far the principle of Righteousness and Moral Virtue was affected in the mixt scenes of Commerce, God only knows." Evangelical Calvinists and conservative Old Lights such as Noah Hobart and Nathanael Hunn charted the fall of righteousness and moral virtue quite precisely. In the first decades of the century, a relatively static, localized economy provided predictable standards for judging price and value. In the new economic milieu, prices fluctuated wildly, debt was an unknown risk, competition drove commerce, and poverty devastated by surprise. Jared Eliot (1685–1763) urged the Assembly to stop printing paper money because its depreciation tended to "destroy the natural notions of *Right* and *Wrong*, to deface the lines between *Good* and *Evil*." Connecticut's election day preachers in 1747, 1748, 1749, and 1751 spoke on inflation. Roger Sherman (1721–1793) sounded a further warning in his *Caveat Against Injustice, or an Enquiry into the evil Consequences of a Fluctuating Medium of Exchange* (New York, 1752). In 1749 Edwards argued that lack of a stable currency "keeps the country in distress" and "threatens us with ruin." The chief calamity, for Edwards, was the temptation to market behavior: "exceeding extravagant" consumption, "continual" indebtedness, "common people" pursuing status through wealth, and "county towns" affecting "to be like the metropolis." Charges of oppression, injustice, fraud, and extortion—standing for unfair prices, variable interest rates on loans, commercial negotiation, and unpaid debts—filled New England sermons, as well as newspaper editorials, through the 1760s.[12]

Certainly, communal control over economic life weakened. Private arbitration and an informal version of party politics overtook customary modes of resolving conflict as the colonial government replaced the town as dispenser of justice. Currency policy, trade, and the land bank replaced ecclesiastical polity and doctrinal purity on the Assembly's agenda; settlement of new lands and border disputes dominated local affairs. The government nonetheless could not protect equity, fairness, and concord. Covetousness and greed had existed in New England from its first settlement, but never had they seemed so self-consciously displayed. Prosperity had exacerbated distinctions between the rich and those of common means, between local elites and newer settlers, and between urban and rural cultures.[13]

Yet commerce did not sweep over New England at once. In fact, competing economies and economic cultures coexisted and clashed throughout the eighteenth century. E. P. Thompson aptly describes how proponents of a traditional "moral economy of provision" resisted "the new political economy" in England; James Henretta demonstrates the existence of similar impediments in New England to the triumph of economic individualism. Americans who wrote in the manner of classical republicanism were as wary of the new economy as were English critics such as Erasmus Jones. In many rural towns, commerce involved only local trading and manufactures, not the risks of intercolonial markets, borrowing, or speculation in large-scale ventures. Christopher Clark explains this small-scale activity as the persistence of a "household economy," the idealization of a modest economic competence focused on provision for the family through limited entrepreneurialism. In country towns, the culture of capitalism appeared as novel—and as foreign—as the luxuries that ended up no further west than Boston or New York.[14]

Bethlehem was just such a town. Situated in the rocky hill country some fifteen miles from the nearest trading center (Litchfield), its economy consisted almost entirely of agriculture: 386 of the 401 taxpayers listed from 1741 to 1774 had income only from agricultural activities. Land and probate records indicate the prominence of woodland, followed by orchards (for fruit and cider), pasture (for cows and sheep), and a few fields for rye, oats, winter wheat, and flax. Until the Revolution, the town also supported the pastor, four physicians, two lawyers (including Bellamy's son David), a cooper, a blacksmith, a shoemaker, two taverns, and one modest merchant's shop, started by an early settler named Francis Guitteau. Every resident, including Guitteau, owned far more in land (an average of 77 percent of each estate) than in goods or money, as shown by samples of probate records that reveal the distribution of wealth in ten estates (Table 1).[15]

With most of their wealth tied to land, and poor soil at that, the people of Bethlehem accumulated scant money. Despite the town's rapid growth from its settlement by fourteen families in 1734 to its sixty-four taxpayers in 1753, the community was indeed money-poor. The church society, for example, paid Bellamy in kind (land, firewood, and grain) despite his desire for cash and struggled for eight years to raise enough funds to build a new meetinghouse in the 1760s. This scarcity of money impeded the development of a mercantile elite and a widely stratified social order. Inheritance practices and outmigration also minimized social stratification. By the late 1740s Bethlehem's founders had ceded much of their lands to their sons and willed much of their moveable estate to their daughters (as a form of dowry). For instance, Hezekiah Hooker, an original settler and militia captain, paid £156 in taxes in 1745, which marked him as the wealthiest man in the town. During the next year the captain handed down more than a third of his estate to his two sons. In 1747 his taxes dropped to £99, fifth on the tax list, while Hezekiah, Jr., and James paid their first taxes (£38 and £40). Hooker was not unusual. Lieutenant John Steel ranked at the top of the tax lists in 1747 and 1749; after giving two thirds of his estate to

TABLE 1. Sample Estates from Bethlehem

Name	Occupation	Total estate (£)	Percent of total in real estate and farm tools
Joseph Bellamy	minister	1,891	96
Daniel Dudley	farmer	600	95
Daniel Everit	farmer	570	86
John Steel	farmer/tavernkeeper	6,345	83
Hezekiah Hooker	farmer	406	77
Peter Garnsey	farmer	1,352	73
John Meigs	physician	442	73
Francis Guitteau	merchant	660	70
Nathanael Parks	farmer	30	63
Elizabeth Church	farmer	67	57

WPR, Vols. 3–10; WLR, Vols. 6, 7, 9.

his sons Elisha and Ezekiel in 1753, he dropped to forty-third on the lists. Similar accounts of redistribution of lands within the family—including Bellamy's—abound. Likewise, children whose inheritances provided only a meager livelihood, such as David and Joshua Hendee, often left the town soon after they reached adulthood. Bethlehem's wealth was widely distributed accordingly. Tax records indicate that the top quintile of taxpayers owned less than 40 percent of the town's taxable estate through the 1740s—and that percentage dropped between 1749 and 1755; the middle three ranks of taxpayers, who owned more than half the property and goods, gained higher percentages of the total wealth during the early 1750s. Even taxpayers in the lowest quintile owned nearly a tenth of the town's taxable estate through the mid-1750s (Table 2). Unlike more developed towns or commercial centers, Bethlehem did not have a large class of tenant farmers or indigents; in 1756 only six out of 108 family heads were so impoverished as to be untaxed.[16]

Bethlehem's social order, then, like those of other small New England towns of the first half of the century, was relatively traditional, stable, and homogeneous. Through the early 1750s the village remained unconnected to the new economy of the market. Entrepreneurial wealth and the private consumption of commodities—important marks of success in a market society—were relatively insignificant in Bethlehem. The bulk of Bellamy's parishioners owned, besides land, a fairly equal amount of very little: bedding and wool clothes, common kitchen utensils, a few pieces of furniture, twenty or so sheep, five or so cows, two horses, tongs, barrels, axes, and other farm implements. Some owned a few luxuries: a gun, a sword, curtains, several sets of silver buttons, extra linen, and two topcoats appear in probate records. Bellamy owned a beaver hat, a silver watch, a looking glass, a huge library, five tables, and twenty-five chairs. These were modest collections of market goods. Certainly no one in Bethlehem matched the reigning merchant in Woodbury, Jabez Bacon, for conspicuous consumption. Bacon's taste for English silk, fine leather, and silver—not to mention the sheer mass of his assets (valued at $266,000 in 1810)—would have struck even the most prosperous in Bethlehem as impossibly extravagant.[17]

Under these conditions, commercial success and the accumulation of wealth did not signify the prerogatives of leadership in Bethlehem; early residence, age, and the proximity of one's home to the town center did. Most of the founders and other early families, who originated not only from Woodbury but also from Farmington (such as Hooker, Steel, and Guitteau), Guilford (Hill, Meigs, and Dudley), and Wallingford (Avered and Munger), grouped themselves into something of a neighborhood, settling in the central, north, and northeast lots. For the first eighteen years, these families formed the town's oligarchy. They occupied the offices of deacon, society moderator, tax collector, school committee, and town clerk. Many of them, such as town committeeman Reuban Avered—who ranked in the bottom third of the tax list—were not rich. They simply were the earliest settlers, whose most obvious sign of rank was their prominent seating in the church. To the outsider, Hooker and Guitteau might have appeared indistinguishable in wealth from Avered.[18]

Despite its yeoman, middle-class characteristics, Bethlehem's social order did show some signs of change during the late 1750s and 1760s. New England's economic depression in that period, which closed off credit and forced indebted farmers to sell their lands, particularly affected the community's lower stratum. A handful of farmers became destitute enough for the first time to receive special relief from ministerial "rates" (payments toward the pastor's salary). During the same period, members of the town's upper tax bracket, often creditors to their poorer brethren, gained an increasing proportion of the community's wealth. The top quintile of taxpayers accordingly paid an increasing percentage of the town's taxes after 1759, while the bottom quintile paid less (Table 2). Bethlehem began to show some slight amount of economic restructuring, an increasing disparity between citizens whose wealth and interests as creditors set them apart from a number of folk whose fortunes and economic power fell as debts rose. Certainly, however, the town developed nowhere near the stratification of urban centers, where members in the top quintile of taxpayers owned as much as 75 percent of the wealth, the middle class shrank, and a new class of landless and unemployed paupers emerged. Bellamy's community continued to be an agricultural village composed chiefly of middling sorts of farmers, with localized trading and minimal affluence.[19]

Yet increasing stratification and poverty, however modest, reflected at least the initial encroachments of the market; they were troublesome in

TABLE 2. Percent paid of total of Bethlehem's taxes

Quintile	1743–45	1747–49	1753–55	1757–59	1763–65	1767–69
1st	38	37	35	37	41	42
2nd	22	24	24	25	25	25
3rd	16	17	19	19	18	18
4th	13	13	14	13	12	11
5th	11	9	8	6	4	4

WTR.

such a small community, especially when accompanied by new forms of contention and competition for leadership of the town. In the late 1740s and early 1750s a second, younger group of settlers (the Minor, Martin, and Kasson families) came from Woodbury and built homes in the southern sections of the town. A disparate group of immigrants (for example, Allen, Camp, Chapman, and Parmelee) and investors from New York and Boston purchased the last bits of the town's lands—lots to the west of the center and on the periphery—in the late 1750s and early 1760s. These newer settlers began to challenge the older leadership in the mid-1750s. William Martin, James Kasson, and David Camp, who became the wealthiest townsmen, repeatedly won elections to town and church offices. New seating arrangements in the church also represented the contest for public prominence. Society notes show that the first debates about church seating—of great symbolic importance to New Englanders—occurred in 1755. A committee consisting of three of the earliest settlers voted that newer leaders should not be given preference, "that no person should be deprived by plusing [placing] of him back from where he has been seated" and that "persons should be seated according to their age" before their standing on the tax "lests." One year later, a different commission, composed of two newcomers and one older settler, reconsidered the issue. In 1761 the debate continued, as another committee made "such alterations with respect to seating the Meeting-House" as it "thought best." When the town began to build its new meetinghouse in 1764, the shift in leadership became obvious. The treasurers for the project were all newcomers such as David Camp. As soon as the society finished the building in 1768, it voted "the old seating . . . Noal and Void"; seats thereafter were purchased according to the economic standing of members.[20]

Bellamy and his parishioners were well aware that the market, with all of its potential for advancement as well as disruption, could challenge customary patterns of life. The pastor knew of the power of distant economic forces not only from his travels and reading (most newspapers recounted economic developments and the fiscal crisis in great detail) but also from his personal fortunes. He was the only salaried person in the town. His yearly "maintenance" was set as a monetary figure even if paid in land and goods. Connecticut's economic policies affected him quite directly, since currency depreciation and price inflation often compelled him, as it did most ministers, to renegotiate his yearly contract. Including firewood, his salary in 1740 was £87; it rose to £164 a year over the next three years. In 1747 a church committee noted that the society originally agreed to fix "his Salary by Silver to the intent it mite be kept from fal[l]ing by the sinking of the credet of our paper money." They recognized, however, that "the prise of Silver is now so unsertan" that a fixed salary was sure to depreciate in value and bring "yearly deficulty." The committee attempted to provide a contract that would adjust his salary according to the going rate for common goods; the church voted to pay him £190 at a time when such "speces [specie]" would "b[u]y wheat at 12 shillings per bushel, rice at 9 shillings per bushel," and so forth. Thereafter, the church raised Bellamy's salary as the price of grain rose, and he was paid £270 in 1755. As depression set in and prices dropped in the 1760s, so too his annual wage. In 1764 he finally protested the decline in salary and was given a modest increase.[21]

Bellamy's salary negotiation was one further instance of the impact of economic change on Bethlehem; it also revealed the ambiguities of Bellamy's personal finances. On one hand, he was the town's spokesman for traditional values. "When the Society of Bethlehem first invited me to be their minister," he wrote in 1764, "I had observed the Difficulties which sometimes had subsisted between Ministers and people. Ministers would go to work because they had not salary enough, and people would complain because their Ministers went to work, and they would blame each other, contend and quarrel." He recalled that, "considering the smallness and poverty of this Society," he took a small salary and vowed never to seek income outside the ministry. He idealized Bethlehem's modest past, when he and parishioners went without contention through "those straits and difficulties . . . for many years, when you were poor, very poor." He maintained that he always avoided "the dreadful Consequences of Ministers asking for more salary." When a New York Presbyterian church offered to make Bellamy the highest paid minister in America in 1754, he declined. Some of his motives admittedly were professional; a large faction that opposed Bellamy's ecclesiology—and call—divided the New York church. Yet Bellamy also believed that a move to New York would have betrayed his community for lucre. "My people give me salary enough" and "are very kind too," he wrote to the Litchfield County Association. In some private notes, Bellamy wrote a dialogue in which he imagined what his people might have said had he accepted the call to New York: "Right or wrong, he's resolved to come [to New York], though his church [in Bethlehem] is ruined! Aha! Aha! Dollars! Dollars! Dollars!"[22]

Religious loyalties strengthened Bellamy's resistance to urban and market cultures. Like other New Light Calvinists, Bellamy associated the mercantile elite with unbelief. His friend in Great Barrington, Samuel Hopkins, claimed to have "lived as cheap and low as" possible, "not seeking *great things* in the world" and remaining "unconnected with the great and rich." Samuel Davies warned Bellamy that rich merchants, who had the "nicest Taste," tended to be the worst "Enemies" to Calvinism. Good Scottish Presbyterians who immigrated to Davies's Virginia inevitably took to emulating the "polite" and "fashionable" wealthy "by turning Deists." Bellamy also eschewed the culture of gentility, quite self-consciously. He made much of his rustic manners, his backcountry accent, and his economic modesty. In fact, he disliked the urbane New Yorkers who tempted him with a prestigious post: "I am not polite enough for them. I may possibly do, to be a minister out in the woods, but am not fit for a city." He therefore turned his back on the city and refrained from asking for a raise from his church as late as 1763.[23]

On the other hand, Bellamy sought all the prerogatives of leadership, including wealth, and could be as ambitious as any merchant. Ezra Stiles counted him among Connecticut's wealthiest pastors. He certainly was one of the town's most prosperous citizens, owning five hundred acres of prime land, much of it at the center. He also thought in 1764 that the time had come for the town to reward "all which I bore so patiently" through the early years. Despite his "trembling for fear of the dreadful consequences, for disaffection and contention are dreadful," he was willing eventually to contend for his salary, even to threaten his resignation. He reasoned that the society was financially secure and, with newcomers joining the tax rolls, could afford "to give an honorable support to a minister." The church raised his salary and doubled the size of his house with an addition in 1767, making it the largest and most elegant house in the town.[24]

The apologetic tone of Bellamy's 1764 letter—he told the committee that he wanted "not to mention any of these things" and did so only after a private discussion with several deacons—reveals his fear of appearing mercenary, but there was little to suggest that Bellamy thought that he had capitulated to the consumerism, individualism, or political economy of a free market. He directed his wealth to public use, not private consumption. Like his lands, his library was, in effect, a tool for production. Church and town meetings gathered in his house, the third floor of which served as a dormitory for theological students. Prosperity and prestige in themselves did not violate the fixed standards of justice, equity, and value upon which New England's social order rested. Within the confines of established hierarchies, a controlled economy, and customary rights, Bethlehem's citizens—including the pastor—could pursue modest affluence without danger to the commonwealth.[25]

Bellamy did fear, however, that his people might succumb to the market. He had some reason to suspect that his orderly and stable town had begun to show the first effects of "contention, strife, and division about society affairs." Edwards informed his friends that this kind of behavior overtook Northampton and spelled the end of revival there. In Bethlehem, the arrival of newer settlers, the growth of competition, and the increasing concentration of wealth in the upper class alerted Bellamy to the reality that the town could not insulate itself completely from Boston, New York, or any other source of the new economy.[26]

From the late 1740s Bellamy had expressed dismay at New England's accommodation to commerce; its appearance in Bethlehem therefore alarmed him all the more. When he turned to economics he employed a republican rhetoric that, as Gordon Wood has put it, revealed "an obsession with America's social development," its maturation into a market economy.[27] Bellamy's weekly expositions of the divine law cautioned against a host of values that had remade Britain, transformed New England, and threatened to undo Bethlehem. Those who worked on the Sabbath, he indicated, foolishly took "their cares—business" to be more worthy than heaven. Contention in the town and disobedience to rulers and parents exhibited, like the search for autonomy in the market, a "self-confidence" that was "the ground of many evils." Bellamy joined others of the period who saw in the parable of Dives and Lazarus a censure of the new class of rich who oppressed the poor through avarice and selfishness. He reprimanded those who spent too much time or money in the tavern, where merchandise and liquor provided a dual temptation to excess consumption. He frequently described the preoccupations of the unconverted with images of the self-serving economic man. The market demanded risk taking such as land speculation or commercial investment and promised luxuries in return; those who took such risks in the search for consumer goods exhibited, according to Bellamy, carnality. Vice, in other words, lay beneath the frantic growth of the 1740s and 1750s:

> [Those in pursuit of wealth] tire themselves, they exhaust their strength, they exercise all their art to be gainers of the world. Honor and profits are in their eye and . . . they will reach at them and approach to them and be in possession of them if it be possible. They will venture any hazard rather than they will be kept from them. And the pleasures of the world are no less charming. They will show the greatest diligence and industry in purchasing the delights and sensual entertainments which are set before them. . . . The worldly man and woman are exceeding busy and industrious about the accomplishing of their carnal desires and appetites.

These people, he continued, were nothing but "covetous and voluptuous and ambitious."[28]

As Bellamy rose to intercolonial prominence in the 1750s, his preaching on economics became more explicit and apprehensive. In 1762 he warned Connecticut's magistrates at the annual election that the spread

of market behavior portended the total collapse of society. In the fluctuating values and prices of the market, merchants filled "their traffic full of
deceit and fraud." Commerce lured people to forgo their stewardship over
and cultivation of the land, only to deal in the chimerical and fabricated
world of money, where "luxury, idleness, debauchery" and "dishonesty"
reigned. In the new economy, people began to "envy the rich, despise the
poor," and foment "perpetual discord," as evidenced by the "multiplied
law-suits" in the land. Moreover, the availability of luxuries and ease of
credit encouraged such degeneracy, tempting people to "spend their time
in idleness, their substance in taverns, in gay dressing, in high living, in
law-suits, until poverty comes like an armed man." Should towns such as
Bethlehem become like the metropolis "and extravagant high living should
so increase," he cautioned, Connecticut's "farmers may soon be obliged
to resign their lands to pay their debts," giving them "nothing to leave to
our children but poverty."[29]

Bellamy spoke here of the deteriorating situation of his own parishioners as well as of other New Englanders. In his worst nightmares, he
envisioned a time "when peace and harmony are clean gone, and jar-
ring, angry passions rage, no godliness, no humanity, sabbaths profaned
. . . hearts and hands unclean, whoredom rampant, no government." As
commercial relations replaced the covenant and civil law as the arbiters
of morality, "distempers" would ravage the body politic, bringing "re-
proach and misery." He concluded with the assertion that "pride, luxuriousness, contentiousness, malice, envy, idleness, dishonesty" accompanied the market, and *that*, "by whatever other name it is called . . . is
sin."[30]

Bellamy's language—the striking reference to the voluptuousness and
whoredom of commercial aspirations, the metaphor of disease in the body
politic, the repeated admonitions against idleness, contention, and luxuriousness, and the alarm at poverty—constituted a philippic against the
culture of the market. The rhetoric also implied the importance of more
fundamental issues. After all, commercialization posed a moral-philosophical question: to what extent could people be trusted to pursue their own
interests in a market unhampered by restraints such as land, custom, and
consensus? The search for answers drove him and his antagonists to doctrinal debates about human nature, the ethical foundation that since has
been called theological anthropology. Arminians, Old Lights, and Calvinists alike feared an unstable economy and social disintegration, but their
ideas about human capacities for virtue implied quite distinct economic
sensibilities.

From the mid-1740s New England's religious liberals argued that incentive for all reformation, individual and social, depended on the principle of moral freedom. They disputed Calvinist notions of a depraved will
and imputed moral qualities—evil and goodness implanted from birth by
sovereign will. Only the assertion of an innate capability of choice or free

agency, Arminians and liberal Old Lights maintained, justified the conviction that God justly rewarded virtue and punished vice. Genuine Christianity, in Lemuel Briant's words, "considers us as moral Agents, and sus-
pends our whole Happiness," which is to say, moral status, "upon our
personal good Behaviour." Therefore, Briant concluded, "we needs must
have an higher Opinion" (than did Calvinists) of the potential for "the
Virtues of good Men," since virtue led to "personal and private, temporal,
spiritual and eternal good Effects." According to this position, people were
naturally capable of choosing the good without external compulsion. The
self-interested character of such choices did not necessarily constrain virtue. Indeed, many liberals held that an enlightened cultivation of self-
interest, extended into social acts, was morally acceptable. It promoted the
commonweal far more than did Calvinism, whose doctrine of a depraved
and predetermined moral will, according to Samuel Mather, contributed
to the economic crisis by removing incentives to "Industry, Frugality,
Honesty, [and] Charity." Arminian rhetoric thus mirrored the Enlightenment moral philosophy of Scottish economists such as James Steuart and
Adam Smith. As much as selfishness determined moral choice, Smith
maintained in his much admired *Theory of Moral Sentiments* (London, 1759),
"self-love" could be the "motive of virtuous action" because economic vices
stemmed not "from a want of benevolence, but from a want of the proper
attention to the objects of self-interest." Samuel Cooper, the liberal pastor
of Boston merchants' favorite church, maintained in his 1753 sermon on
I Corinthians 13:5 ("Charity seeketh not her own") that "Self-love may
be improved as a Motive" to industry because "benevolence" was innate,
a natural part of the human constitution. To love self was to be diligent,
to be diligent was to become prosperous, and prosperity benefited all. Self-
love was a form of virtue since it served the commonweal. "If Charity
seeketh not her own," Cooper claimed, "yet she always finds it."[31]

Many of New England's liberals here affirmed at least one component
of the culture of the free market. Chauncy, Mayhew, and Mather stopped
short of Smith, who invented an economic law out of the necessity of self-
love. Yet some Arminians were optimistic enough to claim that a prudent
and industrious pursuit of self-interest would allow people to act virtuously within the market. The problems of commerce, in fact, "will so easily admit of a Cure," opined one writer; "nothing more is required, than
lodging a [moral] Power" to act with "industry and abate our Extravagance."[32]

A sort of Pelagian economic formula emerged from this line of thought:
prosperity was the individual's reward for the virtues of self-discipline and
industry, poverty the due punishment for the vices of extravagance and
sloth. Encouragements to industry and prudence in the mercantile system accordingly appeared as the best means to moral and economic reform. Liberals put this belief into action by favoring projects such as a pri-
vately funded and owned linen manufacture, begun in Boston in 1753.

The scheme was designed to employ the urban poor, turn a profit for investors, reduce taxes, and improve the balance of trade. Early investors enlisted the support of Cooper, Chauncy, and other liberal ministers such as Thomas Barnard. Boston merchants gathered in Cooper's church in 1753 to hear the preachers encourage investment in the scheme. Chauncy's contribution was a condemnation of the idle poor. He suggested that they be given neither public poor relief nor alms but rather employment in industry, to be "fed and clothed with the Fruit of their own Labour." Barnard's 1758 sermon in support of the society counseled patience and optimism in the midst of an uncertain economy. He urged people to "bear in Mind the Superintendency of God," who gave all people the natural "Instinct" for virtue and instilled in them proper economic motives: "He teaches us our Interest by the Order of Nature." Commerce and trade, according to Barnard, hardly threatened the commonweal. Indeed, they instigated virtue by their laws of reward and punishment; even "Religion will most flourish where the Arts of Peace are cultivated, especially Industry."[33]

Bellamy could not fathom these ideals. No vision of prosperity or the hidden benefits of competition could justify to him such trust in the unrestrained pursuits of fallen individuals. How had Arminianism lulled sinners into such complacence, such self-justification, and such capitulation to market mentalities? According to Bellamy, this undue confidence stemmed chiefly from misrepresentations of moral goodness. Arminians and Calvinists held that love or benevolence, in the language of the current moral philosophy, captured the essence of true virtue. Evangelical Calvinists, however, maintained a peculiar position on the objects and motives of that love. In *True Religion Delineated* Bellamy based his analysis on a distinction between "natural good" and "moral good." The former referred to the relative happiness of created agents, their material and emotional pleasures. The latter referred to the intrinsic "fitness of things," the relation of being and acts to absolute goodness. Love of another moral agent because that agent promoted one's natural good was a form of self-love; love of another because that agent promoted the absolute good, which inhered in God's nature and will (the moral law), was love of moral goodness, that is, true virtue. Genuine benevolence accordingly regarded God's glory above human happiness. "God's honour in the world" and "the interest of his Son's kingdom," as Bellamy put it, "ought to appear infinitely more valuable and precious than our own, and therefore our own ought to seem as a thing of no worth." Rationalist moral philosophers such as Hutcheson, Arminian theologians such as Samuel Johnson, and other liberals such as Chauncy all but disregarded this definition of true virtue by promoting the happiness of people as the chief object of benevolence. They valued natural over moral good as the criterion of virtuous action. They also had a limited understanding of the objects of benevolence, discounting God as more worthy of love than were created beings.[34]

Nothing so indicated the defects of the liberals' notion of benevolence, according to Bellamy, as their resistance to the doctrine of eternal punishment. Moral law, he argued, demanded unmitigated love for God. The human disposition to love self-happiness above the Creator's glory violated the Godhead, since selfish acts elevated the rights of the individual above the moral prerogatives of the Creator. This denial of rectitude was an offense of infinite magnitude. The law's just and warranted sentence amounted to eternal punishment. Thus, sincere religion and genuine ethics entailed, among other things, consent to the justice of every person's condemnation. Arminian protests against this sentence as unjust or inhumane only reverted to the sin of valuing human happiness over God's moral rectitude. That, Bellamy concluded, was illogical, irrational, and damnable. Antinomians, who rejected the preaching of terror, the necessity of repentance, and the value of legal obedience, had an equally perverse understanding of virtue. They believed that the promise of forgiveness was a more worthy catalyst for religion than was the inherent justice of the law's precepts, which displayed "the infinite excellency of the divine character . . . antecedent to any consideration of advantage" to people. Arminians loved their temporal prosperity more than God's justice, and antinomians loved heaven more than God's glory. Bellamy thus perceived a common mentality among the enemies to Calvinism. "The worldly hypocrite" (the religiously indifferent), "the legal hypocrite" (the Arminian moralist), "the evangelical hypocrite" (the antinomian), and "the wild, blazing enthusiast" each feigned love of God while motivated by, and justifying, his own self-interest.[35]

The liberals' hypocrisy, according to Bellamy, extended also to their understanding of secondary benevolence—love to created agents. He here agreed with moral philosophers such as Hutcheson, who insisted on the superiority of communal affections to private interest. In a Hutchesonian vein, Bellamy delineated two sorts of social love, as he had defined two sorts of theological love: the natural and the moral. The lowest form of social affection, in this scheme, came from natural motives. These included "natural compassion," "good naturedness," loyalty to family, "party-spirit" (love for those with similar economic and political interests), allegiance to social class, and gratitude. Scarcely benevolent, natural love merely extended self-interest to others with whom one had common material objectives. "*Natural affection*" for one's children, Bellamy illustrated, seemed at worst an innocent and more likely a good motive for economic ambition, but it was rarely innocent and hardly good. It often prompted parents to sheer avarice, to "go, and run, and work, and toil, by night and day, to the utter neglect of God" and communal duty. So debased, it "commonly" led people to idolize money, to fret over their business, and, worse, to excuse their greed and self-serving neglect of the poor: "They [say that they] have nothing to give to the poor and needy . . . they must lay up all for their children: yea, many times they rake and scrape, cheat and defraud, and, like mere earth-worms, bury themselves in the world." Self-ish at root, natural motives engendered social vice. "A *selfish spirit*, whereby we are inclined only to value . . . our own welfare," Bellamy admonished, "makes it *unnatural*" to love others, "even *natural* to delight in our neighbour's misery. And hence it is, that *revenge* is so sweet, and *backbiting* and *detraction* so agreeable in this fallen, sinful world." With its origins in self-love, natural benevolence degenerated into an objectification of people for one's own advancement. It led to dissatisfaction with one's social position and an attendant maliciousness toward those in other positions and parties. Improper esteem for others, Bellamy observed, disposed people "to despise superiors, scorn equals, and trample upon inferiors; a temper in which men over-value themselves, their friends, and party." Natural love bore all of the bitter fruits of the new economy: ambition, self-aggrandizement, individualism, contentiousness, disrespect for authority, and restlessness. Proponents of the market misidentified natural love as virtuous, when in fact such a base affection fell far short of the "love to neighbour" commanded by moral law.[36]

Bellamy explained that the law required in contrast a genuinely moral disposition toward others, the social virtue of a love of complacence.[37] Originating in an "upright, impartial, candid, benevolent temper," complacence esteemed people as God did—according to their intrinsic moral status. It deemed others as divine creations, not objects for profit but "cordial friends" worthy of care, compassion, and charity. It also esteemed people according to their social positions as settled by providence:

> Now, with a disinterested impartiality, and with a perfect candour, and a hearty good-will, ought we to view the various excellencies of our neighbours, and consider their various stations, characters, and relations; and, in our hearts, we ought to give every one his due honour, and his proper place, being perfectly content, for our parts, to be and to act in our own sphere, where God has placed us; and, by our fellow-mortals, to be considered as being just what we are: and indeed, this, for substance, is the duty of every one in the whole system of intelligent creatures.

The truly benevolent person, according to this scheme, recognized that God instituted social hierarchies based not on wealth but on traditional lines of social authority: "magistrates and subjects, ministers and people, parents and children, masters and servants." Motivated by complacence, people valued others in their social stations. Citizens obeyed a government that instituted benevolent policies. Parishioners deferred to ministers who loved their people. Children obeyed parents who raised them with kindness and wisdom. The lower classes respected the upper, who cared for those in need. Genuine virtue maintained a stable society, the concord of a harmonious system. Had New England followed the "love required in the Divine law," it would have been "united . . . to this Day."[38]

Since Arminianism led New England down the confused and disorderly path of natural motives, Bellamy asserted what he deemed a sheer fact: the sin of self-love debased every human motive before regeneration. He gave systematic expression to this belief in the doctrine of human depravity and its corollary, original sin. Evangelical Calvinists had long held (for more than economic reasons) that the Arminian notion of an undepraved human nature, whatever its putative social implications, was a sham. Throughout *The Law, The Evil of Sin*, and the final three sections of the "First Discourse" of *True Religion Delineated*, Bellamy compiled various biblical and theological substantiations of total depravity and original sin. From an ethical perspective, the doctrines were obviously problematic. Bellamy had to prove the proposition that divine law required what humankind by nature could not do: love and honor God and neighbor above self.

His sometimes contradictory arguments showed determination, if not dogmatic consistency. First, he appealed from a sensationalist position, maintaining that depravity was an unassailable, empirical reality. Each person, he asserted, clearly acted from vicious dispositions. An instinctive motivation "from self-love, and for self-ends" was "evidently [i.e., demonstrably] natural to all mankind." By "natural," Bellamy meant "native," following the "bent of our hearts" as the "very first propensities of the new-made soul . . . from [its] very first motion." The initial choice for self instilled from the instant of birth a disposition toward self-love that determined (or "governed") all subsequent moral inclinations, religious and civil. This universal propensity toward self-love confirmed the doctrine of total depravity, since the moral law decreed love of God and neighbor to be more worthy of our esteem than love of self. Human beings were not as trustworthy or as instinctively benevolent as the liberals claimed.[39]

Second, against Arminian complaints that it appeared unjust for God to punish people for failing to do what they could not do, Bellamy employed the kind of distinction between natural and moral capacity that Edwards more fully expounded in *Freedom of the Will* (Boston, 1754).[40] Bellamy contended that natural capacity referred to the faculty of choice, the ability to love and hate; moral capacity referred to the inner disposition, temper, or inclination of the soul according to which the will chose. The doctrine of total depravity did not imply a natural incapacity, or loss of will. People had free wills in that they willed, or loved, or "chose" that which pleased them and were capable of doing as they pleased. They were naturally free from physical (we might add psychological) impediments to willing and acting; this made them moral agents. Yet they were morally depraved in that they willed according to corrupt inclinations. Whatever their understanding told them about God's law, they loved self to the exclusion of God and neighbor and so willed selfishness, greed, avarice, and dishonesty.

Seen from this perspective, the unregenerate were depraved and guilty. Incapable of not sinning, they were yet free moral agents whose love of sin only exacerbated their culpability. Bellamy's explanation of the relation between disposition and will was obscure, not to mention at odds with his first argument (that depravity followed an initial moment of moral freedom). He tended to explain his point by putting the liberals' protests into the form of a reductio ad absurdum: if the law required us to love God only as much as we were so inclined, then it approved equally of depraved blasphemers and regenerate saints. He surmised that bad choices were free choices and that they were all the more condemnable, not the less, for stemming from evil dispositions.[41]

Third, in a later section of *True Religion Delineated*, Bellamy focused on the question of original sin proper, that is, the doctrine of imputed guilt. Many divines, certainly most Old Lights, did not object to the concept that people were fallen, prone to sin, and in some sense depraved. They rejected the idea that such fallenness could be imputed to individuals apart from their personal, volitional performance of evil. Later New Divinity thinkers also disclaimed imputed guilt. In contrast, Bellamy fastened on the doctrine as essential. According to his version, the instinctual motivation from self-love, which all people received from Adam, was sinful. The fact that it preceded conscious choice, was intrinsic and inevitable, did not mean that it was justifiable or morally neutral. With the imputation of our moral constitution came the guilt of a depraved self-love and thus the liability to punishment.

Technically, Bellamy's argument in defense of this proposition followed the federalism that Edwards later employed in his version of *Original Sin*. Bellamy posited a constitutional connection between Adam and Adam's posterity. It was, he argued, legally just and morally benevolent for the Lord to have "established a constitution," in which Adam's actions "represented" the whole race and so "by ordinary generation" made posterity "legally sinners." It was just in that Adam, born into an innocent creation and immediate fellowship with God, was more likely to obey the law than were any of his posterity. His was more than a fair test of human nature. It was benevolent in that the principle of constitutional representation in Adam established the legal precedent, hence juridical possibility, of salvation. Christ, the Second Adam, "by power and rightful authority" acted as Redeemer in behalf of and imputed his righteousness to humanity on the basis of the prior existence of "a public head and moral representative" for Adam's posterity.[42]

Bellamy crystalized these and attendant arguments in the 1750s and early 1760s, when economic developments throughout New England and particularly in Bethlehem gave public meaning to his insistence on the viciousness of human nature. To be sure, he stayed in character and displayed wry humor about such issues. When he wrote to Hopkins in 1755 to arrange a meeting with Edwards on the subject of the will, he teased his younger colleague: "I am apt to think *your* Moral Necessity will operate the first Monday in Feb." to "have congress at your house." But Bellamy was deadly serious about the practical implications of Arminianism. While Edwards dwelt on a philosophical justification of original sin, Bethlehem's pastor struck quickly (perhaps impatiently, in Edwards's judgment) at its social effects. He informed the Arminians that they ought to abandon their aspersions on Omnipotence, see people for what they really were, and acknowledge the evidence that self-love was both universal and depraved. Edwards allowed for some form of self-love or self-interest as an inevitable, and sometimes legitimate, component of all moral choices. Bellamy was less philosophically precise. To him, virtually all self-interest amounted to the vice of selfishness.[43]

When Bellamy wrote of self-love, it was only to decry its social effects. If our affections, he argued, arose "from *self-love*, or is for *self-ends*, nothing is genuine." According to *True Religion Delineated*, "we ought to be *perfectly benevolent* towards" our neighbors, "to rejoice in their prosperity, and be grieved for their adversity; and all from a cordial love and genuine good-will." Self-love instead bred "a *selfish spirit*, whereby we are inclined only to value, and seek, and rejoice in our own welfare," which led people to "*envy* at our neighbour's prosperity, and *hard-heartedness* in the time of adversity." The confirmation of this depravity was obvious, "a plain matter of fact," observable precisely in the scenes of commerce that so distressed him: "Now, as though in very deed there were no God for us to be in subjection unto, we set up for ourselves, to make our own interest our last end . . . we go every one his way, one to his farm, another to his merchandize, all serving divers lusts and pleasures." All one had to do, in other words, was look at the London stock market, at the clash between the idle rich and the working poor in Boston, at the litigiousness and factions in Hartford, at the fraudulence of business dealings and land speculation, and at the rising contention at home. Bellamy could not "imagine that we are not fallen creatures, universally depraved, when it is, so evidently, a plain matter of fact." It was no surprise to Bellamy that "a flood of Arminianism" carried with it a "deluge" of social "immorality," since the "false religion" of the liberals elevated the "principle of self-love" to a moral axiom.[44]

Bellamy placed the blame for social disaster back on those who legitimated self-love. That, and Edwards's intricate and demanding defense of the idea of moral necessity, roused opponents beyond hints and vague protests to a full-fledged assault on fundamental Calvinist doctrine. Arminians focused not on the philosophical possibility of volition (Edwards either had so settled or so confused the issue that the first thorough response came only in 1770), but on the idea of imputed guilt. They first broached the doctrine by recommending John Taylor's *The Scripture-Doctrine of Original Sin Proposed to A Free and Candid Examination* (London, 1740), which attacked the dogma with scriptural exegesis and ethical logic. Then Samuel Webster produced his *A Winter Evening's Conversation Upon the Doctrine of Original Sin.*

This tract was inflammatory, to say the least. At the outset, it framed the issue circumspectly. The question was not whether people were sinners but whether they were born with sinful natures, *"charg'd by God with this first sin"* of Adam. If so, Webster reasoned, then the tiniest infant was damnable—and that was irreconcilable with a belief in God's goodness. Webster then returned to the Arminian position that *"sin* and *guilt . . .* are personal things"; by definition, they referred to the free choice of individuals. Oblivious to Bellamy's and Edwards's arguments on the nature of moral choice, Webster asserted that all moral predicates implied the willful agency of subjects, so it was logically impossible for anyone besides Adam to be imputed with Adam's sin. It was, he contended, "shocking and monstrous" to believe that people were sinful apart from the volitional corruption of their "natures thro' long *custom* and *wicked habits."* Webster heated his rhetoric. He reiterated the Arminian accusation that the doctrine of human depravity—not, as Calvinists argued, confidence in self-love—extinguished all resolve for social virtue. It provided *"a cloke* for . . . wickedness," an excuse to delay reform. It effaced all gratitude for life, respect for parents, appreciation for marriage, interest in procreation, and, alas, belief in God. One of Webster's defenders suggested that the entire scheme of "Election" was so "friendly to a licentious course of life" that it ought to be abolished as legally, morally, and theologically perverse. As if that were not enough, Webster charged Calvinists with pushing a dogma invented by none other than Augustine—a Catholic, a proponent of purgatory, and a bishop who started a line of monastic houses, one of which was located in Canada. If Calvinists wanted guilt by association, then they had it. They were as damnable as the French papists at war with New England.[45]

Bellamy agreed with Webster on at least one point: nothing less than Christian belief hung in the balance. In one more retort to Arminian logic, he argued that mortality itself proved original sin. Every person was born mortal. Since death was a curse for sin, every person was born with the curse, a fate that was just only if every person were born guilty. A rejection of imputed guilt and declaration of human innocence, then, impugned God. They implied doubt about the justice and goodness of providence, and so defied the divine prerogative to constitute and judge human nature. Liberals loved their own lusts and subjective interests more than God's honor. Furthermore, Bellamy charged, such a "self-justifying spirit" distorted the gospel with market mentalities. Arminians assumed that individuals owned something of moral virtue, as though people could buy their way to heaven with a trifling reformation of manners. This amounted to a denial of the need for *"free grace* thro' Jesus Christ—so that I see no other Way, for a considerate, thinking Man, if he is resolved to be consistent with himself, but to become a *Calvinist,* or else a *Deist,* or rather an *Atheist."* As to Arminians' claim to moral superiority, Bellamy contended that they displayed no more than a self-serving desire to justify their own hardheartedness toward God and neighbor. Arminians, deists, and atheists flaunted their "hatred of the Bible" because therein God denounced their rationalizations for selfishness.[46]

Bethlehem's minister undoubtedly thought that his ad hominum attacks were more than justified since liberals, whatever they claimed, had little to do with "*public love* and *public spirit*". The whole of Arminianism appeared to Bellamy as an accomplice to the market's culture of falsehood. At every turn, his antagonists fastened on some form of self-love as justification for disobedience. They refused to call sin by its name and thereby denied human depravity, leaving people to the devices of their depraved wills. Confirmed in their depravity, the unregenerate would never gain a taste for true virtue. Instead of calling for a self-denying repentance and immediate submission to the law of God, Arminians approved of half-way measures of religious duty. Rather than inculcate genuine benevolence, they legitimated self-interested social activity and called it good. Like their sacramental practices, which claimed a covenantal relationship where none existed, their definition of virtue was misleading at best, disingenuous at worst. Having no appreciation for absolute moral realities, they devalued truth itself. In this climate, as Bellamy put it, "no man's word [was] to be trusted." No wonder that the liberal mentality promoted an economy in which prices and values fluctuated according to demand. All of this threatened to rend New England's civic order and bring down the judgment of God. Bad theology made for bad ethics, and bad ethics made for social disaster.[47]

Bellamy's practical recommendations accordingly followed his critique of liberalism. Although there is little direct evidence of it, he likely sympathized with Edwards, who suggested that a closely watched government regulate the market through price controls and restraints on trade. Bellamy consistently advocated traditional limits to market activity. Through his weekly preaching in the 1750s and early 1760s, he urged his people to forgo the autonomous pursuit of wealth and subject their interests to custom, community, and consensus. In a sermon on Lazarus and Dives, he remarked that "that instinct" for riches which liberals legitimated as "a natural affection" was rather "madness and damnation." In another sermon he maintained that the gospel illegitimated money as a criterion for public respect and prominence; Jesus obviated the artificial distinctions between rich and poor that so divided worldly societies.[48]

Elsewhere, Bellamy recommended the economic merits of "Christianity in the apostolic age," when believers "full of benevolent virtue" emulated "Christ, whose whole life was full of activity from love." These ancient Christians worked for "the good of all" and eschewed "the idleness" so characteristic of commercial speculators and so "contrary to the faith of Jesus Christ." Rather than endorse a prudent industriousness in the new economy and schemes such as the linen manufacture, Bellamy focused his economic admonitions on almsgiving. Preaching on the commandment against stealing, he argued that people exercised only stewardship over their "life" and "property." Because wealth belonged to the God who commanded charity, people should relinquish their possessions without "distress" or "melancholy"; with a due disregard for "our selves, we are to give to those that need our help." In his Boston sermon cited at the beginning of this chapter, he stressed the practice of true benevolence through charity. Our "loves," he reminded the congregation, "ought to be in proportion to the dignity and worthiness of beings." In the hierarchy of social obligations, God came first, then "our neighbor, then our nation [as a whole] more than some part of it, our country more than ourself." Duty to neighbor (by which Bellamy meant humanity as whole) superseded duty to country. How could people not give mere money to "poor people that need our help," when nations demanded an even higher sacrifice—their lives? At home, Bellamy urged his church to institutionalize benevolence. The Bethlehem congregation formed a committee that operated as a sort of bank for needy townsmen. It lent the church's excess money at low interest rates. Encouraged by John Graham, the pastor at Southbury, Bellamy extended the charitable activities of deacons to include a weekly collection for the poor and distribution of monies. In a 1756 sermon he explained that deacons, chosen "to take care of the church's money," should be "wise" in the affairs of society and "gifted" with charitable dispositions toward others.[49]

Here, as elsewhere, Bellamy returned to the source of good dispositions—the release of wills from the bind of selfishness. He agreed with rationalist philosophers such as Mandeville and Smith, who distilled every natural motive for reform, including loyalty to the community or even a desire for paradise, to a form of self-love. He disagreed, however, with the rationalists' acquiescence to nature. Instead, he thought that the human predicament called for an evangelical response. Sinners needed regeneration, a radical change in inclinations. They ought to put off their excuses, admit that Arminian preparationism was merely a stall, and turn to the Lord. Bellamy demanded that people repent immediately for no other sake than for God's glory. Calvinism did not proffer heaven as a reward; its predestining God promised nothing to individuals in return for their efforts. Indeed, true repentants willed their own damnation should it honor God— never mind the irony that they thereby demonstrated their membership in the elect and their citizenship in heaven. This self-effacing affection, Bellamy thought, could not be reduced to self-love. It broke the cycle of natural self-interestedness, regenerated the will's inclination to true virtue, and enabled the individual to act with genuine benevolence. After regeneration, people might will rightly, love God, appreciate his law, repent of evil, trust Christ, follow God's law, and hence love their neighbor.[50]

At the end of his otherwise pragmatic election sermon, Bellamy reiterated his broad moral perspective: the only real hope for the economy lay in spiritual revival. Moral depravity, he insisted, was "the source" of Connecticut's economic "misery and ruin." He contended that "this dreadful monster, this firstborn of satan, this universal destroyer, which we call sin, has entered into this colony! nay, has entered into our hearts, and is the source of all our calamities, civil, ecclesiastical, and domestic." But should New England become a regenerate society, he mused, there would be "an end to all our divisions. . . . Pride and a luxurious disposition" would cease, "in consequence of which our debts would soon be paid." And "should we posses a disposition" to reform, and "a true Christian temper" and "love to God and to mankind" take "full possession of our souls," we would then be "virtuous" as well as industrious and frugal. "Pride, luxuriousness, covetousness, malice, envy, idleness, dishonesty" would all "die" should "righteousness come and reign" in their place. "The duty of each and every one of us," Bellamy concluded, was to "repent and be converted, to give up ourselves."[51]

We should appreciate the extent to which Bellamy applied Calvinism—even its harsh doctrine of human nature—in ways that made sense to New Englanders. The New Divinity originated, matured, and spread as Bellamy extended his legalistic rendition of doctrine and ethics into the public realm. By addressing the economic concerns of the day, he asserted the importance of Calvinism to the commonweal and the church's prerogatives as a social institution. With special attention to the doctrine of disinterested benevolence, Hopkins later led the New Divinity into other issues of social reform, demanding, among other things, that New Englanders renounce commercial sentiments for slavery.

Bellamy also strengthened Calvinism's cultural voice and appeal—its ability to compete with theological alternatives. Although he lived in a geographically isolated town, Bellamy was caught up in major intellectual and social currents.[52] Certainly his defense of the dogma of original sin attracted much attention. Calvinists as far afield as Scotland requested that he write more on the subject. Hopkins consulted with Bellamy before preparing his contribution to the debate on original sin, *A Bold Push* (Boston, 1758), and other New Englanders were equally affected, if not pleased, with Bellamy's performance. When the Yale faculty found out in 1763 that one of its pupils had studied in Bethlehem, it pressured the young man to "give up . . . original sin," the "distinctive feature of [Edwards's and Bellamy's] party."[53]

Closer to home, Bellamy's ideas resonated with yeoman farmers who felt morally and economically threatened by the intrusion of the market. Hezekiah Hooker and Daniel Avered perhaps did not grasp the nuances of pamphlet warfare. They nevertheless must have appreciated Bellamy's association of Arminianism with commerce, since they too could conclude that contentious market behavior and other vices accompanied liberal religious ideas. Bethlehem's folk also perceived the kinship between Calvinist theories of depravity, repentance, self-denial, and concord and a traditional economic culture. The doctrine of original sin, as many have pointed out, appealed to those who had some sense of crisis and disillusionment.[54]

It would be misleading, however, to reduce Bellamy's theology to an assault on the market. For him and his adherents, Calvinism was a complex of doctrine, ethics, and social values; it formed a single culture.[55] In his pronouncements on human nature and critique of self-love, Bellamy took one aspect of Calvinism and addressed but one part of the ensemble of an as yet immature capitalism. He was not an economist but a theologian. (The "dismal science" separated from moral philosophy only toward the end of the eighteenth century.) Indeed, as William Brietenbach has shown, New Divinity ministers such as Bellamy may have contributed in the long run to the culture of capitalism with their belief in the hidden hand of providence and their ethic of moral restraint.[56] But that is to speak of long-range and implicit effects. If capitalism was the unintended and ironic outcome of the Protestant ethos, then the irony seems particularly strong in the case of Bellamy. Moreover, New England's internal social problems provided only one context for Bellamy's theology. Calamities worse than commerce would press him to further defenses of the God, and the churches, of Calvinism. The coming of the market threatened to unravel society thread by thread. The coming of war threatened a conflagration that would destroy all of New England at once.

Notes

1. Bellamy to Samuel Hopkins, Feb. 3, 1758, HSP; Bellamy, Ps. 119:68, June 4, 1758, CHS. Frink's sermon was published as *A King Reigning in Righteousness, and Princes Reigning in Judgment* (Boston, 1758). We have no direct evidence that Bellamy went to Boston before 1758, but he certainly passed through there during his itinerations in the early 1740s; see Anderson, 331–41. For examples of Boston's widespread and somewhat notorious reputation, see Gary B. Nash, *The Urban Crucible: Social Change, Political Consciousness, and the Origins of the American Revolution* (Cambridge, Mass., 1979), 161–97.

2. Bellamy discussed his efforts in Boston in a letter to Thomas Foxcroft, Oct. 25, 1758, Bellamy manuscripts, Houghton Library, Harvard University, Cambridge, Mass. The key publications, in addition to Bellamy's, Webster's, and Edwards's (titled simply *Original Sin* in the Yale *Works*), were Peter Clark, *The Scripture-Doctrine of Original Sin Stated and Defended. A Summer Morning's Conversation* (Boston, 1758); [Charles Chauncy], *The Opinion of One that has Perused A Summer Morning's Conversation* (Boston, 1758); and [Samuel Hopkins], *A Bold Push, in a letter to the Author of "Fair Play"* (Boston, 1758).

3. Alan MacFarlane, *The Culture of Capitalism* (Oxford, 1987).

4. See Erasmus Jones, *Luxury, Pride and Vanity the Bane of the British Nation* (London, 1750). The discussion here of the growth of the English stock market and the moral commentary that followed relies on P. G. M. Dickson, *The Financial Revolution in England: A Study in the Development of Public Credit, 1688–1756* (Lon-

don, 1967), and Pamela Divinsky, "Virtue in Distress: The Discourse on Economy in Eighteenth-Century England" (Ph.D. diss., University of Chicago, 1990). Divinsky makes good use of the pamphlet literature and the following interpretations: J. G. A. Pocock, *The Machiavellian Moment: Florentine Political Thought and the Atlantic Republican Tradition* (Princeton, N.J., 1975); Pocock, *Virtue, Commerce, and History: Essays on Political Thought and History, Chiefly in the Eighteenth Century* (New York, 1985); Caroline Robbins, *The Eighteenth-Century Commonwealthman: Studies in the Transmission, Development, and Circumstance of English Liberal Thought from the Restoration of Charles II until the War with the Thirteen Colonies* (Cambridge, Mass., 1959); and Joyce Oldham Appleby, *Economic Thought and Ideology in Seventeenth-Century England* (Princeton, N.J., 1978). A suggestive theoretical analysis of the relationship between value commitments and economic modernization is Amartya K. Sen, "Rational Fools: A Critique of the Behavioral Foundations of Economic Theory," in *Beyond Self-Interest*, ed. Jane J. Mansbridge (Chicago, 1990), 25–43. In *The Radicalism of the American Revolution* (New York, 1992), Gordon S. Wood shows that the Revolution eventually fused republican sentiments to more liberal affirmations of self-love and commerce. In "Republicanism: The Career of a Concept," *Journal of American History* 79 (1992): 11–38, Daniel T. Rodgers critiques the use of republicanism as an explanatory paradigm, warning against reification. I use the term here and throughout this book merely to identify one strain within Anglo-American social thought at mid-century.

5. Allan Kulikoff, "The Transition to Capitalism in Rural America," *WMQ* 46 (1989): 120–44. New England did not develop a mature market capitalism until the nineteenth century. For debates about definitions and the timing of the emergence of capitalism, see the historiographical essays by James Henretta, Gary Nash, and Joyce Appleby in Jack P. Greene and J. R. Pole, eds., *Colonial British America: Essays in the New History of the Early Modern Era* (Baltimore, 1984), 233–316, and collected essays by James A. Henretta, *The Origins of American Capitalism* (Boston, 1991).

6. For the development of Connecticut's urban centers, secondary market towns, and country towns, see Bruce C. Daniels, *The Connecticut Town: Growth and Development, 1635–1790* (Middletown, Conn., 1979), and Bruce H. Mann, *Neighbors and Strangers: Law and Community in Early Connecticut* (Chapel Hill, N.C., 1987), 47–50. Helpful discussions of New England's rural markets and the economic implications are Gloria L. Main and Jackson T. Main, "Economic Growth and the Standard of Living in Southern New England, 1640–1774," *The Journal of Economic History* 48 (1988): 27–46; Winifred B. Rothenberg, "The Market and Massachusetts Farmers, 1750–1855," *The Journal of Economic History* 41 (1981): 283–314; and Rothenberg, "The Emergence of Farm Labor Markets and the Transformation of the Rural Economy: Massachusetts, 1750–1855," *The Journal of Economic History* 48 (1988): 537–66. Bushman, *Puritan to Yankee*, 107–14, describes the pattern of trade in rural Connecticut. For a discussion of official trade policy, see Glenn Weaver, *Jonathan Trumbull: Connecticut's Merchant Magistrate (1710–1785)* (Hartford, Conn., 1956), 32–40. For a general statement on the growth of the imperial market and its impact on New Englanders, see T. H. Breen, "Narrative of Commercial Life: Consumption, Ideology, and Community on the Eve of the American Revolution," *WMQ* 50 (1993): 471–501.

7. For Connecticut and Massachusetts currency rates and inflation, see Leslie V. Brock, *The Currency of the American Colonies, 1700–1764: A Study in Colonial Finance and Imperial Relations* (New York, 1975); McCusker, *Money and Exchange*

(Chapel Hill, N.C., 1977), 131–55; and Trumbull, *History of Connecticut*, II:11–31. McCusker's figures indicate an inflation rate for Connecticut's currency of 100 percent from 1740 to 1749. Examples of acts by Connecticut's General Assembly may be found in *CR*, 8:14, 352–59, 392; 9:282, 452–53. Bushman, *Puritan to Yankee*, 107–34, describes the regional conflict over currency. For other comments on the crisis, see Weaver, *Jonathan Trumbull*, 11–21; Robert J. Taylor, *Colonial Connecticut: A History* (Millwood, N.Y., 1979), 98–103; and Zeichner, *Connecticut's Years of Controversy*, 29–41.

8. Bruce C. Daniels, *The Fragmentation of New England: Comparative Perspectives on Economic, Political, and Social Divisions in the Eighteenth Century* (Westport, Conn., 1988), 26–37, 137–49; Mann, *Neighbors and Strangers*, 62–63; Bushman, *Puritan to Yankee*, 115–21; Weaver, *Jonathan Trumbull*, 97–98; and Harold E. Selesky, *War and Society in Colonial Connecticut* (New Haven, Conn., 1990), 99–143.

9. Mann, *Neighbors and Strangers*, 43.

10. T. H. Breen, "'Baubles of Britain': The American and Consumer Revolutions of the Eighteenth Century," *Past and Present* 119 (1988): 73–104. Other observations on New England's consumer tastes are made by Bushman, "American High-Style and Vernacular Cultures," in *Colonial British America*, ed. Greene and Pole, 345–83, and by Kevin M. Sweeney, "Furniture and the Domestic Environment in Wethersfield, Connecticut, 1639–1800," in *Material Life in America, 1600–1860*, ed. Robert Blair St. George (Boston, 1988), 261–90. Provocative remarks on the role of consumption in Anglo-American capitalism are given in Grant McCracken, *Culture and Consumption: New Approaches to the Symbolic Character of Consumer Goods and Activities* (Indianapolis, Ind., 1990), 3–30, and MacFarlane, *The Culture of Capitalism*, 144–90.

11. *Boston Evening Post*, June 23, 1755. The 1762 New London broadside "The Poor Man's Wealth Described; In an Epitomy of a Contented Mind" is typical of popular discontent and criticism of the wealthy. For merchants and wartime ethics, see Weaver, *Jonathan Trumbull*.

12. Nathan Fiske, sermon on Eccles. 10:19, Jan. 23, 1757, Nathan Fiske papers, American Antiquarian Society; Stiles, *Literary Diary*, I:92; Jared Eliot, *Give Cesar His Due* (New London, Conn., 1738), quoted in Bushman, *Puritan to Yankee*, 135; Edwards, Sermon VIII [untitled], June 1749, in *Selections from the Unpublished Writings of Jonathan Edwards*, ed. Alexander B. Grossart (Edinburgh, 1865), 208; and Edwards, "The Sin of Theft and Injustice," Sermon XXVIII in *Practical Sermons: Never Before Published*, tr. Jonathan Edwards the Younger (Edinburgh, 1788), 324–25. Other examples of popular suspicion of commerce abound; see, for example, the *Boston Gazette*, April 27, 1747, and the *Boston Evening Post*, July 24, 1749. The economic ethics of earlier divines show a confidence in determining price, wages, etc. See, for example, Cotton Mather, *Debtor and Creditor* (Boston, 1716) and *Concio ad Populum* (Boston, 1719); Peter Thacher, *Fear of God Restraining Men from Iniquity in Commerce* (Boston, 1720); and Benjamin Wadsworth, *Fraud and Injustice Detected and Condemned* (Boston, 1712).

13. See Mann, *Neighbors and Strangers*, 171–86, for figures on law cases and the judiciary. Ecclesiastical records and reports to and from the General Court indicate an increasing reliance on the government to solve church disputes: CA, *passim*.

14. E. P. Thompson, "The Moral Economy of the English Crowd in the Eighteenth Century," *Past and Present* 50 (1971): 76–136, quotation from 136; James

A. Henretta, "Families and Farms: *Mentalité* in Pre-Industrial America," *WMQ* 35 (1978): 3–32; Christopher Clark, "The Household Economy, Market Exchange, and the Rise of Capitalism in the Connecticut Valley, 1800–1860," *Journal of Social History* 13 (Winter 1979): 169–89. Toby L. Ditz reinforces the importance of the household economy and the ideal of competence in his "Ownership and Obligation: Inheritance and Patriarchal Households in Connecticut, 1750–1820," *WMQ* 47 (1990): 235–65. Daniel Vickers argues that the notion of a household economy, even in rural towns, accommodated new economic values such as competition: Vickers, "Competency and Competition: Economic Culture in Early America," *WMQ* 47 (1990): 3–29. For the economic implications of classical republicanism in America, see Gordon S. Wood, *The Creation of the American Republic, 1776–1787* (Chapel Hill, N.C., 1969), 107–18; and *The Radicalism of the American Revolution*, 94–225.

15. Figures on tax rates and number of taxpayers are taken from WTR. Samples of Bethlehem's probate inventories and land records are taken from WPR, Vols. 3–10 (covering the second half of the century), and from WLR, Vol. 6 (1737–1745), Vol. 7 (1741–1750), and Vol. 9 (1743–1755). Probate records in the Woodbury Town Hall are contemporary copies of wills and other records kept in full at the Connecticut State Library, Hartford, Connecticut; I have sampled and consulted the original records in Hartford in some cases. Occupational identities were taken from probate and land records and from Marshall Linden and Linton E. Simerl, eds., *250 Years of the First Church of Bethlehem* (Bethlehem, Conn., 1990), 17–18, 81–90.

16. For soil conditions, see Daniels, *Connecticut Town*, 187–89. Population figures from WTR and *HW*, I: 239–40. Descriptions of Bellamy's salary and records of the church's building project are contained in the manuscript volume of society records for Bethlehem, the "First Book of the Ecclesiastical Society (1740–1825)," kept in the Bethlehem, Connecticut, Congregational Church (hereafter cited as Society Records); see especially years 1741, 1747, 1761–1769. The Society Records note that in 1761 a committee voted no longer to "oblige [Bellamy] to receive grain in payment for his salary." For Bellamy's lands, see WLR, 6:155, 161; 7:16, 17, 21; and 9:12, 137. Inheritance practices are shown in WPR, *passim*. These documents show a patrilineal inheritance pattern as described by Ditz, "Ownership and Obligation." The figure of 108 family heads in 1756 is an extrapolation from the Woodbury census cited in *HW*, I:775.

17. WPR, *passim*: for Bacon, 10:255–64; for Bellamy, 9:113–14. In sum, Bethlehem resembled the rural Connecticut towns of Woodbury and Kent and the Massachusetts village of Chewbacco, as described in Walsh, "Woodbury"; Grant, *Kent*; and Jedrey, *The World of John Cleaveland*.

18. For the discussion of settlement patterns and neighborhoods, I have used WLR; map of Bethlehem tiers and plots, Bethlehem Town Archives; and Linden and Simerl, *First Church*, 11–20. Hooker's estate included a gun and a few silver items but little else to distinguish him publicly from Avered, whose most notable possession was a deck of cards; Guitteau likewise owned nothing ostentatious. See WPR, 3:65–66; 8: 89; for Guitteau, see the Woodbury probate records at the Connecticut State Library.

19. WTR, *passim*. Probate records often list debts owed to wealthier farmers; John Steel, for example, was a creditor to twenty other townsmen, in the total amount of £112; see WPR, 3: 95, 117. Requests for relief from ministerial rates,

usually granted, are contained in the Society Records. For stratification in urban centers, see Henretta, "Economic Development and Social Structure in Colonial Boston," *WMQ* 22 (1965): 75–92, and Allan Kulikoff, "The Progress of Inequality in Revolutionary Boston," *WMQ* 28 (1971): 375–412.

20. Data on newer settlers gathered from WLR; map of Bethlehem tiers and plots; Society Records, 1761–1768; and Linden and Simerl, *First Church*, 11–20. WTR provide evidence of changes in the profile of the upper class. Information on society affairs, the election of church and town officers, the raising of the new meetinghouse, and seating debates is taken from the Society Records, 1755–1775, and Church Records. For a helpful analysis of meetinghouse politics, church seating, and social development, see Tracy, *Jonathan Edwards*.

21. Society Records; Bellamy to the Moderator of the Bethlehem Society, Mar. 8, 1764, HS 81306; see also Bellamy to the Moderator, Mar. 15, 1764, HS 81309. Until 1755 the Society Records note Bellamy's salary in Old Tenor; in 1760 it was £239. From then until 1763 his compensation is listed in a confusing mixture of Lawful Tenor (which came into use in the early 1750s and followed the price of silver) for wages and Old Tenor for firewood, which lowered the total figure to £193 for 1761. When Bellamy wrote to the committee in 1764, he used Lawful Tenor figures only, describing his salary as £80 plus firewood. In 1778 the Society Records switch to "Continental Law money," resulting in a salary of £90. All of this is further evidence of the fiscal complexities of the period.

22. Bellamy to the Moderator of the Bethlehem Society, Mar. 8, 1764, and Bellamy to the Litchfield County Association, Jan. 25, 1754, quoted in *HW*, II:1059–60. Bellamy's dialogue is quoted in *HW*, II:1060. For Bellamy's New York salary, see William Smith to Bellamy, Feb. 12, 1754, YS, and Richard Webster, *History of the Presbyterian Church*, 628–50. Other documents from the New York affair are discussed and quoted in Anderson, 453–504.

23. Samuel Hopkins, "Memoir," in Edwards A. Park, *Memoir of the Life and Character of Samuel Hopkins, D.D.*, 2d ed. (Boston, 1854), 93; Samuel Davies to Bellamy, July 4, 1751, HS 81192; Davies, *The State of Religion Among the Protestant Dissenters in Virginia: In a Letter to the Reverend Mr. Joseph Bellamy* (Boston, 1751), 29; Bellamy to Anthony Stoddard, Jan. 23, 1754, HS 81207. Some New Yorkers agreed with Bellamy's opinion that he was a rustic; see David Van Horne to Bellamy, Jan. 8, 1754, HS 81533. Davies's observation made its way nearly verbatim into Bellamy's *Divinity of Jesus Christ*, 488, which argued that "*deism* has for some time been . . . the most fashionable scheme among the polite and genteel."

24. Bellamy to the Moderator of the Bethlehem Society, Mar. 8, 1764. Stiles's remark comes from *Extracts*, 405–6. For Bellamy's lands, see WLR, 6:155, 161; 7:16, 17, 21; and 9:12, 137. Bellamy's house still stands; it is owned by the New England Antiquarian and Landmark Society, Hartford, Connecticut.

25. Bellamy to the Moderator of the Bethlehem Society, Mar. 8, 1764. Linden and Simerl, *First Church*, 91, describe the dormitory in Bellamy's house. Notes of society meetings and town and church officers are in the Society Records.

26. Bellamy, Personal Account, in *HW*, I:243; Edwards, "The State of Religion in Northampton," in *The Great Awakening*, ed. Goen, 544–47.

27. Gordon Wood thus characterizes "the obsession with luxury, vice, and corruption" as essentially social commentary in the republican strain; see *Creation of the American Republic*, 113.

28. Bellamy: Amos 4:12, Aug. 13, 1749, YS; Phil. 2:12–13, Jan. 30, 1757, YS;

Luke 13:43, c. 1749, HS 81464. Other sermons used here include Exod. 20:8–11, Apr. 23, 1749, YS (on the Sabbath); John 16:26, May 4, 1755, YS (on the foolishness of materialism); Eccles. 12:1, Feb. 1755, CHS (on rebellion against superiors and parents); Luke 16:27–31, Feb. 1757, YS (on Lazarus and Dives); Matt. 24:40, c. 1755, YS (on idleness and consumption); and John 3:19, Sept. 25, 1740, HS 81454 (on drunkenness). Manuscript sermon collections show that interest in economics was widespread in this period among the clergy, including the likes of Ebenezer Gay (a rationalist), Ebenezer Parkman (a rural Old Light), and New Lights such as Bellamy and Edwards; see, for example, Gay's sermons in *Gay Family Sermons*, Folder 2, American Antiquarian Society, and Parkman's sermons in *Parkman Family Papers*, Box 1, Folder 4, American Antiquarian Society. For other preachers, see J. E. Crowley, *This Sheba, Self: The Conceptualization of Economic Life in Eighteenth-Century America* (Baltimore, 1974).

29. Bellamy, *A Sermon Delivered Before the General Assembly* (New London, Conn., 1762) in *Works*, I:528, 531 (hereafter cited as Election Sermon). Bellamy used the same language throughout his weekly sermons at home, e.g., on Matt. 5:43, June 23, 1753, YS (on selfishness); 2 Thess. 3:6, Dec. 25, 1763, YS (on idleness); and Rom. 12:18, June 15, 1768, CHS (on contention).

30. Bellamy, Election Sermon, 528, 540.

31. Briant, *The Absurdity*, 7, 20–21; Samuel Mather, *The State of Religion in New England* (Glasgow, 1743), quoted in Clifford K. Shipton and John Langdon Sibley, *Sibley's Harvard Graduates: Biographical Sketches of those who Attended Harvard College*, 14 vols. (Boston, 1873–1968), VII:225; Adam Smith, *The Theory of Moral Sentiments* (London, 1759; rep. London, 1853; rep. 1853 edn. New York, 1966), 446; Samuel Cooper, *A Sermon Preached in Boston, New-England, Before the Society for Encouraging Industry, and Employing the Poor* (Boston, 1753), 3, 21. Several Connecticut Old Lights argued the case against moral determinism before the General Assembly and the governor; see, for example, Samuel Hall, *The Legislature's Right*; Hunn, *The Welfare of a Government*; and Todd, *Civil Rulers*. For a brief introduction to Steuart and Smith and their currency in America, see Forrest McDonald, *Novus Ordo Seculorum: The Intellectual Origins of the Constitution* (Lawrence, Kan., 1985), 117–33.

32. *Industry & Frugality Proposed As the Surest Means to Make Us a Rich and Flourishing People, and the Linen Manufacture Recommended* (Boston, 1753), 4, 7, 10.

33. Chauncy, *The Idle Poor Secluded from the Bread of Charity by the Christian Law* (Boston, 1753), 17; Thomas Barnard, *A Sermon Preached Before the Society for Encouraging Industry and Employing the Poor* (Boston, 1758), 10, 14. Similar sentiments on the superiority of works projects to poor relief were expressed by Noah Hobart, in his *Civil Government the Foundation of Social Happiness* (New London, 1751).

34. Bellamy, *TRD*, 69, 186; for the full explication, see *TRD*, 54–81. Bellamy also followed this line of argument in his unpublished critique of Hutcheson, "The Religion of (deprav'd) Nature Delineated," and in his letter to Samuel Johnson, Apr. 7, 1747. After he read *The Nature of True Virtue*, Bellamy adopted Edwards's more nuanced analysis of the types of love. "Love," he wrote in 1766, was motivated by, in descending order of virtue, "benevolence, complacence, [and] gratitude." A benevolent love approved of the primary and irreducible quality of being in another agent, or of "Being in general." A complacent love consented to another agent's virtue—as determined by that agent's "universal union [to] being." A love from gratitude regarded another agent as amiable because that agent ef-

fected some natural good in the subject. Gratitude was hardly more than instinct. Complacence was more virtuous, the quality of commonly good people who were motivated by an intellectual perception of moral qualities. Benevolence, the highest virtue, originated only in a love for being itself. Since God was ontologically supreme—the One with the most being and the source of all being (hence, "Being-in-general")—the highest benevolence came only from a direct sensation of God; Bellamy to Punderson Austin, ca. 1766, quoted in Tryon Edwards, "Memoir," xxix; see xxix–xxxi; Bellamy, unaddressed letter, Oct. 20, 1764, quoted in Tryon Edwards, "Memoir," xxix.

35. Bellamy, Deut. 27:26, Apr. 15, 1759, CHS; *TRD*, 229. Bellamy's explications of these points are contained in *TRD*, 143–63, 299–320; *The Evil of Sin*, 497–522; and *The Law*, 32–39.

36. Bellamy, *TRD*, 181–82, 189; see *TRD*, 179–91, for the full explication. In many regards, Bellamy here anticipated the analyses of common morality in Edwards's *True Virtue*.

37. Bellamy used the term "complacency" in *TRD*, 182. He later adopted Edwards's terminology, "love of complacence."

38. Bellamy, *TRD*, 180; Matt. 5:43–48, June 23, 1753, YS. See *TRD*, 185–88, for the extended discussion.

39. Bellamy, *TRD*, 201–5. Edwards also drew upon supposedly empirical evidence for total depravity in *Original Sin*. Much of the philosophical background for these arguments concerning self-love may be seen in the dispute between Hobbesean, Lockean, and Hutchesonian moral philosophers.

40. Edwards also expressed this distinction in terms of the difference between determinism, which he rejected, and compulsion; see Ramsey, "Editor's Introduction" to Edwards, *Freedom of the Will*, 34–47. Hopkins also used the same definitions of moral and natural capacity, e.g., in Hopkins, *The Works of Samuel Hopkins*, III:299, 428.

41. See Bellamy, *TRD*, 143–65, and *The Law*, 40–58. The most helpful of many discussions of these theological points are Guelzo, *Edwards on the Will*, 17–111, and William K. Breitenbach, "Unregenerate Doings: Selflessness and Selfishness in New Divinity Theology," *American Quarterly* 34 (Winter 1982): 479–502.

42. Bellamy, *TRD*, 301, 309. The words quoted above indicate the forensic tone of Bellamy's argument in *TRD*, 301–20. See Foster, *Genetic History*, 121–25, and Breitenbach, "Consistent Calvinism," 251–55.

43. Bellamy to Hopkins, Dec. 22, 1755. Bellamy's urge to gloss over metaphysical intricacies with moral imperatives helps explain Edwards's somewhat qualified recommendation of *True Religion Delineated*. In the "Preface" to Bellamy's work, Edwards described it as "very seasonable at this day . . . although the author . . . has aimed especially at the benefit of persons of vulgar capacity": Edwards, "Preface," in Bellamy's *Works*, I:46. More forthright to Erskine, Edwards confided that "it might have been well, if [Bellamy] had more years over his head" before publishing *True Religion Delineated*; Edwards to Erskine, July 5, 1750, quoted in Sereno E. Dwight, "Memoir," in *The Works of Jonathan Edwards in Two Volumes*, ed. Edward Hickman (London, 1839), I:clx. Conforti's description of Hopkins elucidates differences between the New Divinity doctrine of disinterested benevolence and Edwards's concession to self-love in *True Virtue*. Hopkins and Bellamy applied their theories to social issues with slightly different emphases; Hopkins

stressed the affective nature of benevolence, Bellamy the public nature of adherence to moral law: Conforti, *Samuel Hopkins*, 109–24.

44. Bellamy, *TRD*, 49, 181–82, 184, 190, 194, 199.

45. Webster, *A Winter Evening's Conversation Upon the Doctrine of Original Sin* (New Haven, 1757), 6, 9, 22–27; [Edmund March], *Fair Play!* (Portsmouth, 1758), 18. For background to the debate, see Conrad Wright, *Unitarianism*, 91–114; Smith, *Original Sin*, 13–59; Holbrook, "Original Sin," 142–65; May, *The Enlightenment*, 51–59; Clyde A. Holbrook, "Editor's Introduction" to Edwards, *Original Sin*, Vol. 3 of *The Works of Jonathan Edwards*, ed. Holbrook (New Haven, Conn., 1970), 1–26, 67–85; and Griffin, *Old Brick*, 111–12, 172–75.

46. Bellamy, *A Letter to the Reverend Author of the Winter-Evening Conversation on Original Sin, from one of his Candid Neighbours* (Boston, 1758), 12–13; Matt. 22:37–40, Sept. 12, 1768, HS 81456. Bellamy's *Essay*, 348–76, expands on these points.

47. Bellamy, *The Evil of Sin*, 520; Election Sermon, 528.

48. Bellamy, Luke 16:27–31, Feb. 1757, YS (on the folly of natural instincts to wealth); Luke 14:16–17, Feb. 9, 1755, (on the rich and poor). For Edwards, see Mark Valeri, "The Economic Thought of Jonathan Edwards," *Church History* 60 (1991): 37–54.

49. Bellamy, 2 Thess. 3:6, Dec. 25, 1763, YS (on idleness); Exod. 20:13, c. 1758, YS (on stealing); Ps. 119:68 (on poor relief); Society Records, *passim* (on the church's lending); John Graham to Bellamy, Apr. 15, 1740, PHS; Church Records; and Bellamy, Acts 6:3, July 1, 1756, YS (on deacons).

50. Bellamy, *TRD*, 97–98; *The Evil of Sin*, 527–28. Hopkins notoriously expressed this consent as "that disposition which implies a willingness to be damned, if it be not most for the glory of God that he should be saved," in "A Dialogue between a Calvinist and a Semi-Calvinist," in Park, *Memoir of the Life and Character of Samuel Hopkins*, 150. For Bellamy's fullest explication of regeneration, see *TRD*, 426–62. As Richard Rabinowitz has written about Hopkins and later New Divinity thinkers, they "vowed to live beyond the limits of human nature." While Rabinowitz concludes that this "diminished" the "practical immediacy of the divine in Christian lives," my argument is that for Bellamy the emphasis on self-denial reinforced both spiritual and practical commitments; see Rabinowitz, *The Spiritual Self in Everyday Life: The Transformation of Personal Religious Experience in Nineteenth-Century New England* (Boston, 1989), 63.

51. Bellamy, Election Sermon, 539–40.

52. Conforti nicely demonstrates the frontier origins of New Divinity conservatism, but he slightly exaggerates the social and intellectual isolation of New Divinity preachers. See Conforti, "The Rise of the New Divinity in Western New England, 1748–1800," *Historical Journal of Western Massachusetts* 8 (1980): 37–47, and *Samuel Hopkins*, 41–58.

53. Hopkins to Bellamy, June 21, 1758, HS 81251; William Gordon to Bellamy, July 27, 1763, HS 81603; Punderson Austin to Bellamy, Feb. 25, 1763, HS 81294. The full title of Hopkins's tract, published anonymously, was *A Bold Push, in a letter to the Author of "Fair Play"* (Boston, 1758).

54. H. Richard Niebuhr and Perry Miller particularly insisted on the close relation between Calvinism, an acute sense of the human predicament, and social disillusionment. See Niebuhr, *The Social Sources of Denominationalism* (New York, 1929); Miller, *The New England Mind: The Seventeenth Century*, 3–34; and Miller,

Jonathan Edwards, 265–82. For a suggestive essay on this topic, which somewhat overemphasizes social and political marginalization, see Daniel Walker Howe, "The Decline of Calvinism: An Approach to Its Study," *Comparative Studies in Society and History* 14 (1972): 306–27.

55. I mean to propose that we view Calvinism holistically, in ways suggested in Clifford Geertz, *The Interpretation of Cultures* (New York, 1973), 3–30.

56. Breitenbach, "Unregenerate Doings."

4

The Wisdom of God

On July 8, 1758, more than twelve thousand regular and provincial troops, one of the largest British expeditions ever assembled in North America, attacked the French-held Fort Carillon at Ticonderoga. Defended by fewer than four thousand Frenchmen under the marquis de Montcalm, Ticonderoga lay between Major General James Abercromby's forces and their chief objective to the north, Crown Point, from which French and Indian forces protected the southern entrance to Lake Champlain and terrorized English settlers on the New York and Massachusetts frontier.[1]

The British were desperate for victory. The continuing threat to New England from Crown Point symbolized three years of Anglo-American military frustration during the Seven Years' War. This conflict between an Anglo-Prussian alliance and the combined forces of France, Austria, and Spain was by contemporary accounts a decisive moment in modern history: the struggle of Protestantism and liberty against Catholicism and tyranny. In 1755 Parliament called on Connecticut and Massachusetts to form provincial regiments for the American phase of the contest, the so-called French and Indian War. Buoyed by memories of New England's surprising 1745 victory at Louisbourg (the French fortress on Cape Breton Island),[2] expectations of the expulsion of the French and Indians, and visions of participation in a global—and to some, millennial—victory of the armies of light over the powers of darkness, New Englanders readily enlisted in provincial regiments.

A series of British defeats from 1755 to 1758 stunned these volunteers. In the first widely publicized battle of the war, a French and Indian party in the wilderness of Pennsylvania ambushed and massacred Major General Edward Braddock's force of fifteen hundred men, three hundred of whom were from Connecticut. New England newspapers, which published the battle's shocking mortality figures (more than 650, including Braddock and more than two thirds of his eighty-five officers) described it as a "gloomy" affair; the army retreated in "Confusion" and "Panick" and "the Officers were absolutely sacrificed."[3] During that summer in 1755, Connecticut sent fifteen hundred volunteers along with Massachusetts recruits on expedition to Crown Point. They suffered high casualties on the march, lost more than two hundred men in an indecisive and bloody encounter with the French at Lake George, and, having failed to sight Crown Point, established a small garrison, Fort William Henry, at the south end of Lake George.

In 1756 and 1757 British military fortunes sank even lower. Once emboldened by the prospect of glory, New England soldiers returned home with accounts of the drudgery of long marches into the wilderness, the maladies of camp life, and the horrors of battle. The number of volunteers, who signed on for one campaign at a time, dropped markedly. The appointment of John Campbell, Lord Loudoun, as head of the North American campaign made recruitment more difficult, since Loudoun antagonized provincials with his reliance on regular officers and his use of New Englanders to build supply lines rather than to engage the enemy. In the summer of 1757 French troops took Fort William Henry in a mere six days, after which their Indian allies slaughtered the retreating English.

Only with the accession of William Pitt as Britain's prime minister did British military fortunes begin to match antebellum expectations. Pitt sent nearly twenty-five thousand troops to North America in 1758. He also replaced Loudoun with Abercromby, making him responsible for moving against the French in the west, and put General Jeffrey Amherst and Brigadier James Wolfe in charge of the reduction of Louisbourg and an assault on Quebec. By July 1758, Anglo-American hopes in the western theater thus lay with Abercromby's forces. Financially exhausted and nearly despondent over the disappointments of the past three years, people throughout New England prayed for word of victory over Crown Point.

On July 11 Chaplain Jonathan Ingersoll (1714–1778) of the Fourth Regiment gave Joseph Bellamy the news from Ticonderoga. It was horrid. According to Ingersoll, Abercromby left his cannon "two miles from the fort" and at the crucial moment of the battle sent the bulk of his best troops upon the most fiercely defended French breastwork "with only Small Arms." Colonel George Augustus Howe, virtually the only regular officer liked by the provincials, was killed shortly into the melee. During the "very Sore" fight, as Ingersoll described it, "a dreadful Slaughter was made among us." Dreadful indeed. The *Boston News-Letter* bewailed the more than two thousand casualties, more than three hundred of whom were provincials. Ingersoll's only consolation amidst a "Discouraged army" was that God showed "Distinguishing mercy to Connecticut troops"; the colony's only regiment engaged in the central and ill-fated attack escaped with few deaths. Sadly, Ingersoll continued, one of the fatalities was John Smith, a young farmer from Bethlehem.[4]

Bellamy undoubtedly informed Smith's widow and son that Smith had perished at the hands of the French on a day of universal mortification throughout New England. Ticonderoga was the most widely publicized battle of the Seven Years' War in North America, and it fell to Bellamy to interpret its meaning to a mournful community. He could not have foreseen that by the end of the summer Louisbourg would fall to Amherst, that the next year Amherst would take Ticonderoga and Crown Point, that Wolfe would capture Quebec in September 1760, and that the war would conclude in 1763 with the Treaty of Paris and the triumph of the British empire. Victory seemed elusive in July 1758.

Bethlehem's pastor had long announced that "God's moral perfections may be known by his moral government of the whole world." North America no less than ancient Palestine "was created for a stage" to "exhibit" divine power, justice, and goodness. It was difficult to grasp, however, how God scripted justice, much less benevolence, in the Champlain Valley or the wilderness of Pennsylvania. Certainly, as Bellamy preached about Ticonderoga, one could sympathize with "poor souls in our army" such as Smith, who, the parson hoped, had "prepared for death." Bellamy knew, however, that New Englanders needed more than sympathy. In order to love God for his moral goodness—the only true preparation for death—and to act with courage, they had to understand God's purposes for the evil that intruded into their lives. War forced Bellamy to bring his theology beyond questions of human nature to the problem of divine nature and history. New England's crisis turned Calvinism into theodicy.[5]

Although relatively few men from Connecticut took part in direct engagements with the enemy after 1755, military conflict came home to Bethlehem with frightening effects. At least one in every five families from Bellamy's town had a son, husband, or father in provincial forces; certainly every resident knew someone on campaign. Woodbury sent four companies into the northern wilderness, two of which saw action at the 1755 battle at Lake George. In 1757 two more companies, among which were twelve Bethlehem volunteers, joined the disastrous defense of Fort William Henry. At least two other soldiers from Bethlehem, including the unfortunate Smith, participated in the debacle at Ticonderoga.[6]

Bellamy stayed in close contact with other New Lights stricken by the imperial conflict. Ten provincial chaplains, two of whom were Bellamy's former students, sent word from the front to Bethlehem. On campaign from Greenbush in southern Massachusetts to Crown Point in 1755, John Graham urged Bellamy to visit the regiment and deliver one of his powerful sermons to fortify the troops, who fought on behalf of "all mankind." Later that summer, Bellamy queried Isaac Foot, a major in another Connecticut regiment, about the Crown Point expedition. Foot replied apprehensively. The march had been slow and inefficient, burdened by heavy provisions, desertion, and news of Braddock's defeat. It would be "awfull," Foot wrote, "if God Shold . . . Cause that we return ashamed or fall in the wilderness—the Consequences too Dark to admitt." Inconceivable to Foot, a French victory at Crown Point would disgrace the cause of godliness: "the Heathen" would "ridicule us and prophanely Roar and Say where is your God[?] How would the adherents of Antichrist Triumph and sing *te Deum*. . . . How many of our Dearest friends, mourn the loss of Husband and Children" and others mourn "the Public Danger and Tremble for the Ark of God." The major pleaded with Bellamy to organize "Good ministers" into a "monthly or oftener" meeting for fasting and prayer.[7]

When the French did indeed survive British attacks on Crown Point, through this and the next two years, Calvinists in western Massachusetts were beset with anxiety. In May 1756 Bellamy wrote to Edwards "in pain, fearing" further defeats at Crown Point and, more poignant, for his mentor's life. He implored Edwards to retreat with his family and Hawley from Stockbridge to the parsonage in Bethlehem, lest they "be too venturesome, and fling away" their lives. Hawley and Edwards refused the invitation, yet displayed little optimism. Hawley told Bellamy in 1757 that he would "sacrifice" his "Life" if necessary, but Montcalm's successes and the defection of most of the Iroquois Confederacy, known as the Six Nations, to the French nonetheless left him deeply frightened. He was "in the utmost distress," unable to sleep for nights on end. Hopkins alerted Bellamy to the precariousness of his own and Edwards's position on the Massachusetts frontier as early as 1754; on a summer afternoon in that year, terrified settlers burst into Hopkins's worship service with news that Indians had attacked Stockbridge and, "shooting, and killing, and scalping," had approached Housatonic. Bellamy's friends survived, but Edwards became "more dejected and melancholy" than Hopkins had ever seen him. Hopkins's frequent letters to Bellamy over the next three years revealed anguish, if not desperation. "Remember your afflicted brother," he asked Bellamy in 1756. Removed from Housatonic to Sheffield, Hopkins dashed off word that the siege of Fort William Henry meant "worse news" to come; Albany and Sheffield would "be taken" next. When the fort fell and a French unit set south to Fort Edward, Hopkins confessed that he was "struck with terror unfelt before." After he saw the dejected countenances of the troops to whom he preached, he "went to studying the book of Judges." Even that most martial of Old Testament histories did not steel Hopkins's nerves. Perplexed at the apparent injustice of it all, he lamented that "we live in strange World and in strange Times." Less than a year later, he remarked with a "sorrowful heart" that the death of Howe at Ticonderoga boded the worst: "we have lost all."[8]

New Englanders had cause enough to ponder God's purposes apart from armed combat. Natural disasters such as droughts, about which Bellamy preached frequently, were constant and often inexplicable threats to farmers' livelihoods. More troubling, an epidemic wasted Bethlehem in 1750 and 1751. This "destroying angel," as Bellamy characterized it, within a few months killed more than thirty people, among whom was Isaac Hill, Bellamy's close friend and the town's physician. The plague aroused popular speculation on malevolent visitations; people were awestruck, according to contemporary accounts, when a flock of quail dropped dead out of the sky above the house of an infected Bethlehem man. The epidemic also moved the General Assembly to grant the town temporary relief from taxes and inspired this 1760 poem:

> Poor Bethlehem that little Part
> Was sorely wounded to the Heart:
> For Thirty-four there soon did die,
> So great was the Calamity:
> A swift Disease swept them away,
> They buried four all in one Day.

From 1755 on, Bellamy and other ministers noted that such local adversities signaled the eruption of more ominous, and widespread, events: regional epidemics, a series of earthquakes in Europe and New England in 1755, and a severe drought throughout New England in 1761–1762.[9]

These natural disasters merely compounded the extraordinary afflictions of the war. It seemed to New Englanders that death and sorrow now came with unprecedented harshness, and ministers struggled in sermons, letters, and private diaries to discover the causes for the evil that befell the children of light. At times, even the most theocentric preachers analyzed some adversities in temporal perspective, as the effects of merely human decisions. Thus, Edwards sometimes blamed the war on the machinations of Louis XV, complained to Erskine about the decisions of British field commanders, and deplored what he perceived as London's unwillingness to fund and prosecute a decisive invasion of Canada. While Edwards, Hopkins, and Bellamy discussed military strategy, Erskine informed his New England brethren of political and diplomatic developments on the Continent: the Anglo-Prussian alliance, affairs in Moscow, and a botched attempt to infiltrate the court at Versailles. When Chaplain Mark Leavenworth (1712–1797) gave Bellamy an analysis of the 1760 expedition to Montreal, he mentioned only natural powers; Leavenworth's fears focused on small troop numbers, inadequate munitions, the weather, and smallpox.[10]

Yet the Edwardseans also tried to explain the moral causes behind politics, strategy, and natural disasters. The doctrine of providence taught that natural powers such as human agency were tools for God's work; the

Lord shaped history through corporate affairs to glorify himself, vindicate righteousness, and punish wickedness. Bellamy described the fall of Fort William Henry accordingly as a "secondary cause," one in a series of "public judgments" or natural "evils" that "come upon Nations and countries . . . from God" to enforce the moral law. "Our duty," Bellamy offered, was to trust providence, repent from the sins that occasioned divine judgment, and pray for mercy. Droughts too, Bellamy preached, were "instruments" of "divine moral government . . . bestowed" as tokens of righteous "vengeance." By moral right, God could "fling the whole world into confusion and render the whole miserable." Ever displaying "kindness" and "benevolence," he instead "handed over" droughts only as occasional judgments; his regular and "constant" pattern was to grant "protection from darkness, cold, [and] famine." In a similar vein, Thomas Foxcroft (1697–1769) analyzed Pitt's policies and Amherst's consequent action at Montreal as "subservient and auxiliary Incident[s]" that from a "spiritualized" vantage appeared as mere instruments of providence.[11]

Bellamy's doctrine of moral law thus implied a providential understanding of history and marked a shift from the Augustinian view of history taken by Edwards, and by Bellamy in his revival days. Earlier in his career, Bellamy discerned no visible pattern of justice in temporal affairs; instead, he sought the meaning of history in the invisible outworking of redemption. Now he sought to explain providence as God's execution of justice in earthly events.

Not all providential schemes, however, were alike. From a millennial perspective, the Anglo-French conflict was part of the eschatological struggle between the godly forces of Protestant England and the evil power of Catholic France. God fixed calamities such as French victories into a pattern that ultimately would vindicate Britain and glorify Christ. Attendant earthquakes and droughts portended these events. Millennialist preachers proclaimed the current crises as signs of New England's inevitable victory.[12]

Bellamy eschewed this civil millennialism. As antagonistic as he and other Edwardseans were toward the British, he did not see New England as part of an Anglo-American union arrayed for apocalyptic battle. He predicted no providential intervention on behalf of the national interests of either Britain or America—no cataclysmic judgments or miraculous deliverances. He understood key millennialist passages to refer not to current collectivities but to timeless moral truths. According to the consistent Calvinist reading of history, New England's fate during the war hinged solely on the extent to which colonists upheld common, juridical standards of rectitude. Divine election, the predestination of individuals apart from their moral actions, did not apply to societies or nations. Given this assumption, Bellamy found no rationale for asserting a specific plan of divine intention for the colonies. The only inevitability to history was the conjunction of corporate virtue and prosperity, vice and calamity.[13]

Bellamy's Calvinism drew closer to the tradition of covenant theology, even though he was not strictly a covenantal thinker. According to that tradition, temporal adversities were chastisements appointed to discipline God's favored nation, bring it to repentance, and secure its redemptive destiny. In 1770 Bellamy's colleague in Litchfield, Judah Champion (1729–1810), remembered the 1757 fall of Fort William Henry and "destruction upon destruction" that followed as God's discipline upon a people who broke the covenant and did "sin away" their "privileges" of peace and prosperity. The "continent" was "alarmed" and turned to the Lord. Thus chastised and humbled, they were delivered and set on high ground. To explain Montcalm's victory at Fort Oswego in 1756, Bellamy drew a parallel between New England and the Israelites of Judges 2:14, whom the Lord "delivered . . . into the hands of spoilers" because of their wickedness. "How much our case is like that of old," Bellamy observed. New England, like Israel, "forsook the Lord" despite a century of divine blessings, incurred God's righteous "anger with the land," and desperately needed "repentance." In a 1758 sermon Bellamy warned soldiers against profanity and prostitution lest they forfeit "God's direction." They were to repent "now," since "it may be too late soon."[14]

Yet Bellamy differed from many covenantal preachers in that he thought the reasons of providence more universal than any putatively national covenant. Along with Hopkins, he projected corporate calamities against a greater backdrop, the operation of the moral law throughout history and in every nation. Indeed, as Bellamy rejected a millennial nationalism, so he abstained from a federal nationalism, the assumption that God instituted a particular covenant with New England as a political entity.[15] He based his apology for Calvinism on an argument from natural law: God was sovereign and good by virtue of his enforcement of moral principles that operated absolutely and universally, that is, irrespective of national prerogatives. "*All men,*" Bellamy asserted, "own the law," even if they did not obey it. Bellamy also argued in his sermon on the fall of Oswego that God gave "the law to all nations of the earth . . . to bring them to repentance." From this perspective, Bellamy spoke of ancient Israel, New England, and French Canada as equally subject to the law. That every nation prospered or perished according to its righteousness or iniquity displayed the justice of divine moral government.[16]

While the language of covenant thus remained an implicit foundation for Bellamy's preaching on providence, it yielded to the terms of moral law as an explicit explanation of corporate duties, neglect of which had brought on New England's afflictions. His wartime sermons lacked reference to the peculiar privileges or covenantal status of New England and exposed instead "the divine conduct towards the world as the law" dictated. Transgression of this law "provoked [providence] to destroy" nations "immediately," that is, inevitably—almost automatically—as the followers of Baal and neighbors of Noah knew all too well. Moral reasons for military fortunes "may appear to us ever so dark," Bellamy explained in 1758, but "the dispensations of divine providence" always upheld the "rule of virtue," as impartial observers such as "the inhabitants of heaven" might discern. According to one of Bellamy's 1759 sermons, the law "by nature" and without exception mandated penalties for its violation; only "to do our duty . . . can save us from oblivion." Hopkins too favored the idea of God's rule through law over a millennial or covenantal nationalism that implied an inscrutable and arbitrary divine will. To emphasize the predictability of providential government, Hopkins (with Braddock in mind) suggested that British difficulties on the Ohio frontier followed "the natural course of things." Many "Calamities and Evils" that were mistaken for direct providential judgments were in fact "the Natural Consequence of Corruption" and other legal transgressions.[17]

This explains why Bellamy did not take the occasion of Connecticut's 1762 election to give a traditional discourse on the covenantal foundations of government. Instead, he lectured the General Assembly about the inherent and natural connection between merit and collective prosperity. The Lord, he reminded his audience, ruled nations through the moral law, so that "Righteousness . . . has a natural tendency to make a nation prosperous and happy. . . . For, as virtue and happiness, so vice and misery, are naturally connected together." No pretensions to a favored status as a religiously orthodox people rendered the colonists safe from this moral principle. New England was as vulnerable to total and irreparable destruction as was pagan and papist Canada. Moreover, should New Englanders of every social class attain "moral virtue," Bellamy promised, peace and harmony would follow; "even the most haughty monarchs of the earth, who in the present state of things, summon mighty armies [and] spread war, devastation, and ruin," would be stopped. "Thundering cannons would cease to roar."[18]

The days nonetheless appeared so laden with calamity that Bellamy was driven beyond the formulaic conventions of providential history. The moral law—much less the millennium, the covenant, or any combination thereof—did not in itself account for the ultimate reasons behind the military blows so lamented in newspapers, the casualties so tragic for Bethlehem, Stockbridge, and dozens of other towns, or the frightening prospect of epidemics. As Fred Anderson has shown, the outcome of battles often confused preachers. Bellamy's admirer John Cleaveland allowed that he simply could not understand, much less explain, the defeat at Ticonderoga. "I am at a loss," Cleaveland wrote, to find "encouraging arguments to use" to lift the troops' "spirits up" from "universal dejection." Nor could Samuel Finley account for the unexpected and swift demise of that "incomparable man," Jonathan Edwards, who had escaped Stockbridge in the spring of 1758 only to die in Princeton a few weeks later from a smallpox innoculation. It was "hopeless," Finley wrote to Bellamy, to proffer some reason for such "a loss." David Bostwick, a New York pastor and protégé of

Bellamy's, admitted to his mentor that during times of such widespread misery and "quick" death, the reasons for evil were "mysterious." In the midst of war and personal tragedy, Bostwick could only mourn: "Good God on what a Slender thread / Hang everlasting things!"[19]

The sheer immensity of New England's suffering raised vexatious questions. What were the reasons for the intrinsic conditions that brought exterior threats? Whence the moral evils that occasioned such natural evils? It was one thing to demonstrate the conjunction between iniquities and affliction, quite another to explain the origins of iniquity itself. Even Calvinists could take only so much punishment before they wondered why God allowed sin at all.

The problem of evil sparked controversy, and as Bellamy addressed it he again encountered Arminians who turned their version of the moral law against Calvinism. They agreed with Bellamy that "*palpable* violations of the law of nature," in Mayhew's words, resulted in misery; God "established [the] connextions" between virtue and natural good, vice and natural evil. Arminians claimed, however, that Calvinists misrepresented God's purposes for the moral law. It was given not to demonstrate God's sovereignty but to present free moral agents with choices. Chauncy thus switched metaphors on Bellamy. History was not a stage on which people acted a providential script; it was a school in which they learned virtue by trial and error. As Chauncy explained, "we need a mixture of evil with good" as "disciplinary tryals," which gave "frequent opportunity for the exercise" of moral faculties—the chance to determine one's future by one's actions. From this perspective, people were quite capable of avoiding "habits of vice" and reforming themselves in order to rectify the misfortunes caused by their own bad choices. Moral evil, then, originated with the potential for humans to obey and disobey fair and attainable legal standards. According to Chauncy's and Mayhew's sermons, New Englanders themselves were ultimately responsible for the evil behind the recent crises.[20]

Such arguments, as Robert Ross (1726–1799) notified Bellamy, challenged Calvinists to explain the justice and goodness of a sovereign creator who had authorized *unavoidable* evil and *inevitable* corruption.[21] Bellamy did not need Ross's reminder. He, Hopkins, and the dozens of younger New Divinity men whom they trained knew quite well that the social crises of the late 1750s and early 1760s demanded particularly of Calvinists a vindication of omnipotent providence. As they tried to reconcile the divine government to moral law, they maintained that an Arminian God abandoned people to their enemies without and within. The God of the consistent Calvinists made no such retreat. He permitted the very sin that brought on the present afflictions and used it to further the Kingdom of Christ and human happiness. This affirmation of both the glory and the benevolence of God, Bellamy and other Edwardseans thought, imbued suffering with order and hope. It was comfort and consolation to a troubled New England.

Driven deeper into theodicy, Bellamy once again consulted Erskine and the Enlightenment theologies that he provided. "The dangerous state of our colonies" and the "late earthquakes," Erskine observed, proved as confusing to British Christians as they did to American, and they provoked similar debates about providence and evil. To Erskine's wonder, European Calvinists found great support in the writings of German theologians under the influence of Christian Wolff (1679–1754), whose theodicy nearly duplicated that of the esteemed (even if heterodox) Gottfried Wilhelm Leibniz (1646–1716). Erskine mentioned a pack of Wolffians, including Ludwig Phillipp Thuemmig (1698–1747), Karl von Creuz (1724–1770), Daniel Wyttenbach (1706–1779), and Johann Freiderich Stapfer (1708–1775). Using syllogistic logic and rationalist axioms, these theologians turned theories of natural religion into a variation of Leibniz's theodicy as follows. First, there must be a sufficient reason to affirm the positive existence of anything. Second, evil is primarily a privation of goodness and has no efficient cause. God, therefore, can be said only to permit evil. Third, given that creatureliness necessarily implies imperfection (hence, evil) and that creation (increased existence) is better than nonexistence, it must be affirmed that God necessarily and rightly creates imperfect beings. It was but a small jump, Erskine intimated, from this conclusion to a Calvinist understanding of creation and fall. He informed Bellamy that Wolffian populizers had "made some of the Lutherans more favourable to Calvinism, and some of the Calvinists to defend their system on a new plan."[22]

Erskine recommended especially and sent to Bethlehem the works of Stapfer and Wyttenbach. "I wish," Erskine wrote, that "both you" and Edwards "would glance" at Stapfer's five-volume *Institutiones Theologiae Polemicae Universae* (Zurich, 1743–1747); it "made good use" of the "great principle" of Leibniz and Wolff "that there is nothing without a sufficient reason: and that therefore, there must be a sufficient reason why a system of which the permission of natural and moral evil is a part should be preferred to any other." Bellamy, that is, might do well to adapt the Wolffians' theology to a refutation of Arminianism, Socinianism, and other anti-Calvinist systems. He did indeed take Erskine's advice and acquired the major treatises of Wolff, Wyttenbach, and Stapfer. Since they relied heavily on the natural law theories of Samuel von Pufendorf (1632–1694), who in turn drew on the legal philosophy of Hugo Grotius (1583–1645), Bellamy obtained Pufendorf's *Of the Law of Nature and Nations* (1672; London, 1749) as well.[23]

Although Bellamy read such works in the context of the colonial crisis, he subsequently raised Calvinism above merely New England polemics; armed with texts of the German Enlightenment, he set out to justify the ways of a Calvinist God to man in terms of a transatlantic, European discourse on fundamental theological issues.[24] His efforts were published as a trilogistic discussion of providential rule: *Sermons upon the Following Subjects, viz. The Divinity of Jesus Christ; The Millen[n]ium; The Wisdom of God, in the Permission of Sin* (Boston, 1758).[25] Gleaned from Bellamy's systematic studies, the rhetoric of these treatises reflected Moral Sense ethics, natural law theory, and Leibnizian cosmology throughout. Bellamy attempted to demonstrate that God was responsible for all of history, including its imperfections, and yet good in terms of benevolence—that he created the best of all possible worlds and ruled it through the moral law so as to promote both justice and happiness. As Bellamy claimed in *The Wisdom of God*, "long before the foundation of the world" an infinite variety of universes "equally lay open to the Divine view." Sovereign and omniscient, God "had his choice" of which to create and used his "perfectly good [moral] taste" in the selection: "this he chose; and this of all possible systems, therefore was the best, infinite wisdom and rectitude being judges."[26]

The final clause of this thesis is striking. Bellamy intended to show that external standards of "wisdom and rectitude," that is, the moral law, constrained God's activity. As one unfriendly Scottish reviewer put it, Bellamy was so enamored of "moral fitness" that he vitiated the dynamic self-agency of God and went "so far as to prescribe law to the Almighty, and dictate with assurance what he may do." Edwards had argued in *Concerning the End for Which God Created the World* that God's will was arbitrary in the sense that the internal character of deity, the divine wisdom, mediated God's acts in the world. Taken to extremes, this postion might imply a voluntarism, according to which whatever God did was good by definition. In contrast, Bellamy here maintained that God's will conformed to self-transcendent, external precepts. The law, in other words, did indeed mediate God's response to himself and the world; it defined the character of divine activity.[27] Only that supposition allowed people to attribute to God what they held as moral qualities, to understand divine goodness, appreciate the reasons for evil, and therefore respond to temporal affliction with faith and obedience. So Bellamy rejected an indiscriminate voluntarism. He thought that "the supreme Monarch of the universe" was no "arbitrary, despotic being, conducting without regard to what is fitting and best, having no reason" or "end in view" inaccessible to "our inquiries and researches." In so weighting the moral perfections of God, Bellamy employed an essentially rationalist method against the Arminian claim that only moral freedom legitimated the existence of sin.[28]

From Bellamy's perspective, then, moral law was the hermeneutical key to the three events that registered the problem of evil: the fall of humanity into sin (the topic of *The Wisdom of God*), the death of Christ (treated in *The Divinity of Christ*), and the final judgment (explained in *The Millen[n]ium*).[29] He began his analysis in *The Wisdom of God* with a reiteration of the Calvinist claim that God glorifed himself in history through the moral law. The creation and preservation of the natural world, which in themselves witnessed to the Creator's benevolence, amounted to "a grand and noble THEATRE" for the perennial disclosure of the law and the wisdom of the divine will in its execution. To illustrate, Bellamy drew on the story of Joseph, the Israelite patriarch whose brothers sold him into slavery. "Ye thought it evil against me," Joseph told them toward the end of his life of remarkable success and prosperity, "but God meant it unto good" (Genesis 50:20). The Lord rectified injustice and used evil in like manner throughout history for the cause of righteousness. "To wean the Israelites from Egypt," for instance, God "let Pharaoh loose" upon them, hardened Pharaoh's heart, and allowed the "impious, covetous, [and] tyrannical" Egyptians to oppress the Israelites. This served only as a prelude to the great exodus event, wherein God destroyed the oppressors, saved Israel, and taught all people to depend on and revere him. The Lord thus declared his willingness "to vindicate his own honour at all events, and revenge affronts offered to his Majesty, and carry on his own designs in spite of all opposition." The exodus revealed God's control over history, "how he fore-ordained whatsoever came to pass"; it also illumined how he worked through an inviolable and predictable law of justice. New Englanders could easily read the subtext beneath Bellamy's exposition: if they were a righteous people suffering under the yoke of idolatrous, French tyranny, then God would deliver them, too.[30]

Israel's history, moreover, was simply one instance within a grander scheme. Beneath stories of hostile emperors and godly deliverers lay the premise of the whole moral system: the admission of sin and misery. "God's moral government of the world," Bellamy suggested, included a "great plan" in which "so much sin is permitted, and so much misery endured." Bellamy's "so much" blunts the point; the problem of evil concerned in reality the inescapability of iniquity and the universality of suffering. Bellamy was quite "sensible" of the "many objections which will be apt to arise in the reader's mind . . . and which, at first sight, may seem to appear quite unanswerable." He listed them. How did the fall of "innocent man" serve God's honor? How was it wise or benevolent for the earth to be inhabited by hell-bound, wicked sinners instead of "a race of incarnate angels" who were "for ever holy and happy?" Could God not have found a better "system?" Did a providential consent to evil imply that "sin is agreeable to his will?"[31]

The second half of *The Wisdom of God* answered these questions with four interconnected demonstrations of the positive value of evil. First, Bellamy proposed from a Leibnizian perspective that created agents were by "the nature of all finite things . . . mutable," since "to be, by nature, immutable, is peculiar to the Deity, and cannot be communicated to a creature." This mutability, or susceptibility to change, made finite agents incapable of more than a "partial view of things." So limited, all created beings were liable to mistaken moral judgments and thus to apostasy. The very existence of humanity was morally good, yet implied God's willing-ness to consent to the possibility of temptation and sin. Second, God cre-ated neither sin nor sinful dispositions. His "permitting of sin consists merely in not hindering of it." He allowed created agents to sin, however, because only thereby could they perceive their subordinate and depen-dent status. Without such knowledge they would have dishonored God by their self-righteousness and their ignorance of a need for grace. The existence of evil, then, had the positive effect of allowing created intelli-gences to recognize their inferior rights in proportion to those of the God-head. Third, the fall allowed people to discern the moral perfections of their Creator. Adam's sin and the subsequent depravity of all his descendants threw into relief God's omnipotence, justice, and benevolence. In his con-demnation of sin yet merciful provision of forgiveness and restoration in Christ, God revealed his regard to human happiness and faithfulness to the law.[32]

Fourth, Bellamy argued, the divine inclination "to bring good out of infinite evil" produced more happiness than would have resulted had God simply brought "good out of good." History was wisely designed to show how providence "can and will over-rule" sin "to greater good." God's rec-titude, that is, appeared only in the actual judgment on, hence presence of, both evil and good. This led to joy and holiness among created agents. Bellamy attempted to demonstrate this point by applying a Hutchesonian moral calculus to two imaginary groups of angels.[33] Suppose, he asked his readers, that the first group of angels suffered no apostasy; they would ex-perience a constant amount of happiness. In a second group of angels, a third fell from innocence. The two thirds remaining under grace would experience happiness tenfold that enjoyed by the first, innocent group, since the blessed angels would recognize the preciousness of their preser-vation, appreciate God's saving grace, and delight in the justice of God's punishment on the fallen. In sum, the total degree of happiness in the second group of angels, even subtracting the hundredfold misery of their fallen brethen, would rise dramatically above the happiness in the first group (by a factor of thirty-two). "It may easily be seen," Bellamy an-nounced, that the "proportionable degree of HAPPINESS" of rational agents exceeded both the level of misery in this world and the degree of happi-ness in an innocent world.[34] Bellamy intended this argument, however it might be judged fatuous, to drive home this point: Calvinists could use no less a moral authority than Hutcheson, as they could Leibniz, to subtantiate God's permission of sin.

Fortunately, Bellamy delved no further into mathematical proofs in *The Wisdom of God*. He concluded with an application of his doctrine to the current crises. The world, he admitted, was indeed terrifying; the poten-tial destruction of New England's social order indicated malfeasance on a universal scale. He quoted John Milton to the effect that war exacerbated the fundamental predicament of humanity,

Who live in hatred, enmity and strife,
Among themselves, and levy cruel wars,
Wasting the earth, each other to destroy;
As if, (which might induce us to accord,)
Man had not hellish foes enough besides,
That day and night for his destruction wait.

As New England's battered troops knew only too well, sin was a fact, and "facts are stubborn things." But to claim, as did Chauncy and Mayhew, that sin existed as a contradiction to God's will, that people could willfully flee providence and throw themselves into worse hands, was to lapse totally into hopelessness and inactivity. By their remonstrances against divine sovereignty, Arminians led people to despair and "conceive the DEITY as unconcerned in human affairs" or, worse, as incapable of prohibiting sin. New England desperately needed to hear instead that "how dark soever the present stage of the world," which "has hardly looked like God's world, but rather like a world where satan reigns," yet God decreed and judged all that was: creation and fall, redemption and consummation. Calvinists had "the greatest reason to believe" that "all should issue well." If other New Englanders also confided in "the conduct of infinite wisdom," Bellamy claimed, then they would forswear their fearful self-interest and strike out with "serenity." A "sight of the wisdom of God in the permission of sin," he asserted, "has a great tendency to make us feel right, and behave well"; it was "the greatest inducement to go on cheerfully in the ways of our duty" with "implicit faith in the supreme Ruler of the universe." Fittingly, Bellamy found a martial metaphor the most appropriate expression of this confidence: "You therefore, may . . . have nothing to do but your duty. Nothing, but to attend upon the business he has marked out for you; like a faithful soldier in an army, who trusts his *general* to conduct affairs."[35]

With their flawed understanding of providence, Arminians failed to appreciate not only the reasons for evil but also the means by which God rectified sin and saved people from it. Bellamy elaborated on this in *The Divinity of Christ*. His subject was the atonement, and his legalistic exposition of the doctrine produced some of his more innovative theology. Augustinian schemes of redemption characteristically placed the crucifixion at the center of providential action. According to standard Puritan theologies, Christ's redemptive death was the principal subject of revelation; it provided the interpretive framework for history. This christocentrism allowed mundane events to appear as types or tropes of the spiritual and eternal effects of Calvary, the assemblage of Christ's invisible Church throughout time. Bellamy's understanding of providence yielded a different perspective. The atonement was but one manifestation of the divine government, the chief instance of God's intention to fulfill the law in history. Bellamy read scripture not primarily as a compilation of christic types but as a succession of literal events that in themselves executed God's justice and benevolence. God acted within historical time at the cross to satisfy retributive justice and redeem sinners.

In support of this proposition, Bellamy deviated from traditional Puritan soteriology with an assertion of a governmental and universal theory of atonement. According to tradition, God appointed Christ's death as a propitiary sacrifice, a payment of the debts owed to God by sinners. It personally transformed believers from unrighteous to righteous and therefore was intended only for the elect (a definite or, as detractors called it, limited atonement). This Anselmic theory, it seemed to Bellamy, placed too much emphasis on the legally awkward concept of transferable guilt and innocence, the notion that Christ released people from their legal obligations. It amounted nearly to antinomianism.

Bellamy based his doctrine instead on the legal theories of Grotius and Pufendorf, according to which the meaning of the atonement lay in the impersonal, forensic requirements of moral justice. The moral law obliged God to punish human depravity with eternal retribution, "for if God pardons an apostate world" without retribution, Bellamy wrote, "then it will appear, that he has no regard to his law . . . or to impartial justice." Yet universal damnation likewise demeaned God's character; a resignation of "the whole human race to destruction" would give "eternal consolation and joy" to the powers of evil who so hated humanity. In his later *Essay on the Nature and Glory of the Gospel of Jesus Christ* (Boston, 1762), Bellamy portrayed God as a political ruler on trial. The Lord maintained his rightful authority over his subjects only with a public demonstration of his willingness to condemn violations of the law; he retained their loyalty only by his willingess to effect their redemption. To accomplish both ends, God incarnated himself in Christ, whose death revealed divine judgment on sin and therefore allowed God juridically to forgive whomever he willed. The cross was a "practical declaration, in the most public manner . . . that God was worthy of all that love, honour, and obedience, which his law required, and that sin was as great an evil as the punishment threatened supposed . . . to the end God might be just, and yet a justifier of the believer. And this he did by obeying and dying in our room and stead." Christ's work, that is, satisfied the necessity for divine rectitude. It was a "salvo *to the divine honour*," a manifestation of God's hatred of sin, not a payment for the personal sins of believers.[36]

Such "evidence" of "impartial rectitude" gave God the legal prerogative to redeem all people (hence a universal atonement). Having removed all moral objections, as it were, to salvation, "Christ's merits are sufficient for all the world, and the door of mercy is opened wide enough for all the world; and God, the supreme Governor, has proclaimed himself reconcileable to all the world." In fact, of course, God elected to regenerate and thus to save only believers in Christ, but any gracious act on God's part demonstrated divine benevolence. Bellamy insisted that all people had good cause to repent and pursue moral reformation—in the knowledge that Christ died for every person and in the hope that regeneration might occur in the process. Since God "opened a way for the honourable exercise of divine grace towards sinners . . . on the cross of Christ," Bellamy proposed, "every motive, every encouragement to God, is collected and brought to a point." God's moral perfections and the glory of the law were manifest, "yet we have the fullest proof, that God is ready to forgive . . . all those who repent and return to him."[37]

According to *The Divinity of Christ*, Arminianism undercut the very foundation of the doctrine of the atonement and thus enervated motives to repentance. The infinite punishment required of a depraved humanity, Bellamy reasoned, necessitated a Mediator whose sacrifice was of infinite worth.[38] With their affirmation of moral freedom, Arminians denied the necessity of an infinite sacrifice, hence Christ's mediatorial role. It was no surprise to Bellamy that many Arminians rejected Christ's divinity and tended to deism. Antinomians too were tacitly anti-Trinitarian, since their disparagements of the divine law equally denied the moral rationale for the divine Sonship. When "stupid mortals," Bellamy fumed, "see so little evil" in the human condition, they find themselves without a Redeemer, helpless before the onslaught of malevolence and without reason to resist its temptations.[39]

However much the atonement manifested the wisdom of providence, two problems remained for Bellamy's theodicy. He had to account for the fact that the unregenerate often prospered on earth and appeared immune from the legal punishments they so deserved. Furthermore, he needed to explain the benevolence of a system in which God created so many people who fell outside the bounds of saving election. Bellamy addressed these topics in the final third of his trilogy, *The Millen[n]ium*. Only at the consummation of history, Bellamy argued, would humanity witness the completion of the acts of providence through the moral law. At the final judgment, the Lord would exhibit fully his execution of justice and benevolence. This last act in the divine drama, written in the eschatological passages of the Bible, fell into two parts: the final punishment of evil and the ultimate salvation of a remarkable number of elect.

Bellamy premised much of his analysis in *The Millen[n]ium* on the doctrine of retributive justice. To reconcile "the eternity of hell-torments" with the ideals of natural law, he argued that the Lord's vindictive wrath, by which ungodly nations had been overthrown throughout history, would justly damn unrepentant individuals and demonic powers. Divine retributive justice was not "groundless, arbitrary vengeance" but a reasonable mode of legal justice. Moreover, it was lovable, since vengeance on misdeeds and selfishness upheld the divine honor. "Love to God, to virtue, and to the system" of natural law, Bellamy insisted, "will naturally induce the governor of the world to punish those who are obstinate enemies to God, to virtue, and to the system." He claimed that "it cannot but appear infinitely amiable" for God to so love the law that he destroyed those whose rebellion incurred the law's condemnation. It was "contrary to the universal [moral] sense of mankind," Bellamy wrote, "groundless" and "irrational," not to say "unscriptural," for New England's liberals to protest the doctrine of eternal punishment. While Chauncy and Mayhew could not bring themselves to admit the moral necessities, and divine wisdom, of hell, Bellamy proclaimed it as a rational implication of moral justice. Adherence to the doctrine equally bested the antinomianism of Croswell, Hervey, and Cudworth, who, too proud to view themselves under sin, rejected the law's demand that every person consent to his own damnable state.[40]

The Millen[n]ium, then, admonished saints on earth to find solace in the divine promise to redress all of the wrongs so apparent in temporal history. Bellamy admitted that this required patience; French and Indian raiders still descended on Massachusetts and deists still taught at Harvard because "satan is still walking to and fro through the earth, and going up and down therein." The "downfall of Antichrist" had not been "accomplished." Bellamy would not forecast the time of the consummation and even intimated that it lay at some distance. Yet Scripture predictions and temporal events from the Exodus to the Reformation confirmed God's intention to destroy Satan in a steady, even if apparently gradual, execution of retributive justice. "So," Bellamy concluded, "we may rationally expect" that Antichrist "will continue to fall."[41]

The Last Days, moreover, encompassed more than damnation; they contained unprecedented moral pleasure. A "sincere concern" for equity, Bellamy maintained, would be conspicuously satisfied in the Millennium, when "the cause of virtue shall finally prevail." To reassure those who suffered in the present crises and persuade those who doubted the goodness of a sovereign God, Bellamy again resorted to moral calculus and computed the soteriological effects of the millennial period of peace, prosperity, and godliness. Given a geometric rate of increase and an end to natural calamities, wars, and providential judgments, the human population born during the millennium would far overbalance the number of people born before. All of these would be saved. Therefore, by the end of history, the proportion of those granted everlasting life to the damned would amount to seventeen thousand to one. No one, Bellamy concluded, could properly question the benevolence of this scheme. The present state of the world should not discourage believers, since millennial felicity as well as justice would arrive gradually, in what Bellamy foresaw as a distant future. Between the present and the "fullness of time," he wrote, "days, and months, and years, will hasten along, and one revolution among the kingdoms of the earth follow upon another."[42]

The Millen[n]ium did not convey a civil millennialism, which predicted an imminent fulfillment of national expectations; yet Bellamy's theodicy nonetheless had political implications. He was so oriented to the collective effects of providence that he conceived of the end of the divine moral government as a harmonious body politic. God had "such power and authority" to "over-rule" the anarchy of cosmic rebellion, Bellamy essayed, that he would "finally bring good out of evil . . . order out of disorder, and . . . harmony and peace, out of all the sin, confusion, and uproar." The Kingdom of God was indeed a kingdom, a social order in which God would "establish his throne, confirm his government, make his law honourable [and] his justice appear tremendous." Such rhetoric linked the eschatological dimensions of providential wisdom once again to New England's contest with forces who threatened to rend and annihilate a godly society in North America.[43]

Although Bellamy assured his people of no particular military victory, imminent or otherwise, he nonetheless roused them to war with confidence that sovereign providence still ruled to rectify all wrongs. In his concluding exhortation in *The Millen[n]ium*, Bellamy mustered all of his rhetorical powers to ennoble and fortify hesitant New Englanders. His conflation of the moral with the temporal dimensions of divine government issued in what Alan Heimert has placed "among the most remarkable perorations in the history of American public address." If one "stood at the head" of the millennial and "glorious army [of Christ], which has been in the wars above these five thousand years, and has lived through so many a dreadful campaign, and allowed to make a speech to these veteran troops," Bellamy wrote, then one "might" give the following address—which he now delivered to New England:

> Hail, noble heroes! brave followers of the Lamb! Your general has sacrificed his life in this glorious cause, and spoiled principalities and powers on the cross! and now he lives and reigns. . . . Your predecessors, the Prophets, Apostles, and Martyrs, with undaunted courage, have marched into the field of battle, and conquered dying! and now reign in heaven! behold, ye are risen up in their room, are engaged in the same cause, and the time of the last general battle draws on, when a glorious victory is to be won. And, although many a valiant soldier may be slain in the field; yet the army shall drive all before them at last.

Assured that they "shall reign with Christ" and witness the eventual triumph of the moral law, Bellamy's hearers were to enlist self-sacrifically in the army of God, just as they were called to volunteer for the assault on Canada:

> Wherefore lay aside every weight, and, with your hearts wholly intent on this grand affair . . . and with . . . redoubled zeal and courage, fall on your spiritual enemies . . . labouring to . . . induce the deluded followers of satan to desert his camp, and enlist as volunteers under your prince, MESSIAH. . . . Sacrifice every earthly comfort in the glorious cause! Sing the triumphs of your victorious general in prisons and at the stake! And die courageously, firmly believing that the cause of truth and righteousness will finally prevail.[44]

Bellamy's *Millen[n]ium* was so successful that he preached it frequently throughout Connecticut during the next several years. It was only one of many such sermons in which he prodded New Englanders with a Calvinist vindication of providence. Indeed, in his weekly preaching during the war Bellamy made even more explicit applications of his theodicy. He repeatedly urged moral effort in the public arena, a union of worldly exertion with confidence in the corporate effects of providence. This had little to do with the salvation of individuals, but it had everything to do with the salvation of New England. "If we love our country," he pleaded in 1755, then "we are to own that we have forfeited this good land" and confess that God brought the French and English "governments to war"; repentance and acknowledgment "that we are entirely dependent" on God would bring New England "to obtain victory over" its "enemies." In July of that same year, Bellamy preached to a congregation composed of civilians and a company of Woodbury troops ready to join the first Crown Point expedition. He explained that France and Spain designed to destroy "the state of America and Britain" and institute a "universal Monarchy" of Catholicism. This providential scourge could be averted with corporate "repentance and reformation," since God would vindicate a righteous country. A state, Bellamy continued, was especially accountable for the institution of moral law in the public realm, that is, civil justice. Citizens and recruits were to "examine" their society "for what is amiss," to root out in particular all inequity in civil courts and see to it that "judges and jurors are faithful." These acts of virtue "would engage God to be on our side" and to "inspire the British nations with wisdom and Courage . . . fill our enemies with Terror," and "prosper us in all our enterprises." The concluding exhortation to this sermon may have unnerved Woodbury's troops on that day, but the preacher intended it as an affirmation of divine justice: "God" could so "easily blast our enemies" from their "fort" that "500 Cannon Ball flung" toward the British at close range would kill "not one man . . . if God wills it."[45]

It afterwards became clear that God had not so willed it—at Crown Point or at a dozen other battlefields. Yet New Englanders, Bellamy insisted, still should not doubt God's purposes. As Bellamy preached in 1756, moral resignation receded into cowardice, which explained the paucity of military enlistments that year. This shamed the colonies. "To be backward and refuse to afford . . . help in a war," he maintained, was self-interested defection, "a deserting of your country's cause." Refusal to volunteer tended "to discourage others . . . encourage the enemy" and therefore afflict New England with the Curse of Meroz (Judges 5:23). In contrast, providential trust produced fortitude, "a temper" to deny any "right to our lives" and dispense with "fear." So minded, "able-bodied young men" decided to "resign" themselves to God's call and simply "up and go" to the army.[46]

Other New Divinity men also surmised that assent to God's purposes for evil allowed a corporate activism particularly needed in times of calamity. When Hopkins expounded on the glorification of God "by the sins of men," he emphasized that "were it not for this truth," there "would be no support for Christians, but their minds would be involved in the most painful gloom." Instead of "being overwhelmed in darkness and despair," the believer received "divine support and comfort." Although Samuel Davies was not a self-proclaimed New Divinity man, he was close enough to the spirit of Bellamy's theology that he too espoused a Calvinist interpretation of history as a spur to action. As Davies preached to Virginia volunteers in 1755, "the best Preparative to encounter Dangers and Death; the best Incentive to true, rational Courage" in the face of such horrors as Braddock's defeat, was to "maintain a sense of divine Providence upon your Hearts." Calvinism allowed frightened soldiers to "be of good Courage, and play the Men for the People and Cities" of God. The doctrine of divine sovereignty, Davies counseled in a 1760 sermon, provided "a calm shore" after all the "sickness and pains, losses and disappointments, war and its ravages." The godly soldier knew that life was unpredictable and often harsh but, rested and assured by providence, flung himself into action, while the self-preoccupied person lapsed into "that easy, negligent," and "idle course" of Arminianism.[47]

In sum, Calvinists thought that their doctrine was politically and militarily much more invigorating than Arminianism. As Bellamy suggested in the preface to his 1758 *Sermons*, the liberals' recourse to the idea of human self-determination was discouraging; if people could embrace evil despite God's best intentions, then misery dominated both earth and heaven, not to mention hell. Arminians, he wrote, "can by no means believe that from eternal ages" the existence of sin "was contrived by infinite wisdom and goodness; but are under a necessity to suppose, that they have taken a different course from what God intended; and that he is really disappointed and grieved." If such "grief and sorrow" burdened heaven, then how much more they dampened courage and fortitute on earth. "To rectify these mistaken notions and scatter these gloomy apprehensions," Bellamy proposed a theodicy that afforded hope. His sermons on the widsom of God in the permission of evil, the atonement, and the millennium were "published at this season, when the state of the world and of the Church appears so exceeding gloomy and dark, and still darker times are by many expected"; they were "calculated to give consolation." True "insight into the nature and wisdom of God's universal government," Bellamy contended, will "afford abundant support, let the present storm rise ever so high, and times grow ever so dark."[48]

Old Lights and Arminians had cause to resent Bellamy; he made it appear that they betrayed New England's armies, not to mention the God and churches of Calvinism. Liberals fired back with charges that his confidence stemmed less from true insight than from theological presumption. The most telling liberal response was Samuel Moody's (1726–1795) *An Attempt to Point Out the Fatal and Pernicious Consequences of The Rev. Mr.*

Joseph Bellamy's Doctrines Respecting Moral Evil (Boston, 1759).[49] The danger of Bellamy's speculations on God's purposes for evil, Moody argued, lay in the "full Horror and Deformity" of their "Manichean" conclusions; it was perverse to ascribe the origins of sin to God's will, rather than to human liberty. Moody glossed Bellamy's illustrations with biting sarcasm. Would Calvinists wish "General *Amherst*" to "Plan to lose a great Number of his Troops: (a third Part suppose;) or that they should revolt?" Such military suicide was impeachable. By inference, a God who ordained the fall deserved no honor. The damnation of their fallen brethren pleased the blessed angels in Bellamy's hypothesis; ought we not by extension, then, Moody continued, "Relish" the "Misery" of fellow human beings? Why not simply "erect Wracks" and torture our neighbor to enhance our moral pleasure? *The Wisdom of God* made God the author of sin, Satan a friend to good. Since people cooperated with the schemes of providence by their viciousness, they had no reason to suspect themselves of rebellion, no motives to repent, and no cause to expect retribution. Indeed, Bellamy taught people to cherish their sins as acts of benevolence, since God used sin to enhance the happiness of the moral system.[50]

To Bellamy's argument that an innocent world would have produced less happiness than this fallen one, Moody replied that Bellamy did not appreciate divine benevolence. God intended a perfectly happy and virtuous world without sin: "had all rational Creatures" used their moral freedom for obedience instead of disobedience, "they would have in a voluntary, active Manner" honored God and lived in an earthly paradise, where there would be no death, no natural disasters, "no War, Carnage, and Devastation, with which Europe and America now groan." The facts of sin and misery, Moody contended, did not argue for the wisdom of their existence; they were "from those Lusts which are dishonorary to God." Political sedition and treachery too were facts, but they were not for "the best," as Bellamy reasoned. According to Moody, Bellamy thus collapsed all moral categories into one overwhelming notion of divine sovereignty. *The Wisdom of God* transformed wickedness into a merit and ironically contradicted the rationale for retributive punishment, the atonement, and Christ's divinity. If believed, Bellamy's account would drive people to deism. More likely, Moody asserted, it would offend the moral sentiments of common people and cause them to abandon Christianity altogether. Better no God than Bellamy's God.[51]

It was typical of "Mr. *Bellamy*," Moody suggested, to "be so violently confident" as to attempt a theological demonstration "above . . . any human Talents." A tyrant in ecclesiastical affairs, Bellamy showed himself equally audacious "by being over curious and positive in Doctrines and Dispensations abstruse and mysterious." The Old Light was far more willing than was the Edwardsean to forego a metaphysical resolution to the contradictions of divine omnipotence and historical contingency, the perfections of God and the existence of evil. From Moody's perspective, Bellamy's Calvinism was too insistent on explanations of moral dilemmas.

It was too rational. Israel Dewey, one of Samuel Hopkins's parishioners, complained in 1759 that Bellamy's moral calculus in *The Millen[n]ium* and in *The Wisdom of God* "was obtained by a wedding between a warm imagination, and the goddess of arithmetick." Old Lights identified Bellamy and Hopkins as friends to deism, near-pantheists who equated God's will with mundane events and therefore merged the divine nature and the created world. Worse than innovative, this "New Divinity," as Holly derided it, appeared inhumane and unbenevolent. When Hopkins began preaching a Calvinist theodicy, Dewey protested the notion of divine permission of sin as "pregnant with a train of the most deformed monsters, that ever were born in the kingdom of irreligion." William Hart saw Edwardseanism as a hard-hearted, arbitrary, cruel tyrant, a tormentor of souls. Israel Holly had the Calvinist doctrine of history in mind when he decried the New Divinity as "a vile and hateful novelty" and "a skulking scheme, a pestilence that walks in darkness."[52]

Hopkins and other Calvinists prompted Bellamy to answer Moody's challenge; Bellamy's subsequent *The Wisdom of God in the Permission of Sin, Vindicated* (Boston, 1760) confirmed the debate as a social and political as well as a theological contest.[53] According to Bellamy, Moody asserted that the Lord was unwilling to create the best moral universe and incapable of preventing evil. In character, Bellamy claimed that Moody's impertinence was lese majesty writ large: "The author of the *Attempt* . . . has undertaken to write against—Against *whom*? against *me*? No: rather, to write against his Maker." Bellamy designed his reply "not to vindicate *myself*, but to vindicate the GOD that made us all." Moreover, Bellamy was indignant at the social implications of Moody's tract. The Old Light denied God's omnipotence and gave all people "reason to fear" the "devil or wicked men." At a time of war, this amounted to treason. The whole premise of New England's engagement against the French was God's absolute power over infernal foes. "We have had public fasts, and public thanksgivings, relative to the war," Bellamy alleged, "as though we firmly believed the universal extent of divine providence." Moody would have "all *New England*" in retreat, convinced that it was at the mercy of "wicked men" over whom God had no "control." Bellamy's theodicy provided in contrast "a prospect of success, that encourages men to action."[54]

Bellamy also pursued the logic behind the pragmatic application, and his subsequent vindication revealed how much his critics were right in this respect: he indeed had come to depend on a rationalist apologetic. He maintained in the *Vindication* that Enlightened ethicists and philosophers such as Cudworth, Turnbull, and Chubb realized that God's omnipotence, goodness, wisdom, and benevolence were a priori axioms for theology. From this perspective, history must be seen to "display God's various natural and moral perfections." The natural law moreover defined these perfections, making it "simply impossible," Bellamy wrote, for God "to conduct" himself "contrary to . . . the joint declaration of all" moral virtues. God could not violate his own transcendent laws and fail to "advance his glory and the good of creation." By definition, then, a divinely created world was the "best of all possible systems," as Leibniz and Turnbull confirmed. Furthermore, sin and misery were a posteriori facts. Bellamy concluded, therefore, that belief in a God who created this world necessarily entailed an affirmation that the divine permission of sin wisely served the ends of moral rectitude and benevolence—that God incorporated evil into this best of all possible worlds. Those who rejected this conclusion cast doubt on either God's goodness (which indeed rendered him the author of sin) or existence. It appeared to Bellamy that proponents of natural religion, including Cudworth and Whitby, had "juster notions of God's moral character" than did the Arminians. "Yea," the deist "Mr. *Chubb* himself" was more quotable than were the likes of Moody.[55]

Bellamy even feared that some New Englanders were so shaken by misfortune that they might accept the most absurd and desperate resolution to the problem of evil—to deny that there was a God. He went so far as to attempt from the pulpit what many Calvinists thought a rationalist presumption: proofs for God's existence. His argument from design paralleled Hutcheson's and Butler's, according to which the system of nature rewarded benevolence and thus reflected a morally superior Designer. "The moral world and the natural world," Bellamy asserted, were "best suited to answer the end" of moral virtue and so demonstrated an intelligent and good "Artificer." Bellamy also produced a variation of the Leibnizian cosmological proof, avering that God's existence, omnipotence, omnipresence, and self-sufficiency were deducible from the dependence of all created things upon an exterior Agent:

> Our own existence is a dependent existence: our blood moves, our pulse beats, and we continue to breathe and live, not of our own labours nor in consequence of our own volitions. God makes us live. . . . So we have the same evidence of his existence as we have of our own. All nature proclaims the Creator [in this sense:] there is not an atom in the center of the earth, but that as it exists by him. [God therefore] is absolutely all-sufficient, [the] original fountain not only of Being, but also of all moral existence. [So,] the Universe is the sole property of an absolute Being, for the Universe is the property of him who gave it existence and continues it in existence.[56]

Bellamy here may have realized that the problem of sin implied a theological demarcation more fundamental than that between Arminians and Calvinists. Sixteen years after the Treaty of Paris, a brilliant essay entitled *Dialogues Concerning Natural Religion* notified the Anglo-American world that the existence of evil reduced all philosophical options to two: revealed (hence irrational) religion and stark (albeit rational) atheism. David Hume, it became clear, was a far greater threat to Christianity than was Francis Hutcheson. "On Hume's Scheme," Bellamy wrote in 1783, "the existence of a Creator" was "all delusion."[57] Yet Bellamy did not dwell on the specter of philosophical atheism in the 1750s and 1760s. He criticized Old Light and Arminian doctrines as a halfway house to unbelief, an abandonment of God's sovereignty over evil and by implication over temporal history. According to his persuasion, liberalism was an illogical and dangerous betrayal of New England, Calvinism a reasonable and ennobling source of courage.

While later historians have focused on the consistent Calvinists' understanding of human nature, Bellamy's contemporaries attended more to the New Divinity doctrine of providence and God's purposes for evil. That doctrine was so important to Bellamy that he made it the subject of his standard ordination sermon, delivered several times before his consociation. Bellamy instructed new ministers to link evangelical themes to history and divine justice—to "understand the true state between God and Man, have just notions of the moral perfections of God and of his moral government of the world . . . and *justify the ways of God to Men.*" Bellamy's critics—from Israel Dewey in 1759, Ezra Stiles in 1772, and Israel Holly in 1780 to *The Quarterly Christian Spectator* in 1830—were right to designate a Calvinist theodicy as the center of his system. Their very protests revealed the urgency of the issue in its time. Stiles especially recognized that Bellamy was a popular and important figure because people yearned to understand divine sovereignty in the midst of social crises.[58] So, for all of its severity, Bellamy's system further enhanced Calvinism's public voice; it spoke quite directly to the daily concerns of frightened New Englanders and their perplexed pastors, anxious magistrates and their distressed farmer-citizens, hesitant soldiers and their mournful relatives.

As Bellamy conformed the New Divinity to ethical discourse and theories of natural law, then, he applied a Calvinist doctrine of history to politics. In particular, his theory of providence asserted God's temporal interest in the vindication of national righteousness and judgment against national iniquity. In 1758 he directed this message to members of a provincial colony who fought as subordinates to the British empire. After 1763 he joined other New Englanders who gained a different perspective. Bellamy began to comprehend that America was an independent subject of the divine moral government. As this conviction strengthened, he turned his commentary from the afflictions of French and Indians to evil in the guise of the British empire itself.

Notes

1. My account of the war here and following relies on Fred Anderson, *A People's Army: Massachusetts Soldiers and Society in the Seven Years' War* (Chapel Hill, N.C., 1984), 6–25, 65–110; Selesky, *War and Society*, 102–19, 144–48; and Trumbull, *History of Connecticut*, II:307–29.

2. The fortress at Louisbourg guarded the Atlantic entrance to the Saint Lawrence River and was returned to the French in the 1748 Treaty of Aix-la-Chapelle.

3. *Boston Weekly News-Letter*, Aug. 14, 1755.

4. Ingersoll to Bellamy, July 11, 1758, HS 81582; *Boston Weekly News-Letter*, July 27, 1758. Smith's widow and son are mentioned in WTR and Church Records.

5. Bellamy, *TRD*, 71–72 (see 70–92); Amos 6:3, July 16, 1758, YS. For the publicity surrounding Ticonderoga, see Anderson, *A People's Army*, 147.

6. *HW*, I:777–78; WTR; Linden and Simerl, *First Church*, 184. Anderson, *A People's Army*, 8, 58–60, concludes that every family in Massachusetts had a relation in provincial regiments or militias.

7. Graham to Bellamy, July 28, 1755, HS 81237; Foot to Bellamy, Aug. 19, 1755, HS 81238. Among the dozens of letters to and from Bellamy about the war, none reveal Bellamy's response to Graham's request. Foot's alarm at the prospect of French victory was shared widely. One popular ballad, quoted in Anderson, *A People's Army*, 220, lamented Braddock's defeat: "Their foes rejoice and shout aloud, / And Antichrist grows very proud." Some of Bellamy's correspondence on the French and Indian War is published in Ford Lewis Battles, "Bellamy Papers," *Hartford Quarterly* 8 (1967): 64–91.

8. Bellamy to Edwards, May 31, 1756, Jonathan Edwards Papers, ANTS; Hawley to Bellamy, Feb. 14, 1757, PHS; and the following letters from Hopkins to Bellamy: Sept. 3, 1754, in Park, "Memoir," 41–42; Jan. 18, 1756, HS 81240; Aug. 5, 1757, HS 81246; Aug. 11, 1757, HS 81655; and July 20, 1758, PHS. See also Hopkins to Bellamy, Aug. 15, 1757, in Park, "Memoir," 43.

9. Church Records (with Bellamy's remark on the 1750 plague); Society Records (for popular fears); and *CR*, 9:562 (the Assembly's reaction). The verses, from [Joseph Fisk], *A Few Lines on the Happy Reduction of Canada . . . and Sickness at Woodbury* (New Haven, 1761), and the story of the doves are cited in Anderson, 250–51. During 1750, 1755, and 1761 a striking number of Bellamy's sermons were occasioned by funerals and droughts. His were not untypical concerns; from 1755 to 1759 some twenty sermons were published in New England on the war and some fifteen on earthquakes.

10. Edwards to Erskine, Apr. 15 and Dec. 15, 1755, Jonathan Edwards Papers, ANTS; Bellamy to Hopkins, Dec. 22, 1755, HSP; Erskine to Bellamy, Jan. 24, 1758, PHS; Leavenworth to Bellamy, Aug. 5, 1760, HS 81272. See Edwards to Erskine, Dec. 11, 1755, Jonathan Edwards Papers, ANTS; Bellamy to Edwards, May 31, 1756, in Dwight, *The Life of President Edwards*, 555–56; and Hopkins to Bellamy, Aug. 5, 1757, HS 81246. Chauncy's *A Letter to a Friend . . . Giving A Concise Account . . . of the Ohio-Defeat* (Boston, 1755) provided one of New England's most straightforwardly naturalistic explanations of military defeats.

11. Bellamy, Lev. 26:41, Aug. 14, 1757, YS; Matt. 5:45, June 20, 1757, YS; Thomas Foxcroft, *Grateful Reflexions . . . on Occasion of the Surrender of Montreal* (Boston, 1760), 34–35. In his *Earthquakes a Token of the Righteous Anger of God* (Boston, 1755), Chauncy gave a thorough explanation of primary and second causation.

12. In New England sermons from the 1750s, Nathan O. Hatch discerns the emergence of civil millennialism, according to which the war predictably unfolded as the eschatological struggle between Christ and Antichrist, republican virtue and absolutist vice; see Hatch, *The Sacred Cause of Liberty: Republican Thought and the Millennium in Revolutionary New England* (New Haven, Conn., 1977). In *Visionary*

Republic, Bloch also describes a millennial fervor attached to American fortunes, a heightened apocalyptic sensibility that cut across Old Light-New Light divisions. In his *In the Pursuit of Shadows: Massachusetts Millenialism [sic] and the Seven Years War* (New York, 1989), Kerry A. Trask places war sermons in the context of a general sense of social crisis in the period. As I argue below, Hatch and Bloch so limit clerical interest in politics to millennialism that they underestimate the extent to which Bellamy addressed contemporary political and military affairs through other providential genres.

13. See, for example, Bellamy, Rev. 12:15, June, 1756, YS; Isa. 66:24, Oct. 24, 1758, YS; 2 Pet. 3:7, Aug. 29, 1758, YS.

14. Judah Champion, *A Brief View of the Distresses, Hardships and Dangers of our Ancestors* (Hartford, Conn., 1770), 26, 43; Bellamy, Judg. 2:14–15, Sept. 5, 1756, YS; and Bellamy, Ps. 108:11–12, May 28, 1758, YS (which reflected the common perception that British encampments were rife with swearing, prostitution, and other forms of ungodliness). These are only two of dozens of Bellamy sermons that addressed the war in such terms. Stout has contended that Edwards and other New Lights joined the bulk of New England ministers who drew upon federal theology to interpret Britain's wars with France; see Stout, *The New England Soul*, 233–55, and "The Puritans and Edwards," in Hatch and Stout, eds., *Jonathan Edwards*, 142–59.

15. Earlier Puritans applied the national-covenant scheme to history with much more confidence than did their mid-eighteenth-century heirs, who found it increasingly difficult to define the covenantal community. Was it a voluntary body of saints, all of New England, or—given the war against France—all of Protestant Britain? Bellamy's emergent political ideas and his contribution to this debate, which became especially heated in the 1760s, are discussed in Chapter 5. A helpful analysis of distinctions between natural law and the covenant in Puritan thought is John D. Eusden, "Natural Law and Covenant Theology in New England, 1620–1670," *Natural Law Forum* 5 (1960): 1–30.

16. Bellamy, Judg. 5:2, 9, 18, Apr. 16, 1758, CHS (emphasis mine); and Judg. 2:14–15. See Bellamy, Rev. 16:4–7, Aug. 19, 1759, YS (on Canada); Isa. 66:24 (on Israel).

17. Bellamy, Deut. 27:26, Apr. 15, 1759, CHS; Judg. 5:2, 9, 18; Josh. 7:5, July 16, 1758, YS; 1 Pet. 3:18–20, Apr. 22, 1759, CHS; and Hopkins, Joel 2:20, Aug. 23, 1755, Hopkins sermons, HSP. Many other Bellamy sermons reflect these themes, e.g., 1 Kings 18:21, Jan. 29, 1758, CHS.

18. Bellamy, Election Sermon, 518–19, 528, 532.

19. Cleaveland, July 11, 1758 letter, quoted in Fred Anderson, *A People's Army*, 144; Finley to Bellamy, May 17, 1758, YS; Bostwick to Bellamy, Mar. 19, 1760, HS 81592. The sermons of the Westborough, Massachusetts, preacher Ebenezer Parkman similarly reveal a profound disorientation during the late 1750s. Fixated on corporate crises, Parkman shifted week to week from optimism to despair to detachment. See Parkman Family Papers, Box 1, Folder 5, American Antiquarian Society. Fred Anderson provides other examples of preachers who wavered between fear and trust, confusion and certainty, empirical realism and spiritual reflection; see Anderson, *A People's Army*, 196–210.

20. Mayhew, *Sermons upon the Following Subjects* (Boston, 1755), 51, 52, 494 (see 51–72, 460–510); Chauncy, *Earthquakes a Token*, 15 (see 7–11, 15–22), and *The Earth Delivered from the Curse . . . A Sermon Occasioned by the late Earthquakes*

(Boston, 1756), 12, 17. For discussions of moral freedom, see Mayhew, *The Dissolution of All Things* (Boston, 1755), 65–67, and *Practical Discourses* (Boston, 1760), 6–9, 114–25. On the connection between natural and moral evil, see Mayhew, *God's Hand and Providence* (Boston, 1760), 7–9. For Mayhew's nonprovidential reading of the war, see his *Two Discourses Delivered October 25th, 1759 . . . A Day of Public Thanksgiving for the Reduction of Quebec* (Boston, 1759). As Heimert has pointed out, Arminians so came to associate the doctrine of divine moral government with predestination that they disparaged the doctrine as a Calvinist ploy. See Heimert, *Religion and the American Mind*, 338.

21. Ross to Bellamy, Sept. 29, 1755, HS 81239.

22. Erskine to Bellamy, Mar. 24, 1755, HS 81234, and Apr. 26, 1756, HS 81241. See Erskine to Bellamy, Aug. 8, 1760, PHS, for a subsequent recommendation of German rationalists.

23. Erskine to Bellamy, Mar. 24, 1755; WPR; Anderson, 378.

24. My perspective thus differs from that of other commentators who describe Bellamy as conservative in method and narrow in focus. Guelzo, for instance, argues that Bellamy and Hopkins "no longer required a transatlantic perspective to keep their minds busy" and that such American provincialism set the New Divinity apart from Edwards, who engaged a more profound and international theological discourse; see Guelzo, *Edwards on the Will*, 135–37. I argue nearly the opposite. It was especially Bellamy who took Calvinist discourse after Edwards out of its New England context and set it in transatlantic perspective.

25. Page references for *The Divinity of Jesus Christ* and *The Millen[n]ium* are given for *Works*, Vol. I. Page references for *The Wisdom of God* (hereafter cited as *WGPS*) are given for *Works*, Vol. II. Other Calvinists also wrote theodicies. Hopkins's was *Sin, thro' Divine Interposition*; Samuel Davies's was *Divine Conduct Vindicated, or the Operations of God Shown to the Operations of Wisdom* (London, 1761). Edwards had broached the topic in the first of his *Two Dissertations. I. Concerning the End for Which God Created the World. II. The Nature of True Virtue* (Boston, 1765).

26. Bellamy, *WGPS*, 35.

27. Robert Riccaultoun to John Erskine, n. d., quoted in Webster, *A History of the Presbyterian Church*, 630. In *Churchmen and Philosophers: From Jonathan Edwards to John Dewey* (New Haven, Conn., 1985), 62–63, Kuklick indicates several points in Bellamy's theology that reflect such differences between the New Divinity and Edwards. Broadly conceived, this contrast was one of mere emphases; just as Bellamy had shifted from his evangelical and Augustianian approach to a providential theodicy, so too Edwards—as seen in the different approaches from *A History of the Work of Redemption* to *The End for Which God Created the World*. Fiering demonstrates that Edwards adopted the apologetic agenda of "theocentric, rationalist metaphysicians" such as the Cambridge Platonists and Malebranche. Fiering's description of this agenda provides an apt characterization of Bellamy's view of history: "because God is an infinitely wise spirit, as well as being omnipotent, all of the creation must be ultimately explicable as an expression of His purposes, which in large part are intelligible to man." See Fiering, "The Rationalist Foundation of Edwards's Metaphysics," in Hatch and Stout, eds., *Jonathan Edwards*, 73–101, quotations from 79, 93. Whereas Edwards drew more heavily on philosophical idealists, however, Bellamy relied extensively on the Wolffians' natural law theory.

28. Bellamy, *WGPS*, 52; see 39–53. Heimert interprets Bellamy's theodicy as an application to liberal society of the evangelical critique of Old Light religion, a polemic against rationalism and Arminianism rendered political through an emphasis on moral government. Identifying Bellamy with later New Divinity theologians, Breitenbach maintains that the Calvinists asserted that the prerogatives of divine will were inaccessible to rational and legal reproof or exoneration. Both Heimert and Breitenbach underestimate the extent to which Bellamy adopted the philosophical ethics of the liberals. Progressively radical Arminianism and the turmoil of the French wars pushed Bellamy to accommodate his conception of divine action to the common idea that God ruled, or governed, according to a clear and logically consistent moral law. See Heimert, *Religion and the American Mind*, 339–50, and Breitenbach, "Consistent Calvinism," 252–55. My analysis aligns more closely with those of May, *The Enlightenment*, 59–65, and Haroutunian, *Piety Versus Moralism*, 30–35, who argue that Bellamy used the Enlightenment's standards to defend Calvinism.

29. Although Bellamy placed *The Wisdom of God* last in his trilogy, it may be analyzed first, as the logical foundation (the temporal past) for his discussion of the work of Christ (the temporal present) and the final judgment (the temporal future).

30. Bellamy, *WGPS*, 18, 32, 53; see 12–28, 41–54. Jeffrey H. Richards shows that the metaphor of *theatrum mundi* served many colonists who struggled to grasp the meaning of historical events in this period. See Richards, *Theatre Enough: American Culture and the Metaphor of the World Stage, 1607–1789* (Durham, N.C., 1991).

31. Bellamy, *WGPS*, 38–39.

32. Bellamy, *WGPS*, 11, 57–58; see 38–74.

33. In the second treatise of *An Inquiry into . . . Beauty and Virtue*, 4th ed., Hutcheson explained and modeled a quantification of moral properties, a moral calculus similiar to that made famous later by Jeremy Bentham.

34. Bellamy, *WGPS*, 67; see 64–67.

35. Bellamy, *WGPS*, 11, 111 (quoting John Milton, *Paradise Lost*, II:500–505), 113, 115; see 106–17.

36. Bellamy, *The Divinity of Jesus Christ*, 490; *Essay*, 378; *TRD*, 349. For Bellamy's use of Grotian and other natural law theories, see Foster, *A Genetic History*, 113–15; Haroutunian, *Piety Versus Moralism*, 160–69; and Doris Paul Rudisill, *The Doctrine of the Atonement in Jonathan Edwards and His Successors* (New York, 1971), 36–47. Other New Divinity men and many liberals adopted this governmental/unlimited theory of the atonement; see Breitenbach, "Unregenerate Doings," 248–50; Guelzo, *Edwards on the Will*, 131–35; and Wright, *Unitarianism*, 219–21.

37. Bellamy, *The Divinity of Jesus Christ*, 492; *TRD*, 391; *Essay*, 399; see *TRD*, 380–402, and *Essay*, 395–402, 427–38.

38. Bellamy, then, did not underpin his doctrine with ontological or metaphysical arguments; he focused on the christological implications of the ethics of mediatorial sacrifice.

39. Bellamy, *The Divinity of Jesus Christ*, 492–93; *Essay*, 381–89. Bellamy elaborated on this argument in an unpublished essay on "The Trinity," YS.

40. Bellamy, *WGPS*, 102, 109, 107. See *The Millen[n]ium*, 498–504, and *Essay*, 413–87.

41. Bellamy, *The Millen[n]ium*, 503.

42. Bellamy, *The Millen[n]ium*, 495–96, 508–09; see 510–12. Affirming Christ's postmillennial advent, Bellamy omitted references to an imminent *parousia* and to a cataclysmic, divine intervention. His emphasis on a gradual coming of the Millennium set him apart from a more fervent, national millennialism. As many scholars have indicated, Bellamy's millennial speculations represented an accommodation to several Enlightenment ideas of divine-human interaction in history, among which were the benevolence of the deity and an optimism towards worldly affairs. See Bloch, *Visionary Republic*, 80–86; Conrad Cherry, *Nature and Religious Imagination: From Edwards to Bushnell* (Philadelphia, 1980), 71–80; and James H. Moorhead, "Between Progress and Apocalypse: A Reassessment of Millennialism in American Religious Thought, 1800–1880," *Journal of American History* 71 (1984): 524–42.

43. Bellamy, *The Evil of Sin*, 511–12.

44. Heimert, *Religion and the American Mind*, 346; Bellamy, *The Millen[n]ium*, 514–15. Bellamy, of course, was not the first Calvinist to link providence to worldly warfare. His exhortations fit neatly into Michael Walzer's analysis of Calvin, Huguenot resistance to the French monarchy, and the Puritan Revolution. See Walzer, *The Revolution of the Saints: A Study in the Origins of Radical Politics* (Cambridge, Mass., 1965).

45. Bellamy, text. illeg., 1755, YS; sermon on "At Crown Point" (no text given), July 9, 1755, YS.

46. Bellamy, Judg. 5:23, Nov. 7, 1756, YS.

47. Hopkins, "God is Glorified in the Sins of Men," Sermon XX in *Twenty-one Sermons, On a Variety of Interesting Subjects, Sentimental and Practical* (Salem, Mass., 1803), 344–45, 354–55; Davies, *Religion and Patriotism the Constituents of a Good Soldier* (Philadelphia, 1755), 11, 24; Heb. 4:11, Dec. 1760, Samuel Davies Papers, Webster transcriptions, Presbyterian Historical Society, Philadelphia. See also Davies's *The Curse of Cowardice* (Boston, 1759).

48. Bellamy, "Preface" to *Sermons Upon the Following Subjects*, in *Works*, II:vii–viii. To compare Bellamy's use of theodicy for consolation to that of other New England ministers, see Davidson, *The Logic of Millennial Thought* (New Haven, Conn., 1977).

49. Moody's tract was published anonymously.

50. Moody, *Joseph Bellamy's Doctrines Respecting Moral Evil*, 7–9, 27.

51. Moody, *Joseph Bellamy's Doctrines Respecting Moral Evil*, 22–23.

52. Moody, *Joseph Bellamy's Doctrines Respecting Moral Evil*, 6; Dewey, *Letter, By a Layman, to Samuel Hopkins, D.D.* (n. p., 1759; 2d ed. Dedham, Mass., 1809), 6, 12; Holly, *Old Divinity*, viii, 28; Hart, *Brief Remarks on a Number of False Propositions* (New London, Conn., 1769). For Old Calvinist reactions to the New Divinity, see Kuklick, *Churchmen and Philosophers*, 50, and Guelzo, *Edwards on the Will*, 140–75.

53. Hereafter cited as *Vindication*, with page references to *Works*, Vol. II.

54. Bellamy, *Vindication*, 121, 151, 178–79.

55. Bellamy, *Vindication*, 129, 137; see 132–38.

56. Bellamy, Gen. 1:1, ca. 1760, HS 81458. Bellamy tried to prove God's existence also in his preaching on Heb. 11:13–16, Oct. 15, 1757, CHS; Rom. 8:6–9, ca. 1760, CHS; and Ps. 119:68, June 4, 1758, CHS. Edwards attempted variations on the ontological and cosmological proofs in *The End for Which God Created the World* and in his private writings; see Wallace E. Anderson, "Editor's Introduc-

tion" to Edwards, *Scientific and Philosophical Writings*, Vol. 6 of *The Works of Jonathan Edwards* (New Haven, Conn., 1980), 53–75.

57. Bellamy to Stephen West, Sept. 29, 1783, Park Family Manuscripts, Sterling Memorial Library, Yale University, New Haven, Conn. Hume's *Dialogues* were published in London in 1779.

58. Bellamy, Jer. 3:14, also titled "On Ministers of the Gospel: to Consociation, Ordination serm.," ca. 1760, YS (emphases Bellamy's); Dewey, *Letter, By a Layman*; Stiles, *Literary Diary*, I:279–80; Holly, *Old Divinity*; *The Quarterly Christian Spectator* 2 (1830): 529–40.

5

Revolution

Bellamy's sermon text on May 16, 1776, "as the clay is in the potter's hand, so are ye in mine hand" (Jeremiah 18:6), provided him with yet another occasion to speak on the divine moral government and temporal history. He explained that providence enforced the moral law on nation-states: "[T]he divine administration towards Nations is suited to countenance virtue and destroy vice. God loves righteousness and hates iniquity." Since "the governance of the world belongs to himself," Bellamy reiterated, "God is able to do as he pleases with the nations of this world. Nations are apt to think that they are independent [from] God . . . and can escape his rule, his will. This emboldens wicked nations in their wickedness. But every nation is subject in the hand of God," who "is wiser than politicians [and] has all nations in his hand." Preaching in a prophetic vein, Bellamy then emphasized the militant import of this message. In previous years he might have produced a jeremiad on New England's sins. Now he delivered a concluding exhortation as remarkable as it was terse: "The British Empire is ripe for destruction."[1]

Two months after hearing this sermon, forty-eight leading townsmen in Bethlehem swore with their pastor to arm themselves in defiance of Parliament and king. A mere twenty years before, Bellamy's parishioners had fought as natural allies of the British. Now, as their oath attested, the "householders in Bethlem" regarded the British as "unnatural Enemies." In "great Danger" from tyranny, the signatories did "voluntarily Ingage" to form a company and equip themselves as soon as they could "with a good Gun, Swoard, or Bayonet, and Carterage Box . . . for the Defence of" their "Invaluable Rights, and Privileges." They furthermore promised "to support the same" with their "Lives and fortunes." These farmers joined other revolutionary forces as well. The government in Hartford allowed them to assemble a militia unit, under their own Captain Elias Dunning, which fought alongside fellow Litchfield County patriots in the Champlain Valley. Other townsmen enlisted in the Continental army. Indeed, nearly all of the town's able-bodied men committed themselves to independence; at least 111 of the town's 159 freemen belonged to the Continental army, the state militia, or the town's volunteer company.[2]

It was no idle boast when these patriots pledged their lives in defense of politically virtuous causes—their "Rights and Privileges." Less than one month after Bethlehem's July oath, Bellamy informed his son Jonathan that "6 of our people who went up" with "the Northern Army" toward Canada died on campaign. Other soldiers from Bethlehem perished in New York, New Jersey, and the Wyoming Valley of Pennsylvania. Patriotic sacrifice, in fact, touched Bellamy's own family. His eldest son, David, fought as a lieutenant in the Connecticut militia at New York, and his other adult son, Jonathan, named after Jonathan Edwards, accepted a commission as an ensign in the Continental army. With tragic irony, Jonathan Bellamy and his namesake met the same nemesis: both fatally contracted smallpox in New Jersey. Whereas Jonathan Edwards, however, died in the service of theology—victim of a vaccination taken to demonstrate its effectiveness to college students—Jonathan Bellamy died in the service of George Washington's army.[3]

Bellamy's theology of law thus came to fruition in revolutionary conflict, the willingness of his sons and other Bethlehem patriots to risk their lives in opposition to British rule. The above account, to be sure, foreshortens into a few months a development that encompassed the final two decades of Bellamy's career. From the early 1760s through the early 1780s, when he retired from the pulpit, Bellamy poured his energies into debates about the nature of virtue, providence and historical causation, the covenanted church and corporate reform. As he had done in the 1750s and early 1760s, he also continued to drive doctrine to its social implications. He gradually concluded that God willed to enforce the moral law with American independence. Despite the claims of scholars who have interpreted his New Divinity as apolitical, Bellamy's theology in fact culminated in a validation of worldly activism and armed rebellion.[4]

Far from a merely dogmatic extension of Edwards or a duplication of covenant theology, Bellamy's blend of doctrine and public ethics signified remarkable and widespread changes in Calvinism during the Revolutionary period. Many scholars have noted implicit connections between New Light theology and civic rebellion. Yet few have explained the transformations within evangelical Calvinism that allowed sometime critics of worldly preoccupation to embrace independence in alliance with non-

Calvinist patriots who defended the Revolution as the cause of reason, toleration, humanity, and social virtue.[5] Bellamy's career provides a case study of this transformation. It shows how Bellamy and his New Divinity followers rendered evangelical doctrine explicitly political and republican. This theological development, reflected in Bellamy's claim that the empire was "ripe for destruction," gave Calvinists throughout New England reason to believe that armed resistance was a moral duty.

Although that particular duty did not become apparent to Bellamy until the mid-1770s, he applied his doctrine of moral law to social issues long before Anglo-American tensions erupted in outright war. His ideas on sin and self-interest, for example, implied a republican critique of an alliance between magistrates and commerce. His theodicy during the French and Indian War asserted God's sometime judgment against the national iniquities of Britain. In the 1760s and 1770s, moreover, New Divinity men such as Bellamy participated in and contributed to revolutionary discourse with their assertion that God was, as Bruce Kuklick has put it, "a constitutional monarch who ruled according to law." As Bellamy encouraged people to measure God's perfection by the fundamental moral constitution of the universe, so he exhorted them to assess human rulers by their fidelity to legal principles.[6]

Those principles, as Bellamy understood them from a Moral Sense perspective, obliged governments to rule benevolently. He explained this point to Connecticut's magistrates at the 1762 election convention. Elected officials and princes were to subject their personal welfare or the aims of their party to the needs of the body politic. "God," he maintained, "loves to see rulers more concerned about their duty than about their private interest," motivated by "a benevolent, generous frame of heart." In political terms, such benevolence led rulers to expedite social harmony and prosperity, which depended on the virtue of citizens. All persons in the colonial government, from governor to local justices, were accordingly to enforce laws that promoted "virtue." Equally important, the highest officials—particularly king, members of Parliament, and royal officers—were to model virtue by reforming themselves, so that "brotherly love . . . spread through all their royal families, among their privy counsellors, through their parliaments, and to their courts of justice . . . into all their distant colonies." No ruler, not even the king himself, was free of these obligations. Bellamy denied any claim to political authority on the basis of high social standing or hereditary right apart from civic virtue. Rulers were to earn their subjects' love, respect, and obedience by being "naturally affected toward the community as a father toward his children." On a provinical level, the election represented a *"voluntary"* submission to men who had consented "to be our fathers."[7]

Bellamy suspected that Anglo-American rulers rarely lived up to these ideals. Surveying Connecticut's social order, he foresaw the possibility that governmental vice would lead to the demise of the commonweal. The colony was in danger of falling into "poverty and slavery," indebtedness, tenancy in place of ownership of land, and bankruptcy. One could have accounted for these problems with reference to natural disasters such as the 1761–1762 drought, social forces such as population increase and the lack of available land, or financial exigencies such as Connecticut's war debts and paucity of good currency. Bellamy probed instead for moral causes. In republican fashion, he found evidence of economic enslavement, self-interested parliamentary and royal officers, and malfeasance in the court itself. He did not delineate the specific policies that gave rise to his suspicions; he delivered a somewhat jumbled, but fervent, philippic in a republican vein. Spreading corruption through the body politic, "civil rulers" oppressed their subjects with bad laws, inequitable law courts, and capricious wars. Having no "regard to the public weal," many authorities "act an arbitrary and tyrannical part" and "often abuse their power and their supremacy to mischievous purposes." Such despots, "without moral rectitude," had neither the "dignity" nor "lustre," whatever their office, to rule.[8]

Bellamy did not name the culprits, but he implied that the British government could not legitimately rule America if it continued to "act in an arbitrary" manner. To maintain its authority, it ought to govern in a non-arbitrary fashion, according to moral law. More specifically, as Pufendorf and Hutcheson had taught Bellamy, governments were to submit to moral and natural law as expressed in constitutional principles. This connection between moral law and constitutional restraint of rulers provided Calvinist and non-Calvinist New Englanders with a method of detecting governmental corruption and legitimating resistance to it. Thus Bellamy united his theology of law to republican politics.[9]

The extent to which constitutionalism permeated Bellamy's theology is evident in the two major ecclesiastical disputes that occupied him from 1765 to 1770. The first of these concerned the activities of Sandemanian and other separatist congregations in Connecticut. Robert Sandeman (1718–1771), whose *Letters on Theron and Aspasio* (Edinburgh, 1757) appeared in New England as *Some Thoughts on Christianity* (Boston, 1764), was a leader of the Scottish separatist movement founded by John Glas (1695–1773). Sandeman contended that true faith was a simple, notional assent to the historical fact that in Christ's resurrection God revealed the divine will to save all people. Such trust had nothing to do with reason, doctrinal demonstration, moral reformation, or subjective persuasions of being forgiven. The implications of this view were antinomian; regeneration did not change the behavior or emotions of sinners. "My religion," Sandeman professed, "is founded . . . not on feeling any change in my heart to the better, or on the remotest good inclination of my will. [It has no] regard to any difference by which one man can distinguish himself from another." Sandeman accused English Methodists and Scottish Calvinists of Arminianism, since they spoke of visible evidences of regeneration; he accused even James Hervey—otherwise reputed to be an antinomian—of Arminianism, since Hervey stressed emotional transformation as the key to faith. Sandeman's followers denied orthodox conceptions of regeneration and refused to proscribe such traditionally censured activities as dancing and Sabbath-breaking.[10]

For a brief period Old Calvinist, New Divinity, and liberal pastors in New England (and New Jersey) were united in an almost frantic effort to prevent the spread of Sandemanian, or Glassite, churches in America. Sandemanians founded congregations in Connecticut in the 1760s, the largest of which was at Danbury. Several Congregational pastors adopted the sectarian doctrine, including Ebenezer White (1709–1779), James Taylor (1729–1788), and David Judson (1715–1776). As small and scattered as they were, these churches aroused widespread animosity because their adherents proposed an extreme antinomianism when both liberal and orthodox clergy demanded moral reformation on a social scale. Sandemanianism appeared all the more menacing when other separatist groups such as the Rogerene Baptists, who like the Glassites rejected state intrusion into religious affairs, took root in New England. By seeming to encourage quietism at best and immorality at worst, Sandemanians distressed Bellamy, Chauncy, Stiles, and the tolerant Baptist Isaac Backus (1724–1806) alike. Political sentiments eventually marked the Sandemanians as enemies to America. Their churches forbade members to take civil oaths, denied the legitimacy of armed rebellion, and turned Loyalist during the Revolution.[11]

Few sects could have been more an affront to Bellamy's moral theology; yet whiggish convictions tempered his reaction to Sandemanian congregations in western Connecticut.[12] From 1763 to 1764 Bellamy moderated a Fairfield Eastern Association council that adjudicated disputes involving the Sandemanian White, orthodox members of his Danbury congregation, and neighboring clergy who wanted White removed. Bellamy surmised after several consultations that he had convinced White of the difference between a proper critique of Arminian preparationism and an improper rejection of moral reformation and repentance. During the next year the association nonetheless rebuffed Bellamy's attempts to arrange a reconciliation between the factions. It censured White, after which the Danbury congregation separated itself from the hostile association. When the association then called for a General Association council to prohibit the separatist meeting, Bellamy informed prospective members of the council that the association had mistakenly forced the separation and now threatened to deny White's parishioners their civil and religious liberties under the Saybrook Platform.[13]

Bellamy's attendant exposition of the Platform drew on progressive theories of natural law, constitutional rights, and civil liberties. In trenchant letters to the council and unpublished essays on ecclesiastical discipline and religious toleration, he argued that New England pastors ought to be the first to uphold the dissenters' legal and "Natural rights" to private conscience, just as Parliament and king were obliged to allow New Englanders the right to choose their own church practices. The Platform, he held, was designed to assure concord by granting "every man for himself, and every body of men, whether greater or smaller," the "right to judge for themselves what is the true sense of Scripture. Nor can this right of private Judgment be lawfully taken away from one individual by any power on Earth, whether Civil or Ecclesiastical." Should the General Association deny this right, it would implicate itself in political tyranny, the type of dangerous and arbitrary presumption so often assumed by Parliament. "This," Bellamy warned, would "condemn all Protestant Dissenters in the British Dominions" and "Justify the High Tory Party and all other Enemies to Tolleration."[14]

Bellamy did not intend to undermine the principles of congregational discipline; he was an energetic proponent of the use of associational authority against Arminian and antinomian heterodoxy. His juridical logic, however, led to a civic assertion of moral rights. The Platform, he argued, was "binding simply on the fact of a voluntary Agreement." The Danbury separatists had renounced the Platform and no longer were subject to associational rule. Unfortunate as their dissent and doctrines were, Bellamy asserted, White's people should have been allowed to meet as they pleased. The Fairfield East Association had wrongly exacerbated tensions in the Danbury community.[15]

According to Bellamy, the Litchfield Consociation was a model for how the rule of charity and right of private conscience might inhibit the sort of rancor suffered in the Fairfield East Association. "In Litchfield County," he claimed, "we do not think Say-Brook Platform in its peculiarities *Jure Divino* but look upon it merely as an Agreement between Neighbour Churches, voluntarily come into . . . for the Sake of Mutual Benefit." Bellamy and his colleagues thought that natural and constitutional principles, the "peculiar Civil Privileges" of Connecticut, superseded ecclesiastical privilege: "[A]ll the Ministers in Litchfield County are to a man united in these Principles, and no doubt by far the greater part of the colony are in these Sentiments, if they deserve to be called generous, manly, Christian."[16]

In a second controversy from this period, Bellamy took a different approach to the relationship between religious and civic virtue. His last six publications concerned the Half-way Covenant and the consistent Calvinists' reinstitution of regenerate qualifications for communicant privileges in their churches.

Highly visible during the Northampton affair that eventuated in Edwards's dismissal in 1750, questions of sacramental qualifications had receded from public debate during the war with France. They resurfaced, however, in Connecticut in 1767 with the organization of a new parish near Bethlehem, the Litchfield South Farms church, whose members quarreled over the Half-way Covenant until 1775. The majority of the congregation proposed to call a Stoddardean pastor, while the minority followed the prevalent sentiment in the Litchfield Consociation, which under Bellamy's leadership discouraged the Half-way practice.[17]

To win the argument for the minority in South Farms, Bellamy wrote *The Half-way Covenant* (New Haven, 1769), an imaginary dialogue between an unregenerate member of a Stoddardean church who had just moved into a New Divinity parish and his new minister, who refused to baptize the new parishioner's child. Bellamy recapitulated here many of his previous criticisms of Old Light—what had become known as Old Calvinist—patterns of religious life: the putative Arminianism of churches that allowed the unregenerate access to the covenantal prerogatives of baptism and the Lord's Supper. He went beyond charges of Arminianism, however, to an analysis of the moral obligations of "owning the covenant." The minister in Bellamy's dialogue observed that nearly all church covenants required people to "avouch the Lord Jehovah to be" their "sovereign Lord and supreme Good" and "devote and give up" themselves "to his fear and service, to walk in all his ways and keep all his commands." This language, he maintained, conveyed the necessity of spiritual rebirth. Owners of the covenant claimed to have experienced regeneration in the form of self-denial and devotion to God; they also swore to fulfill the divine commands to repent and turn to Christ. None of this was possible without grace. Those who took this oath thus promised that they were to the best of their knowledge regenerate. Properly observed, the covenant belonged only to saints.[18]

If such were the case, the parishioner admitted, then he indeed was not entitled to own the covenant, have his child baptized, and attend the Lord's Supper, despite his communicant membership in his previous church. He was innocent of any intentional deception, since he had assumed (falsely, as he now learned) that the oath required only a profession of moral sincerity: "I never knew what I was about, nor considered the import of the words I publicly gave my consent unto" in order to join "in full communion." Nonetheless, the new minister warned, the parishioner's Stoddardean presumptions had led him "to make a false and lying profession," which was "inexcusable wickedness." The parishioner now had all the more sin from which to repent and seek conversion.[19]

After consultation with his previous pastor, the parishioner returned to the New Divinity man with the proposition that church covenants duplicated not the covenant of grace but the Old Testament covenant of works. God gave the latter to all Israelites, many of whom were not genuine believers. It appeared from this perspective that God obliged whole societies to endorse a covenant into which even the unregenerate might enter. The church, then, properly provided baptism and the Lord's Supper as seals of a covenant that confirmed its members' intentions to seek grace, whether or not they were regenerate.[20]

New England divines had long postulated the existence of several covenants, but Bellamy so objected to Stoddardeanism that he denied the assertion of any covenant but that of grace. According to the dialogue's New Divinity parson, God never sanctioned the covenantal presumptions of graceless Jews; he punished them for their hypocrisy in claiming to be holy when they were not. "God never proposed any covenant to mankind, but what required real holiness" and therefore regeneration "on man's part." True enough, "Scripture language" spoke of "*the law of works and the law of faith*" as universal codes; however, "there is but one covenant," given solely to saints. Therefore, "the doctrine of an external covenant, distinct from the covenant of grace, is not from heaven, but of men."[21]

Bellamy's *The Half-way Covenant* incited a near riot in print. Old Calvinists had complained previously that his ideas were overly popular, especially among the host of young students who streamed out of Bethlehem; John Devotion had warned Ezra Stiles earlier that "Bellamyan Notions" of communicant membership might spread throughout Connecticut, alienate hundreds of sincere but nonregenerate people, and lead to a mass defection to the Church of England. This private protest yielded to public outcry when Bellamy published his dialogues. In little over a year, he and his Old Calvinist opponents produced twelve lengthy treatises on the two most controversial aspects of his argument: the distinction between moral law (by which God ordered all societies) and covenantal privileges (which God gave only to the regenerate), and the claim that Stoddardeanism encouraged people to violate the meaning of public oaths or contracts.[22]

Bellamy's critique, then, provoked some Old Calvinists to reaffirm and defend the doctrine of a social or national covenant. In a *A Second Dialogue, Between a Minister and His Parishioner, Concerning the Half-way Covenant* (Hartford, 1769), Nathaniel Taylor (1722–1800) maintained that Bellamy had some reason to question open communion but no cause to overthrow such a common practice as the Half-way Covenant or such a time-honored doctrine as New England's election to covenantal privileges. While Taylor branded Bellamy a separatist, Moses Mather (1719–1806), an Old Calvinist in what became the town of Darien, wrote a thorough explication of the Stoddardean notion of covenants. In *The Visible Church, in Covenant with God* (New Haven, 1769) and *The Visible Church, in Covenant with God, Further Illustrated* (New Haven, 1770), Mather set out to demonstrate the divine institution of a covenant that bound sinners and saints to external duties such as infant baptism. He grounded his argument, according to Puritan tradition, on the premise that ancient Israel was a national church, an elect people of whom some were unregenerate. Since Israel was a type of the Christian community, the church rightly administered an external covenant that commanded at least superficial obedience to the moral law—hence sacramental participation—and an internal covenant of grace that required regeneration.

In several replies to Taylor and Mather, Bellamy denied the accusation of separatism yet persisted in his assertion that the Bible offered no covenantal promises to unbelievers. According to Bellamy, Taylor recognized as much when he admitted that churches ought to place at least some restrictions on the Lord's Supper; it was inconsistent, Bellamy charged in *The Inconsistence of Renouncing the Half-way Covenant, and yet Retaining the Half-way Practice* (New Haven, 1769), to close communion and open baptism. To the Old Calvinist argument that custom and precedent legitimated Stoddardeanism, Bellamy responded in *That there is but One Covenant* (New Haven, 1769) with a lengthy discussion on the primacy of moral law over historical practice as a rule for doctrine. He argued that requirements for church membership were biblically sanctioned, whatever some ministers held as common practice in New England, only to the extent that they incorporated the covenant of grace, "upon which God's visible church is founded." Any policy that invited the unregenerate to own the covenant was a fabrication, "devised by men" in contrast to the designs of God. Stoddardeans, Bellamy repeated, thus encouraged their people to swear falsely: to lie and say that they fulfilled the covenant when in fact they did not. The assertion of an external, "graceless" covenant—that is, a covenant offered to temporal societies—condoned sin, promoted falsehood, and rewarded hypocrisy.[23]

Old Calvinist ecclesiology, Bellamy concluded, debased social discourse and made for bad public ethics. As he wrote in *A Careful and Strict Examination of the External Covenant* (New Haven, 1770), the Half-way practice violated moral "LAW," plain and simple. In this light, Mather and his type were worse antinomians than the dreaded Sandeman. The law required repentance; Old Calvinists recommended the opposite, proposing instead a sacramental theory that legitimated lying and insincerity. No wonder, Bellamy exclaimed, that when "the true Gospel of Christ is explained" to such men, they "cry out, 'this is *new divinity* to me.' For it may truly be quite new" to reprobates; "the true Gospel of Christ" would not "appear to be *new divinity* to an old saint."[24]

Bellamy's opponents were quick to resist his charge of ethical, as well as doctrinal, deviation. Ebenezer Devotion (1714–1771) argued that if the sacramental debate turned on the issue of social and political purity, then strict Calvinism was untenable. According to Devotion, Bellamy's appeal to honesty and virtue belied his disrespect for liberty; he refused people their "visible rights" to own the covenant according to their own consciences. The New Divinity campaign threatened to expel three fourths of Connecticut's church members and subject those remaining to ministers who autocratically set the terms of communion. This tyranny signified an "infringement upon our religious liberties" at least as odious as Britain's threat to "our civil ones."[25]

Furthermore, according to Devotion, Bellamy taught that people could enter into covenants properly only if convinced of their own moral sincerity. An upright man whose scruples prevented him from an assurance of regeneration had less right or obligation to own the covenant, by Bellamy's logic, than a self-deceived rogue who thought himself godly. This was, Devotion suggested, a "dangerous doctrine in all visible communities . . . bad in common life" and "worse in politicks," since it located the meaning and authority of social contracts not in their explicit language but in the subjective states of subscribers. It was Bellamy's policy, then, not the Old Calvinists', that devalued the significance of public oaths and threatened the very concept of contractual fidelity.[26]

The sacramental controversy had become a forum on political virtue. Increasingly drawn to an alliance between Calvinism and republicanism, Bellamy would not concede to his adversaries. His response to Devotion drew several parallels between strict observance of the sacramental covenant and proper fulfillment of civil contracts. In *A Careful and Strict Examination*, for example, he agreed with Devotion that the meaning of social compacts—whether church covenants, political constitutions, or civil documents such as deeds and bonds—inhered in "the contents of the written instrument." Devotion, however, mistakenly assumed that merely external or verbal assent implied concurrence with the terms of contracts. The subjective state of parties to "written instruments" was indeed crucial in this sense: the validity of consent to those agreements depended on a proper understanding of and assent to the terms therein. "Sealing," as Bellamy put it, "denotes a present consent of heart to the contents," or the "whole transaction would be a perfect trifling" and mere "hypocrisy." He contended in *That there is but one Covenant* that "there are thousands of professed Christians" who claimed to "believe the bible" and belong to "the visible church" and yet patently embraced Arminianism, deism, and antinomianism. Insisting that the Bible contained "their own scheme," they twisted its meaning to suit their own creed. Certainly they were not entitled to their claims. Godless Israelites proclaimed their covenantal fidelity, but they "made a false profession" and "lied to GOD with their tongues." Moses and the prophets rightly condemned them. By inference, it was no "tyranny" for New England's ministers to attempt to distinguish between true and false consent to church covenants, whose meanings were codified in Calvinist creeds such as the Westminster and Savoy Confessions and the Saybrook Platform. Ministers had no "right . . . to combine to set aside truth and strictness, and to introduce error and looseness, in order to please a wicked world."[27]

Judgment of public professions, Bellamy emphasized, protected civil as well as ecclesiastical order. A man might well "swear allegiance to the king and renounce" a wicked pretender, but the magistrate "who administers the oaths . . . judges" their worth according to the man's intention—not to "what outwardly appears." To forgo this assessment was "a short and easy method for dishonest, cheating, promise-breaking" people to violate their word. With their remonstrances against covenantal integrity,

Old Calvinists sanctioned public vice, "for every one of [Mather's] objections against a profession of godliness are full force against a profession of a disposition to honestly pay our debts, and act up to our word and promise in our dealings with our fellow men." From Bellamy's perspective, consistent Calvinism upheld the moral law against perjury and thus reinforced republican vigilance, New England's safeguard against official dissimulation and betrayal.[28]

Despite his attenuated doctrine of social covenant, then, Bellamy did not sever divine command from political institution. To be sure, he asserted that no community to which unrepentant sinners belonged—no Arminian church and no temporal society or nation—should claim the prerogatives of covenantal promise. Since he supposed that the only genuine covenant belonged to believers who understood and accepted its premises, Bellamy rarely drew on covenantal language to explain temporal affairs. Even as he anticipated a war for independence, he deemphasized the federal notion of an elect America. Yet Bellamy still held that secular bodies were accountable to the moral law, through which divine commands came universally and intelligibly to every person and nation. Natural law rhetoric, as Bruce Mann, John Eusden, and James Kloppenberg have shown, obligated civil authorities to impersonal precepts codified in political constitutions; it denoted standards of legitimacy more fixed and more absolute than the unique conditions of divine ordination as posited in traditional covenant theology.[29]

The principle of moral law thus allowed Bellamy to apply his Moral Sense ethics expansively to social and political affairs. The need for honesty and truth in covenantal practice could be translated into a republican tenet. Bellamy held that fealty to public promise—right motives in assent to social contracts whose language was pure—defined the conditions of corporate authority. Those who distorted the intent of contracts (be they constitutional, legal, or covenantal) and thereby claimed undue prerogatives violated not only the meaning of words but also moral law. They were unfit for public trust and destined for judgment, just as the unregenerate were unfit for sacramental trust.

That same moral law also demanded the subjection of private interest to social solidarity. As the sacramental debate in western Connecticut wound down, Bellamy yielded to the will of the Fairfield Eastern Consociation. When George Beckwith (1703–1794), the pastor favored by the majority, settled in the South Farms parish, Bellamy tried to end the dispute amicably. He asked the minority in South Farms to rejoin the church and wrote a conciliatory, if overly formal, letter to Beckwith. In 1770, when a fellow New Divinity minister took the occasion of an ordination sermon to denounce the Half-way practice, Bellamy chastised him for publicly raising the issue again. He, insisted Bellamy, ought to have focused his sermon on "charity, love, and concord." In this case, benevolence meant respect for the right of a community to choose its religious principles, even if they were not strictly Calvinist. This was especially important, Bellamy emphasized in 1776, during a rebellion premised on political virtues such as benevolence. Even Ezra Stiles conceded that the "Pope of Litchfield County," despite his autocratic instincts, had begun to display democratic principles.[30]

In the ebb and flow of antagonism between London and the colonies during the 1760s, Bellamy drew on moral law as a standard by which to measure civil rule, and he increasingly detected corruption. It has become commonplace to note that New Lights in Connecticut were spokesmen for popular opposition to British policies. They protested royal intervention in border disputes between colonies, official prohibitions against the settlement of lands in the west, and Parliament's trade and tax measures, all of which seemed to bring economic devastation and thus roused republican resentment.[31] Connecticut's Sons of Liberty, agitators against the Stamp Act and against officals who supported it, had their greatest following in Litchfield, Fairfield, and Windham counties—where evangelical Calvinism dominated. In February 1766 a convention of Litchfield County towns, including Bethlehem, declared the Stamp Act "unconstitutional" and thereafter met regularly to support patriot activities throughout New England. Governor Thomas Fitch, who regarded Bellamy as politically dangerous, urged him to refrain from stirring up opposition to the colonial government. In spite of such requests, Bellamy and other New Divinity preachers encouraged many of the oppositionist political movements that in Connecticut went under the name of "New Light" politics. They resisted British agents, loyalist magistrates, colonial officials who were responsible for implementing parliamentary policies, and local groups that sympathized with the imperial government. Anglican proposals for an American episcopate especially angered Bellamy, who decried them as "dangerous to the body politic" and to the constitutional principles of civil and religious liberty. He was persuaded to become a leading proponent of the Plan of Union (an attempted coalition of the Presbyterian Church in New York and New Jersey and the Congregational churches of Connecticut) in defense of the rights of congregationalism against episcopacy.[32]

Such conflicts during the mid-1760s marked a turning point in Bellamy's understanding of Anglo-American relations; he began to perceive Britain and New England as moral adversaries. Suspecting that the British government as a whole was corrupt and that the king himself—not just his bishops, ministers, and local officials—harbored malicious intentions toward New England, Bellamy called on his British correspondents for further evidence of imperial designs and motivations. Erskine and William Gordon, an English dissenter, provided him with detailed explanations of elections, parliamentary debates, and British perceptions of events in America. Bellamy shared this transatlantic correspondence with Hopkins and Hart, who characterized it as commentary on "the dark state of publick affairs in America."[33]

Gordon's and Erskine's commentary traced corruption on high to London. Many colonists found signs of encouragement in the fall of the ministry of George Grenville in 1765 and in the revocation of the Stamp Act the following year. Gordon's letters, in contrast, were anything but sanguine. According to him, Pitt's accession to power—applauded by most colonists—merely disguised widespread villainy. He and Erskine repeatedly warned Bellamy that English policies would ruin the colonies economically and destroy their liberties. In 1770 Erskine described politics in Britain as "gloomy" and parliamentary laws as "imperfect"; every British colony was in great danger. Bellamy continued to press Gordon for his opinion of the crisis, while complaining of Parliament's dishonesty, abuse of the law, and refusal to reform. Gordon agreed that imperial statutes were "oppressive tyrannical arbitrary and slavish" and stressed the "wickedness, bribery" and general degeneracy of politics in Britain, where "boroughs" were "bought and sold" and "magistrates" were "a vile set of men." Nonetheless, he surmised, Americans might find relief from oppression, and even achieve independence, through republican virtue—"a prevailing zeal for religion and virtue . . . accompanied with a like zeal for liberty and the good of ones country." Gordon and Erskine confirmed Bellamy's suspicion that imperial powers had violated their public trust. British rulers lied and deceived, committing a political version of the linguistic fraud that Bellamy had condemned in the midst of the sacramental controversy.[34]

In 1765 Bellamy was hardly as radical as James Otis or Jonathan Mayhew. Yet his interpretation of moral law, even if less than a full-fledged theory of political rebellion, provided a critical perspective on political affairs. In that year he introduced into his preaching his first explicit condemnations of royal and parliamentary policy, and thereafter he applied the doctrine of the divine moral government with increasing boldness to themes such as governmental deception and vice, the dangers of political prerogative, and the primacy of a constitutional conception of civil and religious rights.

Bellamy used his idea of providence also to contrast the justice and benevolence of divine rule with current manifestations of human misrule. The civil turmoil of the 1760s and early 1770s, so presented, was all the more lamentable in light of the excellencies of Christ's kingdom. In conclusion to one of his many sermons in response to the Stamp Act, Bellamy opposed human "sovereigns who afflict" their subjects to God, who "offers to be King and protector and to do all things for them." Some British magistrates might have cried "foul" at such a straightforward contrast between God and lords temporal. Bellamy nonetheless insisted on the moral excellencies of God the true King and perfect Lawgiver in such a way that Hanoverian monarchs and Parliament appeared unworthy of New England's political loyalties. The Exodus and the end of the Jewish exile in Babylon, he argued in a 1770 sermon on Isaiah 40:1, showed that monarchs universally oppressed their subjects, whereas God acted "to support and comfort his people under these trials."[35]

The conflict between Great Britain and America, like the earlier war between France and Britain, set the stage for a providential vindication of justice. As Bellamy anticipated divine judgment on despotism, he drew additional analogies between ill-fated biblical dynasties and existing political regimes. This homiletical strategy could convey as bitter a denunciation of political authorities as could any secular opposition rhetoric. Bellamy likened America to Israel in Babylon, waiting to "return to liberty and their land" while the Lord destroyed their evil captors. In employment of this particular trope, he joined American radicals of various theological positions. The songwriter William Billings, for instance, turned Psalm 137 (a lamentation for the Babylonian exile) likewise to New England's captivity:

> By the Rivers of Watertown
> we sat down and wept
> we wept, we wept
> we wept
> when we remember'd thee
> O Boston.[36]

Bellamy, however, tended less toward plaintiveness than toward confidence in God's purposes. Preaching in May 1769, he took as his topic "the dispensations of Divine providence," which were "designed for the instruction of men"; "this world is God's School." Bellamy's interpretation of this image turned on the idea that the Lord manifested divine justice by the temporal operation of the law. Observing that Israel was sacked by Shishak because of Jewish wickedness (1 Kings 14:25, 26), he maintained that "it was for God's honor in the sight of the nations" to uphold the universal dictates of the moral law and consequently to allow Israel to suffer at the hands of the Egyptians. Bellamy made a salient application of this exegesis. As it was with Israel and the ancient heathen empires, so "'tis probable it will be so with Great Britain." He described at length the immoralities of British policy, including "a national rejecting of the gospel" since the time of Charles II and "open profligacy to the dishonor of Christianity." These vices, he argued, would eventuate in political disasters for the empire. He listed "the national Debt," "their divisions," and "their enemies" as factors that would bring about the downfall of Britain. Bellamy interpreted Christ's command to the disciples to have faith (Matthew 8:26) as a call to collective confidence and concluded that "while in the way of duty, [we] have no reason to be afraid in the evidence of the apparent dangers. . . . God governs the world, everything, in the wisest manner."[37]

Predicting God's judgments on political corruption could encourage the colonists; it also could convey their precarious position. Assured that Britain would be punished, Bellamy still appeared tentative during this period about the juridical status of New England, whose people had acted both virtuously and viciously. Citizens and assemblies authorized religious orthodoxy yet permitted the spread of infidelity, encouraged the settlement of new lands yet instituted inflationary monetary policies, provided for widespread civil liberties yet tolerated the enslavement of Negroes.

Many of Bellamy's sermons lamented developments on both sides of the Atlantic and, following fast-day proclamations, emphasized the necessity of discipline and cohesion. New Englanders were not only to watch for dangers coming from Britain but also to scrutinize their own activities, to "mortify all the seeds of discord" as a defense against "afflictions and ill treatment" by foreign enemies. Protection of constitutional rights in ecclesiastical affairs was only one form of such vigilance. In a 1766 sermon Bellamy observed that Anglo-American tensions placed New Englanders in moral combat; severed from their historic ties to Britain, they witnessed "the world in a miserable state" and themselves "in the wild," confronted by "dangers all around"; "multitudes" were "like to perish." Since political fragmentation and isolation manifested the corporate effects of original sin, he continued, people were to eschew in particular economic temptations to individualism, the pursuit of "a jolly life" and "a contentious life." Even the unregenerate "ought to try" to reform, as well as pray, for the common good. Assuming that the imperial crisis would be resolved according to the divine government, Bellamy stressed the nationally impartial nature of the moral law and consequently the duties of all Americans to uphold political justice and social benevolence.[38]

Bellamy's preaching accordingly oscillated between denunciations of the British government and warnings against American sin—until the critical summer of 1774, when, as he put it, "talk over the politicks of the times" consumed his attentions. The recalcitrance of the British ministry during that spring and summer undoubtedly alarmed him and Hopkins, who described the hold of politics on the minds of people: "Our religious disputes in New England seem to sleep at present. Political affairs have engrossed our attention. . . . A considerable number of ministers and churches in Connecticut have agreed to spend some hours . . . every week in social prayer, on account of the present state of our public affairs." In a letter to his son Jonathan early in April 1775, Bellamy attempted to give spiritual advice but could hardly refrain from comment on political events in America; he did not relish the thought of "civil war," but he realized that "if matters" were "pushed much further" there would be "the dissolution" of Anglo-American union.[39]

Two weeks after this letter was written, New England patriots and British regulars clashed at Lexington and Concord, which was evidence enough that "matters" had indeed been "pushed" too far. Such acts of violence, coming after the Stamp Act, the Boston Massacre, the Coercive Acts, and the blockade of Boston Harbor, clarified Bellamy's interpretation of political events. He began to direct his moral critique almost exclusively against Great Britain. Unable to resist the temptation to make political commentary out of any number of biblical villains, he often cited Nebuchadnezzar and drew parallels between the Babylonian and British despotisms. Like the "tyrant" Nebuchadnezzar, Britain's king would be utterly destroyed because of his unredeemable wickedness. Bellamy also compared the British ministry to the leaders of Capernaum, for whom Jesus predicted horrible punishments (Matthew 11:20–24): "The degree of criminality [in Great Britain] is more criminal than the most profligate and the heathens. . . . No doubt the British Empire are as guilty as Capernaum."[40]

Bellamy previously had seen economic, military, and political misfortunes not only as the results of royal and parliamentary misrule but also as moral punishments to which the colonists were to submit. He had argued in his election sermon of 1762, however, that British rulers had a duty to behave as charitable parents toward their colonial children and were under moral obligation to promote virtue and happiness in America. They had failed both duty and obligation.[41] He now could find no cause for God to tolerate such perfidy. Good had to be secured, evil punished; that was the law by which God produced equity in temporal affairs.

During 1775 and early 1776 Bellamy discontinued his warnings against American vice and began to stress the virtue of the patriot cause. He concurrently focused on the prospects of divine deliverance from the empire. In October 1775, to cite but one of many sermons, he took Jeremiah's condemnation of Israel's apostasy (Jeremiah 8:6) to be a model for God's judgment on America's oppressor. British monarchs and members of the government, as he described them, had courted disaster by decades of vice, including "bribery in parliament." Bellamy surmised that the moral law hung heavy upon Britain: "The empire is now on the edge of des[truction], from the National and internal divisions and external Crimes. Now is the proper time for judgement. . . . [T]he cloud over the B[ritish] Empire grows blacker and blacker. Every thing joins to Confirm this Column . . . to exasperate the Ministry." That being so, the colonists had neither moral nor legal cause to obey or love a king who resembled "Ahab, the worst King [Israel] had had." Bellamy urged his people to resist Britain and trust in divine judgment; George III, like Ahab, would be destroyed.[42]

His sermon on June 25, 1775, further revealed Bellamy's shift in perspective as he embraced the moral cause of a victimized America. He explained to his parishioners that the battle at Lexington and Concord was unavoidable. "The [British] ministry," he observed, "are angry with us, more than with any part of America, because we are puritans and particularly of the old puritans. . . . The ministry is angry with us because they would have our money in ways which we ask to be independent." The colonists, Bellamy concluded, now had no option but to take up arms: "It was not safe to submit [to British troops]. There was no way but to fight at Lexington. We are now declared rebels. They will subdue [us] if they can." In subsequent orations Bellamy assured his congregation that God would release them from the oppression of king and Parliament, despite the apparent power of imperial forces:

> They [the British officials] think themselves superior [and] expect we will divide. But God loves to conduct things so as to abase the proud and let it be known that he is the Lord. . . . It is an easy thing for God to deliver us next year . . . it is a wise thing for these colonies to prepare for next year.[43]

Bellamy's resentment of political vice, linked to his doctrine of the moral government of God, had solidified into active opposition to the mother country. He took up the theme of providential theodicy to encourage New Englanders accordingly. In a June 1775 sermon, for instance, he reasserted the critical thesis of *The Wisdom of God*, that God was "unobliged to his Creatures" yet bound to the moral law—"not at liberty to act arbitrarily, without wisdom." Bellamy thought that God, "according to his own self-knowledge," had a "perfect plan of conduct" in the fight against Britain. Trust in "Divine providence" to "execute justice" in temporal affairs, as he emphasized in another sermon that spring, should "animate" patriot resolve and action. Bellamy furthermore applied his doctrine quite explicitly to the military exigencies in February 1776: "[T]he power of God is so universal that it extends to all the exercises of strength and might in the midst of battle, to give Courage and Prudence. . . . It is God that decides the fate of battles." In its political position vis-à-vis Britain, he observed in November 1774, America was like Jerusalem under Roman siege, even if it could not claim Israel's status as a divinely favored political order. "The roman army took Jerusalem," he preached, "because the Jews refused subjection" to imperial tyranny; God vindicated the oppressed Jews by destroying Rome. Likewise, "God hath sent the [British] army to Boston," yet he would ultimately overthrow the unjust empire.[44]

Unlike some more fervently nationalistic patriots, Bellamy did not turn such comparisons to millennial predictions. He exhorted his hearers to fight despots—even if fighting led to a "fiery" martyrdom—but as he consoled patriots he refrained from speculation about an imminent conflict of eschatological proportions. Nothing in Daniel 2:44 or Revelation 21:2— favorite passages for civil millennialists—revealed to him the eschatological roles of Britain or America. He made no applications of such texts to contemporary societies, save to stress the steady and universal workings of the moral law and the importance of social cohesion in the face of temporal adversities. By his lights, the Kingdom of God manifested itself chiefly in terms of moral dispositions and social behavior. The Millennium was the ultimate establishment of benevolence and peace; looming larger than any one political order, it lay in the distant future as a universal reality. For the present, Bellamy could tell his people only "to prepare for trials that we might be ready for the worst" and to consider "martyrdom" as more blessed than "a natural death."[45]

Although his interpretation of the moral law disinclined him to bestow the mantle of divine election upon America, it did reinforce Bellamy's zeal for rebellion. He became an active proponent of rebellion because he thought that British policies violated America's legal rights and threatened New England's corporate order. American independence came as a predictable consequence of the moral law: the divine intention to destroy vice and thereby manifest the virtue and wisdom of providential government.[46] Thus, British Major Harry Rooke's 1775 complaint was not altogether misleading. "It is your G-d Damned Religion of this Country," Rooke raved at an American prisoner caught with a book of presumably Calvinist theology, "that ruins this Country." From a quite different perspective, one awed soldier, on hearing Bellamy preach to a Continental regiment on its way through Litchfield to Massachusetts, remarked that he had "never heard" any sermon "outdone by anybody in my life for liberty."[47]

Extending his consistent Calvinism into politics, Bellamy became a leader of what Tories reviled as the "Black Regiment" of Americans: ministers who presumed to be agents as well as theologians of divine law and thus collaborated with armed rebels. To be sure, his Revolutionary sermons contained an eclectic combination of unoriginal ideas: exegeses of biblical history through the moral government theme, principles of Moral Sense ethics, whig rehearsals of English constitutionalism, appeals to republican theories, and opposition rhetoric linked to effusive declamations against loyalism. However unoriginal in political ideology, his preaching fortified New England patriots. As the historians Ruth H. Bloch, Richard D. Brown, and Charles Royster have demonstrated, ministers like him were crucial to the dissemination of ideas that infused collective action with transcendent purpose. His system, with its republican applications, convinced not only his parishioners in Bethlehem, who volunteered their lives for the Revolution, but also a host of patriot preachers throughout the colonies. The New Divinity movement, in fact, spread most rapidly and widely during the War for Independence. Stiles, ever fascinated and irritated by Bellamy's popularity, admitted that by 1770 Bethlehem's was one of Connecticut's "most eminent ministers," who in the previous year had assisted in twenty-two ordinations of consistent Calvinists in Connecticut and New York. Bellamy's reception of an honorary doctorate from the University of Aberdeen in 1769 only confirmed his transatlantic reputation.[48]

As he reached the height of his influence as both a leader of ecclesiastical affairs in western New England and a teacher of ministerial candidates, Bellamy trained some twenty-five ministers between 1760 and 1774. His closest and most forthrightly patriotic pupils were Levi Hart and

Jonathan Edwards, Jr. Graduated from Yale in 1760, Hart spent the following next year in Bethlehem, writing student essays that reflected
Bellamy's theology of law as well as his penchant for moral philosophers
who were known for whig political views. After his licensure in 1761 and
a few weeks of preaching at Bellamy's church, Hart settled in Preston,
Connecticut, quickly became involved in consociational politics and local
civic affairs, and began to take in his own students. During the 1770s and
1780s he was a popular speaker on social issues, known better for his
politics than for his theology. If there was such a person as a moderate,
nondisputational New Divinity man, he was one.[49]

Edwards the Younger also developed his theology under the influence
of Bellamy (and Hopkins) during the 1760s and 1770s. Following his gradu-
ation from the College of New Jersey in 1765, he studied for a year with
Hopkins and then for six months with Bellamy. His first sermons, composed in Bethlehem in 1766, emphasized the moral government of God,
the necessity for social relations to be structured by law, and the rule of
providence over temporal affairs. During his first three years in New
Haven's White Haven Church (1769–1772), where he preached for much
of his career, Edwards took even the most ostensibly Pauline-evangelistic
texts to be prescriptions for lecturing his congregation on the social obligations of the moral law.[50]

Hart and Edwards applied, as Donald Weber has written, the "rhetorical balm" of the Calvinist doctrine of divine moral government to the
emotional wounds and psychic anxieties of New England revolutionaries.
Like their mentor Bellamy, moreover, they explicated the moral differences between godly and ungodly rule. Hart focused on "the Liberty of
Christ's kingdom" in contrast to monarchies that "are frequently encroach-
ing on the Rights of their subjects" and "have always enslaved mankind."
Edwards similarly pitted the "perfect laws" of Christ the King against unjust human laws, which merited no obedience. Edwards's most popular
sermon of the Revolutionary era—written in 1766 and first preached in
Bethlehem—also mirrored Bellamy's historical teleology, which consoled
patriots with a vision of providential justice. Virtually quoting the "Preface" to Bellamy's 1758 *Sermons* and the conclusion to *The Millen[n]ium*,
Edwards predicted that "however now things may look dark and gloomy;
how[ever] Satan and his emissaries now rage" and God's people are "im-
prisoned, tormented, put to death," yet "the cause of the church . . . shall
be safely defended."[51]

The younger New Divinity men, echoing Bellamy, also turned their
republican rendition of the moral law to revolutionary purpose after 1773.
Hart's *Liberty Described and Recommended* (Hartford, 1775) contained the
most extreme condemnations of "the horrors" of political tyranny. Drawing on whig expositions of civil rights and republican theories of government, he, even more than his mentor, rationalized armed resistance in

terms of just-war theory. "As the peace and happiness of mankind depend on being free from oppression and violence," he contended, "our duty and that in which true religion consists . . . implieth vigorous opposition" to all "oppression and violence." Clearly the British "system of Tyranny," assisted by the "venal house of commons," constituted a *causa bellum*. Parliament sent "a fleet and army" to Boston, ready "to murder" citizens throughout New England, chiefly to enforce unjust policies of taxation. "It is this body of crimes," Hart urged, "you are going to resist and if possible, to put a stop to their violence and robbery—The cause must be good for it is the cause of truth, Justice and of humane nature." Hart applauded rebellious acts such as the 1775 jailing of a loyalist sheriff in Cambridge and gave God's blessing to a hastily organized group of Preston townsmen-in-arms who in the summer of 1775 were ready to march at any sign of British troops.[52]

Edwards attempted to justify the rebellion within the scope of English constitutional history, which he pictured as little more than legislative conspiracy since the Restoration. In August 1774 he railed against acts issued from London. Their rights as English citizens and their duties as Christians, he maintained, obliged the people of Connecticut to support the upcoming Continental Congress and commit themselves to nonimportation of English goods. In April 1775 he argued that parliamentary violation of New England's prerogatives had rendered submission to the British government treacherous. Recent taxation robbed colonists of their property, royal judicial appointments denied justice to the people, crypto-Catholics in Parliament intended to destroy New England's power of religious self-determination, and "an army . . . introduced into our land . . . by which we are likely to be butchered" threatened the very lives of Americans. In defense of their rights, Edwards concluded, citizens had an obligation to take military training and to secure arms and ammunition—the location of which he divulged in the midst of his sermon—even if they had to sell land or livestock to do so. By December 1775 he had begun to give astonishingly pragmatic military advice from the pulpit, proposing that Connecticut ships "seize many of our enemies vessels, and with them much of their property and supplies." He suggested that "the community" depose local officials still loyal to the crown, detect hidden loyalists, imprison known tories, and punish suspect actions such as providing provisions to the enemy, rejecting continental currency, raising fears of British military strength, or refusing to declare for independence.[53]

Other Connecticut Edwardseans also adopted Bellamy's rhetorical strategies and improved Calvinist doctrine to the end of outright sedition. John Graham, a long-time admirer and colleague in neighboring Southbury, exhorted the local militia and blasted "wicked rulers" who in 1775 imposed "the impoverishing burden of exceeding and heavy taxes" for no other reason than commercial greed, "making Merchandize of the people for their worldly interest." Most of Bellamy's students joined the patriot ranks. Ammi Robbins, for example, recorded in his student notebook the virtues of liberty over and against "Monarchical Government." Settled in the northern Litchfield town of Norfolk, he became a chaplain in the Continental army in 1776. Ammi's father, Bellamy's friend Philemon, also sent another son, Chandler Robbins, to Bethlehem, rounding out the Bellamy-Robbins circle of patriots imbued with both consistent Calvinism and republicanism. Nathaniel Niles (1741–1828), another of Bellamy's charges, became a lawyer in eastern Connecticut, a pastor in New Hampshire, and an instrumental supporter of nonimportation. His *Two Discourses on Liberty* (Newbury-Port, 1774) reflected Bellamy's critique of economic individualism and enslavement; like his teacher, Niles contrasted the standards of divine law to "the scheme" of British rulers—their "horrid attack" on "the body of a community plundered for the sake of indulging individuals in pride, luxury, idleness and debauchery."[54]

Indeed, dozens of consistent Calvinists throughout New England followed Bellamy's lead. Samuel Sherwood (1730–1783) and Israhiah Wetmore (1728–1798), whose 1773 election sermon duplicated Bellamy's doctrines of history, announced the glories of independence. Samuel Spring (1749–1818), whom Bellamy taught in the early 1770s, was a zealous patriot in Newburyport, Massachusetts. Bellamy's influence reached also to the Middle Colonies. Jedidiah Chapman (1741–1813) and Joseph Periam (1742–1780), both of whom imbibed Bellamy's doctrines in Bethlehem, served the Continental forces in New Jersey. Memorialized as a patriotic preacher in several poems, James Caldwell (1734–1781)—an ardent New Divinity man and a correspondent of Bellamy's—served as an intelligence officer for George Washington in New Jersey and later joined the Continental forces as a chaplain. Some forty members of his Elizabethtown congregation also took commissions as Continental officers.[55]

Calvinist patriotism took shape equally under the influence of Hopkins, whose doctrine of disinterested benevolence called on Americans to place corporate, Revolutionary loyalties above self-interested, commercial pursuits. In the wake of the Stamp Act crisis, Hopkins had antagonized many leaders in his congregation with his republicanism. "The *tories*," he wrote to Bellamy, "have got all the town offices in their hands" and, angry with Hopkins's politics, intended to force him "out of town." When his opponents succeeded, Hopkins departed western Massachusetts for Newport. There he was more successful in promoting a politics of disinterested benevolence. He led an effort to resist importation of English goods and began a noted campaign to abolish the slave trade. One of his followers, Lemuel Haynes (1753–1833), an African-American minister to mostly white churches in New England and New York, also linked disinterested benevolence to American patriotism and abolition.[56]

New Divinity theology clearly had militant implications. As Bellamy spoke of the "heroic deeds" of King David and numerous other biblical figures, he prompted quite explicit acts of rebellion. He, like Hopkins and other New Divinity men, encouraged New Englanders to forswear British consumer goods, since, as Timothy Breen has argued, they symbolized economic and political dependence. The town of Woodbury, which administratively encompassed Bethlehem during the war, became a hotbed of radicalism; noted for its observance of nonimportation, it assembled a local committee of correspondence that sent relief to Boston in 1774, took possession of the large quantity of salt owned by merchant Jabez Bacon, and disciplined locals who disregarded requests from the Continental Congress. In 1774 Woodbury's town meeting proclaimed its animus toward "enemies to American Liberty" and bound itself "to break off all Dealings with Such Persons and also with all Persons in other Towns and Citys who shall be found Guilty" of importation or of hoarding provisions. In August 1774 a mob of patriots from Litchfield County took part in the kidnapping of the cousin of Jared Ingersoll, the colony's tax collector. Woodbury's Episcopal priest fled to New York soon thereafter.[57]

Litchfield County, in fact, was so fervently engaged that one rather resentful loyalist thought it capable of raising some forty thousand patriot troops on short notice. In August 1775 Bellamy and the lieutenant of a Litchfield militia unit made arrangements for the time and place of an artillery sermon that would be given in case of an urgent call to arms. Bethlehem's parson exhorted his parishioners to enlist in the militia and instructed recruits in their duties to defend the rights and liberties of the colonies. Citizens in Bethlehem and the rest of Woodbury heeded his counsel; by the end of the Revolution, more than twelve hundred Woodbury men had volunteered, one of highest levels of enlistment in the colonies. Bellamy's parishioners and his sons in particular, as previously described, took his call to arms with utter seriousness.[58]

The Revolutionary spirit so captured Bellamy's people that in some measure they even extended the fight for home rule to a contest for rule at home; in the 1780s they began to assert their independence from Woodbury. As early as 1770, militia volunteers from Bethlehem expressed resentment at their inclusion in Woodbury units. Service under "officers" from the larger town, according to Amos Martin, Andrew Baldwin, and Barzilla Hendee, led to "unease" and "discord" among the troops. The General Assembly granted the volunteers' petition, but Bethlehem citizens continued to assert local independence. In 1780 Bethlehem began a campaign to incorporate. Society meetings at Bellamy's church thereafter voted to "be made and set off to be a Town of only this Society" as distinct from "the old society" of Woodbury—language that mirrored New England's more extensive desire for freedom from the Old World across the Atlantic. Agents from Bethlehem filed petitions with the General Assembly in 1781 and 1784, but both were contested by Woodbury and

denied by the Assembly. In 1786, after five years of negotiation over boundaries and taxes, selectmen from the two towns finally agreed to terms of
incorporation, which the Assembly approved in 1787.[59]

Even on such a local scale, then, Bellamy's amplification of Calvinism into
Revolutionary discourse proved immensely popular. He legitimated the
aspirations of hundreds of patriots from Bethlehem, the rest of New England, and other parts of colonial America. This political engagement,
however, should not be read as the providential nationalism of republican preachers who anticipated the fulfillment of covenantal promises or
millennial prophecies in the American nation. Bellamy needed no chiliastic
scenarios, no national millennialism, to posit a religious teleology of the
crisis. He had long struggled to assert the providential vindication of independence without submerging providence itself in the stream of patriotic
triumphalism.[60]

Nor did Bellamy's preaching signify the secular nationalism of less theologically insistent patriots. His advocacy of republican virtue remained
highly charged with, and dependent on, theological assumptions. Republicanism, hence civil rebellion, appealed to him because he was convinced
that the moral law, which transcended national interests, lay embedded
in the will of God. That was the constant refrain in his civic preaching from
his entry into politics in the 1750s to his support of the Revolution. In this
respect, he and his New Divinity adherents joined a long line of Calvinists
who took opposition to tyranny to be a theological, because it was a moral,
necessity.[61]

Indeed, Bellamy showed less interest in any single, sustained theory
of politics than in his theological message: the conflict between America
and Britain as a platform for a demonstration of the divine law in action.
That doctrine was a two-edged sword. During the fight against imperial
power, it implied that an American victory would demonstrate the wisdom and justice of God's governance over temporal affairs. But it also
implied that America, if corrupt, would be as vulnerable to destruction as
were the armies of George III. Independence was a great burden, since it
meant that the new republic was responsible, without British oversight,
for upholding corporate duties of equity and benevolence.

From this perspective, Bellamy and other New Divinity men began to
turn their ideas of moral virtue against self-interested policy within American civic life soon after the signing of the Declaration of Independence.
Bellamy's sermon on May 30, 1777, typified this mentality. He interpreted
Isaiah 40:1—a text he previously had used to comfort the patriots—to be
a warning against America. He admonished his congregation "to put implicit trust in [God] for the accomplishment" of moral justice; the divine
administration of law could not be frustrated. Although "it is easy for God
to deliver us" from the overwhelming numbers of British and Hessian
troops, he cautioned, "it is the mind and will of God" that corporate vir-

tue be rewarded, and vice punished, since moral rectitude was God's "interest in the world." Bellamy sharpened his point. If "we deserve destruction for our sins . . . God can destroy by the sword." In similar fashion, he warned American troops against the twin maladies of camp life—overconfidence and debauchery: "No accursed thing ought to be in the camp, no profaneness, no traitors, no pride or impudence," since "God can make the country depend on him to be."[62]

Pressing upon their congregations the urgency of conducting public affairs in accordance with the moral law, other Edwardseans promoted several projects for social and moral reform, the most prominent of which was their campaign against slavery. Hopkins, who convinced Bellamy to free his own Negro servant, emerged as a leading abolitionist with his *A Dialogue, Concerning the Slavery of the Africans* (Norwich, 1772). He insisted that genuinely revolutionary sensibilities would not countenance slavery and that disinterested benevolence should force slave owners and traders to sacrifice their own interests for the common good. Americans, he argued, could not consistently complain against imperial oppression while trading and owning slaves. Hart contended that virtuous people would outlaw slavery as "*a flagrant violation of the law of nature, of the natural rights of mankind.*" The Edwardseans declared furthermore that slavery was the most prominent, but only one, of many symptoms of immorality in America. Alarmed at the prospect of greed, infidelity, and individualism, they assailed self-indulgence, chastised social vanity and other forms of worldliness, and lamented political factionalism.[63]

In targeting American as well as British social vices after 1776, Bellamy and other New Divinity men attempted to be as consistent in their political ethics as they were in their theological orthodoxy. According to them, the moral law that legitimated the Revolution also proscribed any presumption that providence ordained the prosperity of America. This explains in part why consistent Calvinists appeared as the critics of populist and democratic nationalism during the 1780s and 1790s. During the early years of the Republic, it became increasingly evident that orthodox Calvinists and liberal political and religious thinkers held different positions on the meaning of republican virtue. Defending experimental Calvinism, New Divinity ministers continued to maintain that humanocentric ethics severed the moral life from its ultimate objective: obedience to the divine law as benevolence to the divine being. In one of his last extant sermons, Bellamy lamented the moral character of the nation and criticized an unbridled enthusiasm for freedom as representing a political form of antinomianism. He returned to the themes of "regeneration and repentance," calling for corporate "subjugation to [divine] law." In an extended polemic against the idea that genuine liberty meant freedom from the restraints of social and moral obligations, Niles succinctly expressed the opinions of most New Divinity pastors. "Liberty," he wrote, "does not consist in persons thinking themselves free" or in "private interest" but "in the being and due administration of such a system of laws, as effectually tends" to the "highest good of the community."[64]

Other New Divinity preachers turned their social critique into Federalist politics, but Bellamy's public voice grew silent during the 1780s.[65] His correspondence after 1781, addressed chiefly to his closest friends and family, contains mostly complaints of lethargy and declining health. When Stephen West, for example, asked Bellamy to write further on sacramental issues and the covenant, Bellamy declined: "Times are hard. . . . My heart is grieved. My wife is very sick. I have no time." Bellamy occasionally preached, but even in the pulpit he withdrew from public issues. His post-Revolutionary sermons are fragmentary lists of evangelical tenets. There is virtually no record of his pastoral or ecclesiastical activities save his account of securing a regular preacher for the Bethlehem church in 1786 (predictably, one of his students, Daniel Collins [1739–1822]).[66]

It was perhaps fitting that Bellamy's advocacy of the Revolution entailed the last forceful statement of his career. He began his ministry in the midst of evangelical revival and ended it in the midst of political revival. Bethlehem's oath of 1776 and the muster of patriot units throughout Litchfield County culminated his attempts to transform evangelical Calvinism into a moral authority over corporate life. Moreover, Bellamy might well have rested from his labors confident that he had taught and inspired an array of younger New Divinity men called to authenticate the doctrines of Calvinism in the midst of new social crises.

Notes

1. Bellamy, Jer. 18:6, May 17, 1776, CHS.

2. Andrew Martin, Enos Hawley, et al., July 18, 1776, in Connecticut Archives, Revolutionary War Records, Series I, Vol. 5, Part 1, Connecticut State Library, Hartford; *HW*, Vol. I, 779–87; WTR; Connecticut Archives, Colonial Wars, Series II, 1541ab, Connecticut State Library. For the formation of Connecticut militia units in the Revolutionary War, see Richard Buel, Jr., *Dear Liberty: Connecticut's Mobilization for the Revolutionary War* (Middletown, Conn., 1980).

3. Joseph Bellamy to Jonathan Bellamy, Aug. 12, 1776, HS 81380, and Anderson, 143–46, 305–9. Jonathan died on January 4, 1777.

4. Historians have given little attention to Bellamy's career in this period, in part because from 1763 to 1770 he published essays only about ecclesiastical controversies; after 1770 he published nothing. Even interpreters more narrowly focused on the social reformism of the Edwardseans have overlooked the explicitly political dimensions of this social vision. They have made no analysis of Bellamy's participation in civic affairs after 1770. See Breitenbach, "Unregenerate Doings"; Conforti, *Samuel Hopkins*, 125–41; Ferm, *Jonathan Edwards the Younger*, 76–96; Guelzo, *Edwards on the Will*, 112–39; and David S. Lovejoy, "Samuel

Hopkins: Religion, Slavery, and the Revolution," *New England Quarterly* 40 (1967): 227–43. For an older view of the Edwardseans as impractical and reactionary metaphysicians, see Morgan, "The American Revolution Considered as an Intellectual Movement."

5. Focused broadly on the political effects of the Great Awakening, Heimert argues that evangelical preaching promoted an ethos of resistance to established authorities and therefore was more revolutionary than other forms of piety. Like many such studies, Heimert's *Religion and the American Mind* does not account for changes in the attitudes and activities of individual ministers from the period of the revivals to the civic turmoil that erupted more than two decades later; see also Bushman, *From Puritan to Yankee*. Bonomi, *Under the Cope of Heaven*, 161–216, concurs with Heimert's thesis (that evangelical religion energized anti-British sentiment) but emphasizes controversies over Anglicanism rather than theological differences between Calvinists and liberals. Jon Butler, "Enthusiasm Described and Decried," criticizes Heimert's thesis by pointing to the time lag between the Awakening and the Revolution. A provocative and highly nuanced study of Calvinist preaching and the Revolution, which discusses Bellamy and his New Divinity students Levi Hart and Jonathan Edwards, Jr., is Donald Weber, *Rhetoric and History in Revolutionary New England* (New York, 1988). Weber provides a textual analysis focused on the internal and psychological dynamics of sermons written in the 1770s; he does not assess the process by which evangelicals such as Bellamy were transformed into political preachers from the 1760s through the 1770s.

6. Kuklick, *Churchmen and Philosophers*, 61; see 60–65. Fiering, *Jonathan Edwards's Moral Thought*, 69, also indicates the connection between the Edwardsean doctrine of the divine moral government and political constitutionalism.

7. Bellamy, Election Sermon, 517, 524, 534, 536.

8. Bellamy, Election Sermon, 520–21, 528, 531–32. In his sermons throughout the 1760s, Bellamy repeatedly contrasted divine rule, which was benevolent by nature, to corrupt, self-interested, human polity. Introductions to the extensive historiography of republican ideology are provided by Robert E. Shalhope, "Toward a Republican Synthesis: The Emergence of an Understanding of Republicanism in American Historiography," *WMQ* 29 (1972): 49–80; Shalhope, "Republicanism and Early American Historiography," *WMQ* 39 (1982): 334–56; and, with dissenting perspective, Isaac Kramnick, "Republican Revisionism Revisited," *American Historical Review* 87 (1982): 629–64. The best recent discussion is Rodgers, "Republicanism," which surveys the historiography of the term and critiques its usefulness as an interpretive paradigm. A classic statement on the relation between the New England pulpit and opposition ideology (one strand in the larger fabric of republicanism) is Bernard Bailyn, *The Ideological Origins of the American Revolution* (Cambridge, Mass., 1967).

9. For an analysis of the various ways in which Revolutionary writers blended whig ideas about natural law, political rights, and rationalist ethical theories, see Kloppenberg, "The Virtues of Liberalism," and Morton White, *The Philosophy of the American Revolution* (New York, 1978). For Hutcheson's radical politics, see Robbins, "'When It Is That Colonies May Turn Independent.'"

10. Sandeman, *Letters on Theron and Aspasio*, 2 vols. (Edinburgh, 1757), I:70; see 250–98, where Sandeman also credited his views to Thomas Boston (1677–1732) and Ralph Erskine (1685–1752)—seceders from Scottish Presbyterianism.

See Williston Walker, "The Sandemanians of New England," *Annual Report of the American Historical Association for the Year 1901* 1: 133–62.

11. Bellamy corresponded about Sandeman with his Scottish friends, with Finley and Dickinson in New Jersey, with Hopkins, and with many Connecticut ministers. He owned Sandeman's *Letters on Theron and Aspasio* and commented extensively on Sandeman in the *Essay*, 397, 408–9, 537–38. For Stiles's and Chauncy's alarm, see Chauncy to Stiles, Nov. 10, 1764, in Stiles, *Extracts*, 441–42, and Stiles, *Literary Diary*, I:516. Backus denounced Sandeman in his *True Faith Will Produce Good Works* (Boston, 1767). For Sandemanian loyalism, see Jean F. Hankins, "A Different Kind of Loyalist: The Sandemanians of New England during the Revolutionary War," *The New England Quarterly* 60 (1987): 223–49. As Breitenbach points out, Old Lights often accused the New Divinity of Sandemanianism on the grounds that Hopkins especially criticized the moral worth of preparatory strivings—despite the fact that Hopkins did not take the intellectualist position of Sandeman; see Breitenbach, "Piety *and* Moralism," 192–94. The chief Rogerene tract was [John Bolles], *Concerning the Christian Sabbath* ([New London, Conn.], 1757); see M. Louise Green, *The Development of Religious Liberty in Connecticut* (Boston, 1905), 161–64, 204–6.

12. Bellamy's reactions may have been tempered also by the fact that many Sandemanians, such as Judson, had once been New Divinity men and still shared many beliefs with Bellamy, including their critique of Arminianism.

13. Bellamy to Mr. Smith of Sharon, Mar. 8, 1770, in Tryon Edwards, "Memoir," xxxvi–xxxviii, illustrates Bellamy's doctrinal hostility and political tolerance toward the Sandemanians; for background to and documentation of the White controversy, see Anderson, 550–64.

14. Bellamy and David Brinsmade to Samuel Dickinson and T. Benedict, Mar. 10, 1764, HS 81616. This letter, in Bellamy's hand, recapitulates several of his manuscript essays on these principles. He drafted a lengthy exposition of religious and civil liberty in terms of "inalienable rights," entitled "The Character and Rights of a Christian," ca. 1765, HS 81471.

15. Bellamy and Brinsmade to Dickinson and Benedict, Mar. 10, 1764.

16. Bellamy and Brinsmade to Dickinson and Benedict, Mar. 10, 1764.

17. The following discussion of background to Bellamy's sacramental treatises of 1769 and 1770 draws on Anderson, 569–74, 808–41, and James Patrick Walsh, "The Pure Church in Eighteenth-Century Connecticut," Ph.D. diss., Columbia University, 1967, 189–216.

18. Bellamy, *HWC*, 399.

19. Bellamy, *HWC*, 399, 401.

20. See Bellamy, *HWC*, 407–11.

21. Bellamy, *HWC*, 408, 420, 442.

22. John Devotion to Ezra Stiles, Mar. 17, 1768, in Stiles, *Extracts*, 472–73.

23. Bellamy, *That there is but one Covenant, Whereof Baptism and the Lord's Supper are Seals*, in *Works*, Vol. III, 136 (hereafter cited with reference to this volume).

24. Bellamy, *A Careful and Strict Examination of the External Covenant*, in *Works*, Vol. III, 237, 318 (hereafter cited with reference to this volume); for Bellamy's reliance on moral law and comparison of Mather's position to Sandeman's, see 209–15, 252–54, and 261–65.

25. Ebenezer Devotion, *The Half-way Covenant, A Dialogue between Joseph Bellamy, D.D., and a Parishioner* (New London, Conn., 1769), 5; *The Parishioner having studied the Point . . . on the Half-way Covenant* (Hartford, 1769), 3.

26. Ebenezer Devotion, *A Letter to the Rev. Joseph Bellamy, D.D. Concerning Qualifications for Christian Communion* (New Haven, Conn., 1770), 12. Devotion also wrote *A Second Letter, to the Rev. Joseph Bellamy* (New Haven, Conn., 1770), in which he contested Bellamy's critique of Arminian soteriology. One did not need regeneration, Devotion here argued, for the moral sincerity required by church covenants.

27. Bellamy, *Careful and Strict Examination*, 206; *There is but One Covenant*, 144, 175, 198–99. The other relevant treatises from Bellamy are *An Answer to a Dialogue concerning the Half-way Covenant* (New Haven, Conn., 1769) and *The Sacramental Controversy Brought to a Point* (New Haven, Conn., 1770). For background to the relation between covenant promises and issues of language and truth, see Grasso, "Between Awakenings."

28. Bellamy, *There is but One Covenant*, 177, 190.

29. In *Edwards on the Will*, 126–28, Guelzo mistakes Bellamy's crusade against the Half-way Covenant for separatism. True, Bellamy rejected the organic covenantalism of Old Calvinists on the grounds that their "church-in-society" scheme had no regenerative value; he also jettisoned the national-covenant position, which regarded all temporal events as instruments for the foreordained, covenantally sealed vindication of America. Bellamy's confidence that God enforced the moral law on a corporate, civic scale, however, reflected something of the nonseparatist assumptions of federal theology. As he replaced the explicit terms of covenant with natural law as the basis for collective ethics, he indeed stressed the importance of common virtue and the social—even political—dimensions of the reign of God and duties of the church. Analyses of the relation between covenant and natural law thought are given in Eusden, "Natural Law and Covenant Theology"; Kloppenberg, "The Virtues of Liberalism"; and Mann, *Neighbors and Strangers*. Influential discussions of the covenant and national election are Bercovitch, *The American Jeremiad*, and Lowance, *The Language of Canaan*.

30. Bellamy to Mr. Smith, Feb. 26, 1770, HS 81418; Bellamy to Beckwith, Feb. 26, 1776, Henry M. Dexter Manuscript Book, Beinecke Library, Yale University. During the Revolution, Bellamy frequently preached on the necessity for unity and concord: see, e.g., his sermon on Prov. 3:17, Oct. 29, 1777, CHS. Stiles admitted that Bellamy had become one of most democratic moderators of ecclesiastical societies in western Connecticut; see Stiles, *Extracts*, 182, 456.

31. Connecticut's financial crises in the late 1760s and early 1770s, many of which were brought on by the crown's closure of the Vermont frontier, are described in the following studies: Jackson Turner Main, *Connecticut Society on the Eve of the American Revolution* (Hartford, 1977); Main, "The Distribution of Property"; and Waters, "Patrimony, Succession and Social Stability." See also Kenneth Lockridge, "Social Change and the Meaning of the American Revolution," *Journal of Social History* 6 (1973): 403–39. Zeichner, *Connecticut's Years of Controversy*, 44–48, points out that trade restrictions depressed agricultural prices after 1763. Bushman has shown that Massachusetts farmers feared on the eve of the Revolution that poverty and slavery would attend self-interested political rule; see Bushman, "Massachusetts Farmers and the Revolution," in Richard M. Jellison, ed., *Society, Freedom, and Conscience: The American Revolution in Virginia, Massachusetts, and New York* (New York, 1976), 77–124.

32. William Gordon to Bellamy, Aug. 21, 1764, HS 81311; see Hopkins to Bellamy, July 27, 1766, cited in Conforti, *Samuel Hopkins*, 87. See *HW*, I:173–75, for the Litchfield County resolution of 1766 and subsequent activities. On

Bellamy's political reputation, see Fitch to Bellamy, Feb. 1, 1762, CHS. Anderson, 585-605, documents Bellamy's support for the Plan of Union. Near Bethlehem, the towns of Roxbury and Woodbury had Church of England parishes by 1771: *HW*, I:287–97. For New Lights and the Stamp Act, see Bushman, *From Puritan to Yankee*, 267–88; Edmund S. Morgan and Helen M. Morgan, *The Stamp Act Crisis: Prologue to Revolution* (Chapel Hill, N.C., 1953), 280–300; and Zeichner, *Connecticut's Years of Controversy*, 44–77. In *Mitre and Sceptre: Transatlantic Faith, Ideas, Personalities, and Politics, 1689–1775* (New York, 1962), Carl Bridenbaugh provides an overview of the controversy over the Church of England in New England; see also Bonomi, *Under the Cope of Heaven*, 161–216.

33. Hart, Diary, May 1769 to May 1771, HSP. William Gordon (1728–1807) was a well-known dissenter from the London area who later immigrated to America and wrote a history of the Revolution. Bellamy and Hart sent copies of Connecticut election sermons to Erskine, who was interested in colonial policy from the perspective of a Scottish opponent of Parliament.

34. The following letters from Gordon to Bellamy: Sept. 9, 1766, HS 81621; Oct. 14, 1767, HS 81623; July 14, 1769, HS 81349; and Jan. 27, 1769, HS 81628; also Erskine to Bellamy, Mar. 16, 1770, HS 81355. For further evidence of this transatlantic castigation of British politics, see Erskine to Bellamy, Aug. 8, 1760, HS 81273, and Mar. 17, 1770, HS 81355.

35. Bellamy, Ps. 81:8–12, Aug. 3, 1765, CHS; Isa. 40:1, Nov. 3, 1770, YS. Bellamy addressed the Stamp Act in several other sermons, e.g., Gen. 3:19, May 18, 1765, CHS.

36. Bellamy, Matt. 8:26, Mar. 5, 1769, CHS; Billings, "Lamentation Over Boston," in *The Singing Master's Assistant* (Boston, 1778), 33. In another sermon on the Babylonian captivity Bellamy emphasized the same dynamic of divine judgment: Ezek. 37:3, Jan. 20, 1770, YS.

37. Bellamy, 1 Kings 14:25, 26, May 14, 1769, YS, and Matt. 8:26.

38. Bellamy, Rom. 12:18, June 15, 1765, CHS; 1 Thess. 5:17, Feb. 9, 1766, Henry M. Dexter Manuscript Book, Beinecke Library, Yale University. Robert Ross, "Minutes of the Fairfield Eastern Consociation," Dec. 4, 1765, HS 81328, contains Bellamy's comments on fast days.

39. Bellamy to Jonathan Bellamy, May 12, 1772, HS 81371; Hopkins to Erskine, Dec. 2, 1774, HSP; Bellamy to Jonathan Bellamy, Apr. 3, 1775, in Tyron Edwards, "Memoir," xl.

40. Bellamy, Lam. 3:33, Dec. 31, 1775, CHS; Matt. 11:20–24, May 17, 1776, CHS.

41. In "The American Revolution: The Ideology and Psychology of National Liberation," *Perspectives in American History* VI (1972), 167–306, Edwin G. Burrows and Michael Wallace analyze the pervasiveness of patriot literature that employed the theme of alienated affections between child (the colonists) and parent (England).

42. Bellamy, Jer. 8:6, Oct. 15, 1775, YS; 1 Kings 20:13–22, Dec. 17, 1775, CHS.

43. Bellamy, Hos. 2:5–8, June 25, 1775, YS; 1 Kings 20:13–22.

44. Bellamy, Matt. 20:15, June 18, 1775, YS; Dan. 2:2–5, May 7, 1775, YS; Exod. 17:8–13, Feb. 1776, YS; and Matt. 22:7, Nov. 27, 1774, YS.

45. Bellamy, Dan. 3:19–20, Mar. 12, 1775, YS; Dan. 2:44, Oct. 10, 1772, YS; Rev. 21:1, Dec. 5, 1773, YS; and Luke 3:2–6, Jan. 14, 1769, HS 81457. Edwards,

Jr., Bellamy's student, likewise refrained from civil millennialism. In commenting on Daniel 7:14, for example, he asserted that Christ ruled over "kings and emperors" by modulating the flow of history according to providential justice. He read Revelation 14:4 as teaching only "a high regard for the righteousness of God—his law." New England communities, Edwards taught, were obliged to exhibit the very "love to man" and "justice" that characterized Christ's kingdom: Edwards, Dan. 17:14, Jan. 5, 1772, Jonathan Edwards, Jr., Papers, Case Memorial Library, Hartford Seminary, Hartford, Conn., Box 166, Folder 2731, Item 75600 (this collection cited hereafter by item number); Edwards, Rev. 14:4, Mar. 3, 1774, Jonathan Edwards, Jr., Papers, ANTS.

46. In this sense, the link between Bellamy's evangelical doctrine and patriotism lay not merely "on the level of rhetoric itself," as Donald Weber contends, but also in an elaboration and extension of fundamental theological convictions that Bellamy forged in the 1750s. I do agree with Weber, nonetheless, on the import of New Divinity political rhetoric, which, in his words, drew "assurance out of anxiety" and thus helped to effect an emotional and cultural break from Britain as well as an ethical rationale for rebellion; see Weber, *Rhetoric and History*, 58, 116, 155. In "The Puritans and Edwards," 143, Harry Stout maintains that "federal theology enabled evangelicals and rationalists to come together on a common footing when faced with external enemies." Bellamy's doctrine of covenant, however, had little in common with liberal theologies. What he and rationalist patriots such as Chauncy shared was the conviction of providential rule through the moral law; see, e.g., Chauncy, *Trust in God, the Duty of a People in a Day of Trouble* (Boston, 1770).

47. John Leach, "A Journal Kept by John Leach, During His Confinement by the British, In Boston Gaol, in 1775," *The New England Historical and Geneological Register* 19 (1865): 255–63, quotation from 256; Simeon Lyman, "Journal of Simeon Lyman of Sharon," Connecticut Historical Society, *Collections* 7 (1899): 113, quoted in Charles Royster, *A Revolutionary People at War: The Continental Army and American Character, 1775–1783* (Chapel Hill, N.C., 1979), 19.

48. Stiles, *Extracts*, 300–301; Bloch, *Visionary Republic*, 63; Richard D. Brown, *Knowledge Is Power: The Diffusion of Information in Early America, 1700–1865* (New York, 1989), 65–81; Royster, *A Revolutionary People at War*, 3–24. The reference to a "Black Regiment" comes from loyalist Peter Oliver; see *Peter Oliver's Origin and Progress of the American Revolution*, ed. Douglas Adair and John A. Schutz (San Marino, Calif., 1961), 73. Donald Weber provides a provocative discussion of how Calvinist preachers came to see themselves as "historical agent[s], engineering for America"; see his *Rhetoric and History*, 33–34, 47. Stiles was so struck by, and perhaps envious of, Bellamy's D.D. that without comment he quoted the full text of Bellamy's diploma (Stiles, *Literary Diary*, III:5).

49. For Hart's studies in Bethlehem, see Chapter Two, especially note 38. Ferm, *Jonathan Edwards the Younger*, is the most recent biography; sketches of Edwards and Hart are provided in Sprague, *Annals*, 590–93, 653–60.

50. Edwards's focus on the moral law is shown in his Bethlehem sermons on 2 Pet. 2:22, Aug. 1766, Jonathan Edwards, Jr., Papers, Case Memorial Library, Hartford Seminary, Hartford, Conn., Box 165, Folder 2725, Document 75454 (this collection hereafter cited in the following manner: JEHS 75454); Edwards, Rom. 3:24, Oct. 1766, JEHS 75455. His preaching in New Haven on the law and the moral government themes is illustrated by his sermons on Matt. 23:29, 30, June

1769, Jonathan Edwards, Jr., Papers, ANTS; Rom. 5:8, Mar. 1772, JEHS 75610; and Rom. 6:23, May 24, 1772, JEHS 75607.

51. Weber, *Rhetoric and History*, 82; Hart, Ps. 97:1, June 1766, Levi Hart papers, Connecticut Historical Society, Hartford; Edwards, Rev. 17:14, Jan. 5, 1772, JEHS 75600; Edwards, 2 Kings 6:16, 1766, quoted in Weber, *Rhetoric and History*, 57–58. For fuller documentation and analysis of Hart's and Edwards's revolutionary preaching and its dependence on Bellamy's, see Weber, *Rhetoric and History*, 47–90, and Mark Valeri, "The New Divinity and the American Revolution," *WMQ* 46 (1989): 741–69.

52. Hart, 1 Kings 8:24–25, May 24, 1775, Connecticut Historical Society; Judg. 11:27, May 24, 1776, Connecticut Historical Society; Diary, 1774–1775, HSP.

53. Edwards, Luke 22:36, Apr. 30, 1775, JEHS 75758; Judg. 12:5–6, Dec. 22, 1775, JEHS 75816. Edwards discussed English lawmaking, the cause of Anglo-American enmity, at length in his sermons on 1 Sam. 7:12, Nov. 24, 1774, JEHS 75765, and on Eccles. 4:1, Feb. 1, 1775, JEHS 75777.

54. Graham, Lam. 3:39, May 14, 1775, uncatalogued sermons, Connecticut Historical Society, Hartford; for his sermon to a militia unit, see *HW*, I:199. Robbins's "Question Book," in the Robbins Family Papers, Connecticut Historical Society, is quoted in Weber, *Rhetoric and History*, 179–80. For a full discussion of Philemon Robbins and the Revolution, see Weber, *Rhetoric and History*, 14–46. See also Niles, *Two Discourses*, 19; for a short biography of Niles, see Shipton and Sibley, *Harvard Graduates*, 16: 390–97.

55. Wetmore's sermon was *A Sermon Preached before the Honorable Assembly* (Hartford, 1773); for him and Sherwood, see Heimert, *Religion and the American Mind*, 347–48 (Heimert cites many other Calvinist patriots, 351–453). Spring instigated a remarkable incident among Continental forces mustered in Newburyport in 1775. He and several army officers gathered in the basement of Spring's church at the crypt of George Whitefield—whose evangelical ministrations had provided a model for Bellamy some thirty-five years before—and there cut off pieces of Whitefield's clerical collar and wristbands, which accompanied the officers on their march to Quebec; see Royster, *Revolutionary People*, 23–24. For Chapman, see Dexter, *Sketches*, II:737–39; for Caldwell and Periam, see James McLachlan, *Princetonians, 1748–1768: A Biographical Dictionary* (Princeton, N.J., 1976), 259–62, 399–402. Caldwell suffered a rather inglorious fate; he was shot by a drunken American sentry at the Elizabethtown docks. In his Apr. 14, 1774, letter to Caldwell, PHS, Bellamy wove social commentary into a discussion of providence and theodicy.

56. Conforti, *Samuel Hopkins*, 95–141; John Salliant, "Lemuel Haynes and the Revolutionary Origins of Black Theology, 1776–1801," *Religion and American Culture* 2 (1992): 79–102. In 1771 Hopkins demonstrated a new style of spinning wheel to his Newport parishioners, to encourage nonimportation; Mary Alice Baldwin, *The New England Clergy and the American Revolution* (Durham, N.C., 1928), 105–33, 154, documents this and other revolutionary acts by New Divinity pastors.

57. Bellamy, Ps. 115:54, Nov. 24, 1774, YS; Woodbury Town Meeting, Nov. 17, 1774, quoted in *HW*, I:177; Breen, "'Baubles of Britain,'" 90; Breen, "Narrative of Commercial Life." For Woodbury's committee of correspondence and local radicalism, see *HW*, I:173–215. Nonimportation was commonly practiced throughout Litchfield County. For the kidnapping incident, see Buel, *Dear Liberty*, 27.

58. Eli Catlin to Bellamy, Aug. 10, 1775, HS 81375, includes the arrangements for Bellamy's artillery sermon, to which Bellamy appended notes on the meeting

of the militia. For Woodbury and Bethlehem regiments, see note 2, above, and *HW*, I:194–215. The loyalist Samuel Peters claimed (without convincing evidence) that in response to a 1774 rumor of Boston's invasion, Litchfield County quickly raised forty thousand men, to whom Bellamy preached; see A Gentleman of the Province [Samuel Peters], *A General History of Connecticut . . . wherein new and the true Sources of the present Rebellion in America are pointed out* (2d. ed. London, 1782), 416.

59. Martin, Baldwin, and Hendee to the General Assembly, in Connecticut Archives: Militia Records, Ser. 2, Vol. 7, 1541ab, Connecticut State Library; Society Records.

60. Weber thus overemphasizes the attachment of New Divinity preachers to the new republic itself; see *Rhetoric and History*, 10–11, 73. The large amount of literature dealing with providential nationalism can be sampled in Catherine L. Albanese, *Sons of the Fathers: The Civil Religion of the American Revolution* (Philadelphia, 1976), and John F. Berens, *Providence and Patriotism in Early America, 1640–1815* (Charlottesville, Va., 1978).

61. Bernard Bailyn has described the language of patriotic sermons as a rhetorical and emotionally charged vehicle for arguments that appealed to essentially secular logic. According to this interpretation, adopted in an otherwise fine essay by Melvin B. Endy, Jr., republican preachers focused on the mundane workings of political corruption, drew upon a religiously indifferent group of political theorists, used rationalist ethical arguments for civil rebellion, and thus took the goal of the Revolution to be quite simply the establishment of a republican nation. From this vantage Revolutionary preaching has appeared as secularization and nationalization, since it reduced supernatural intervention into history to divine immanence within history. It is misleading, however, to construe all participation in republican politics as growing out of a divergence between political and religious intentions. For many clerical patriots, genuine religion necessarily involved social morality. When social and moral questions implied political outcomes, preachers engaged in political debate as a matter of religious concern. Whether or not they conceived of those outcomes in millennial terms, they nonetheless viewed a divinely ordained moral law at work in them. See Bailyn, "Religion and Revolution: Three Biographical Studies," *Perspectives in American History* 4 (1970): 85–169; Endy, "Just War, Holy War, and Millennialism in Revolutionary America," *WMQ* 42 (1985): 3–25.

62. Bellamy, Isa. 40:1, May 30, 1777, YS; Josh. 7:10–12, Jan. 21, 1776, YS.

63. Hart, *Liberty Described and Recommended* (Hartford, 1775), 16; Hopkins, *A Dialogue, Concerning the Slavery of the Africans, Shewing It to be the Duty and Interest of the American States to Emancipate All Their African Slaves* (Norwich, Conn., 1776). Much of the New Divinity literature that called for the abolition of slavery and for widespread social reform is summarized in Conforti, *Samuel Hopkins*, 109–58; the relation of such activity to New Divinity ethics is also discussed in Breitenbach, "Unregenerate Doings." Bellamy's manumission of his servant is documented in Anderson, 301–2.

64. Bellamy, John 5:40, Feb. 20, 1780, CHS; see John 16:9, Feb. 22, 1780, CHS; Niles, *Two Discourses*, 7, 26. Despite his overall thesis that Calvinist evangelicalism eventually fostered American nationalism under Jefferson, Heimert shows that Edwardsean New Lights were intensely aware of distinctions between their values and the ideals prevalent among democratic nationalists and that they ex-

pressed their discontent in the form of jeremiads; see Heimert, 454–509. Fiering discusses some of the essential differences between Calvinist and rationalist notions of virtue in "Benjamin Franklin and the Way to Virtue," *American Quarterly* 30 (Summer 1978): 199–223. Mark Noll provides a general description of ways in which theological loyalties frequently determined the extent of patriotic enthusiasm. He also shows that many Calvinists did not embrace a secular nationalism; see Noll, *Christians in the American Revolution* (Grand Rapids, Mich., 1977). In *The Creation of the American Republic*, Wood delineates further differences between the social ethics of the liberal Republicans and conservative Federalists during the formation of the Constitution.

65. Many of Bellamy's parishioners and students—as well as his son David—became active in Federalist politics within the state legislature. The Bethlehem farmer Daniel Everit was a Connecticut delegate to the Constitutional Convention. Niles became a Federalist judge in Vermont before his apostasy to Jeffersonianism in 1794. See *HW*, 793–94; Linden and Simerl, *First Church*, 36, 85; Shipton and Sibley, *Harvard Graduates*, 16: 390–97. Litchfield County as a whole, which was strongly New Divinity, overwhelmingly went Federalist; see Richard J. Purcell, *Connecticut in Transition, 1775–1818* (Washington, D.C., 1918). For New Divinity Federalism, see also Mead, *Nathaniel William Taylor*, 38–53, and James M. Banner, *To the Hartford Convention: The Federalists and the Origins of Party Politics in Massachusetts, 1789–1815* (New York, 1970).

66. West to Bellamy, Nov. 16, 1781, Joseph Bellamy Papers, Yale Divinity School Library. See also the letters in Tryon Edwards, "Memoir," xli–li, and in Anderson, 160–63, 856–66.

Epilogue: The New Divinity

On July 27, 1789, Ezra Stiles visited Bellamy in Bethlehem, where the two men spoke heart to heart. "I asked," Stiles wrote, "if he had Faith and Grace of Assurance? He said 'yes,' he had had it for many years. [I then asked him] whether he still has it. [Again, he replied] 'Yes.'" Stiles laid aside doctrinal differences and assumed the role of pastoral advisor because he recognized that his long-time adversary was near death. Bellamy had suffered a variety of ailments during the 1780s, undoubtedly exacerbated by the loss of his first wife in 1785. In one of his few appearances outside Bethlehem, he addressed Yale's class exercises and advised the board of trustees on ministerial training in 1781; in 1786 he returned to New Haven for the last time, to preach at chapel. Shortly after his marriage that year to the twice-widowed Abiah Burbank Storrs (1731–1806), he suffered an incapacitating stroke. At the end of a prolonged decline, he died on March 6, 1790.[1]

When newspapers announced the death of Bethlehem's pastor, it fell to his colleagues and former students to comment. On March 21, Jonathan Edwards, Jr., preached about his mentor's accomplishments. He allowed that Bellamy had foibles. An unhappy childhood, the traumas of collegiate education at an unusually young age, and the hindrances of rural life had tainted Bellamy's theological "Genius" and "metaphysical" originality— reflected in the transatlantic repute of *True Religion Delineated*—with personal and intellectual irascibility. A more genteel upbringing might have polished his manners and his prose. Yet Bellamy's liabilities were also his strengths. Never an engaging communicator, Edwards marveled at Bellamy's ability to make doctrine accessible to common folk. One of New England's best preachers, Bellamy had "a lively strong imagination" and "a *faculty of striking* representation and familiar illustration," of bringing theology down to "clear and distinct" truths. Bellamy's people were extraordinarily "fond of him" because he "was free—open—sociable, *communicative* and *fond of society and conversation*, and could adapt himself to every person, even the lowest." Moreover, he could illumine the practical and social implications— what New Englanders knew as the "improvement"—of doctrine. "Benevo-

173

lent" and "ready to assist and promote charity," he had "a happy talent" for "getting improvement from his reading." He was "not a mere bookworm." Edwards derided Bellamy's critics as men who merely envied "his talents" and, most of all, "his popularity."[2]

Stiles also observed the passing of Litchfield County's celebrated divine. He agreed with Edwards that Bellamy was one of New England's most favored, "powerful," and "active Advocate[s] for Calvinism," whose "Fort was in preaching and Instruction of Candidates in Divinity." Yet however much Stiles recognized Bellamy's "considerable Attainments" and "Eminence for real Erudition," he could not bring himself to more than a grudging acknowledgment that Bellamy's "numerous noisy Writings have blazed their day." Stiles in fact anxiously predicted the irrelevance of consistent Calvinism. He hoped that "one Generation more" would put Bellamy's New Divinity doctrines "to sleep."[3]

These hopes were fulfilled, by most accounts, in the liberal, populist, and pragmatic ethos of the early Republic. Nineteenth-century opponents of what one critic labeled "the most repulsive inferences" of American Calvinism heralded the demise of the New Divinity. Early twentieth-century historians such as Frank Hugh Foster and Joseph Haroutunian buried Edwardseanism in the abstractions of New England's theological genealogy. Recent scholars have dismissed consistent Calvinism as the reactionary fixation of a few isolated clerical elites.[4]

Since the 1980s, however, there has been a recovery of the New Divinity and a reassertion of its importance to American religious life. Joseph Conforti and William Breitenbach have uncovered the social and intellectual contexts for consistent Calvinism in the early national period, exploring Edwardsean contributions to social reform and America's Second Great Awakening. The cultural historian Richard Rabinowitz has discussed the impact of New Divinity religiosity on the everyday spirituality of rural New Englanders. From a literary-critical perspective, Donald Weber has demonstrated a dynamic political consciousness in New Divinity preaching during the Revolution. A recent collection of essays on the significance of Jonathan Edwards repeatedly highlights the transmission of his thought to American culture through his successors. Moreover, Bruce Kuklick locates Edwardsean thought, which he views as "the most sustained intellectual tradition in the United States," in the mainstream of American theological history. Allen Guelzo describes the work of Bellamy and Hopkins similarly as "the first indigenous American theology"—prologue to nineteenth-century revivalism and attendant debates about the nature of moral responsibility and freedom.[5]

Yet not all of these commentators resist the temptation to portray the New Divinity as a movement at odds with common sentiment and a doctrine divorced from social reality. Kuklick, for one, maintains that Edwardsean theology "seemed to elevate truth over social usefulness." Guelzo insists that Bellamy and Hopkins stood "outside of society" as forlorn prophets whose implicit separatism inclined them to "political indifference." Even Weber holds that the Revolution only temporarily shook the Edwardseans "from the atemporal sequence" of their true theological preoccupations; their occasional sermons on politics had little to do with their more consistent preaching and writing about eternal verities. From this perspective, the decline of the New Divinity and its alienation from the mainstream of Jacksonian America appear as the result of a tendency on the part of Bellamy, Hopkins, and their followers to metaphysical abstraction.[6]

Edwards's and Stiles's comments lead to nearly the opposite conclusion. Although they differed on the value of Bellamy's theology, neither Bellamy's student nor his adversary doubted his popularity and the currency of his ideas. Both men explained them with reference to Bellamy's ability to "improve" the doctrine—to connect fundamental Calvinist affirmations quite poignantly to the real social and political crises of his day. They readily would have recognized Harriet Beecher Stowe's portrait of Grandmother Badger. Even Charles Chauncy, in a backhanded way, complimented Bellamy on the impact of his sermons and treatises. Scandalized by the popularity of Bellamy's New Divinity among Yale undergraduates and tutors, Chauncy warned Stiles in 1771 against Bellamy's nearly fatalistic confidence in God's control over mundane events and human destinies: "['T]is bad, if not worse than paganism" and "the very quintessence of pagan fatality." Yet Chauncy nonetheless resorted to that very Calvinist tenet of Bellamy's, the doctrine of divine sovereignty, as the key to American confidence in the midst of political dangers: "The Colonies are in a bad state in regard of both their civil and religious affairs. Our only comfort is, 'the Lord reigneth,' and 'whenever he pleases, he will so order things.'"[7]

Twentieth-century Americans might think it incredible that theological dogma spoke to the concerns of common people, but Bellamy's version of Calvinism did just that. Granted, Bellamy immersed himself in the sometimes abstract writings of Puritan divines, Edwards, and European moral philosophers who hardly knew of the existence, much less identified with the aspirations, of Connecticut farmers. Yet the ordinary, and sometimes extraordinary, afflictions of everyday life provided Bellamy with his theological agenda. He moved back and forth between theological discourse and his people's struggles, searching for a language to convey the truths of Calvinism as responses to New England's social crises. Bellamy's ideas, in fact, resonated particularly well with participants in the collective traumas of the late colonial period. The doctrines of law and providence—perfect justice and divine omnipotence—consoled, encouraged, and motivated people who faced social and political upheaval. This, as Michael Walzer has asserted on behalf of sixteenth-century French Huguenots and seventeenth-century English Puritans, was the characteristic strength of Calvinism.[8]

The very salience of New Divinity doctrine, rather than its putative remoteness, explains not only its popularity but also, somewhat ironically, its eventual decline some half a century after the Declaration of Independence. America emerged from its Revolution confident and expansive: in the words of Gordon Wood, "the most egalitarian, most materialistic, most individualistic . . . society in Western history." Since these social conditions called less for consolation and communalism grounded on divine sovereignty than for an ideology of opportunity grounded on human autonomy, Bellamy's shared the fate of other apologetic systems that came to appear out of date when crises passed and cultural presuppositions changed. His discourse of moral law left the New Divinity in the lurch when post-Revolutionary Americans either jettisoned its theological foundations or adopted, as Martyn Thompson has described it, a voluntary, social-contract notion of law at odds with the fundamental and moral law tradition. The New Divinity, for all of Bellamy's efforts to nurture experimental religion, was thereafter constrained by a legal paradigm that future generations of Americans increasingly found anachronistic. In the competitive, individualistic ethos of the early nation, non-Calvinist ideas replaced the doctrines of divine sovereignty in the hearts and minds of most Americans. This was as true for fervent Protestants as it was for secular democrats. The Second Great Awakening was premised more on Arminian notions of human effort and moral freedom than on strict Calvinism. When nineteenth-century evangelicals embraced the memory of Jonathan Edwards, they selected his counsel on pious exercises and largely ignored his pronouncements on human depravity.[9]

Thus, in the long run, Bellamy's successes came at some cost to the New Divinity. While other Calvinists stuck closely to Edwards's moral psychology in *Freedom of the Will*, Bellamy followed the trail of Edwards's ethics of creation—the common morality recommended in Edwards's *Two Dissertations*—and went beyond Edwards in defining the relation between providence and moral law. Bellamy muted the more evangelical themes of Edwards's theology—the transcendence of God, the soul's union with Christ, and the inner experience of grace. Edwards's philosophic apology for Calvinism had more affinities with the aesthetic sensibilities of evangelical preaching than did Bellamy's schemes of providential rule. In this respect, Haroutunian was not altogether mistaken to speak of a drift from (Jonathan Edwards's) piety to (New Divinity) moralism. Haroutunian's formulation may mislead; Edwards and Bellamy both took ethics seriously and linked a Calvinist doctrine of God, an evangelical message of conversion, and a call for a moral discipline. Yet Bellamy (and for that matter Hopkins) did produce doctrinal systems that failed to capture the brilliance of Edwards. Edwards's theology is regarded as the more enduring because it united evangelical and Calvinist convictions with philosophical themes that transcended the social and cultural presuppositions peculiar to Anglo-America in the eighteenth century.

Stiles thus believed by 1787 that their students could not appeal to the culture as successfully as had Bellamy and Hopkins; later Edwardseans would find it impossible to match their achievements. With his comments on the first generation of Yale Calvinists in the new nation, Stiles in effect wrote an epitaph on the New Divinity:

> It had been the Tendency to direct Students in divinity these 30 years past or a Generation to read the Bible, President Edwards, Dr Bellamy and Mr. Hopkins Writings—and this was a pretty good Sufficiency of Reading. Now the younger Class . . . suppose they see further than these Oracles . . . and wish to write Theology and have their own Books come into Vogue. . . . Imitation may rise to something above laudable and very useful Mediocrity, but can never reach Originality.

It was nonetheless a mark of Bellamy's public stature that Yale's president not only befriended him in his decline but also lamented the prospect of a New Divinity movement robbed of one of its originators. Edwards's death and Bellamy's and Hopkins's illnesses, Stiles observed, deprived that system of thinkers who had imbued it with considerable power and integrity in their day.[10] Following on Stiles's appreciation for Bellamy's "originality" and on the younger Edwards's assessment of Bellamy's gifts, I have attempted to account for the remarkable vibrancy of his version of Calvinism in the Revolutionary period: the ways in which Bellamy captured so many adherents (not the least of whom were his parishioners), achieved notoriety from Vermont to Georgia, and led a widespread network of consistent Calvinists who virtually dominated western New England and were an important force in eastern Connecticut, Massachusetts, and New Jersey.[11]

Bellamy began his career committed to evangelical revival. After initial successes in Bethlehem, he became convinced that New Light extremists threatened to bring disorder to New England communities and discredit evangelical preaching as antinomian. In an attempt to defend evangelical Calvinism as theologically and ethically sound and to assert its authority over common life, he shifted the focus of his theology. Reading Enlightenment ethicists such as Francis Hutcheson, he adopted the concept of moral law as a paradigm for Calvinism and emphasized Christian duties to social benevolence. During the 1750s internal and external threats to New England's social order drove Bellamy to assess the corporate implications of doctrine; he asserted that Calvinism, rendered in the discourse of moral law, best answered the moral questions raised by these social challenges.

As New Englanders faced the prospect of economic life in the free market, Bellamy provided a defense of the Calvinist position on original sin that stood as a critique of commerce. The Anglo-French conflict in America pressed ministers to explain God's purposes for natural and moral evil; Bellamy contended that God had wisely permitted sin, justly condemned it, benevolently procured redemption from it, and as Moral Governor would uphold the rule of justice in temporal history. Only this Calvinist conviction of an absolutely sovereign God whose actions were mediated by the moral law, he maintained, encouraged New England-ers. When it later appeared that the British government had degener-ated into vice and tyranny, thereby violating the rights of the colonists and transgressing the moral law, Bellamy again responded with a Cal-vinist doctrine of history. He exhorted people to enlist on what he per-ceived to be the ultimately triumphant side of virtue: the divine punish-ment of imperial misrule. Revolutionary preaching consummated his attempts to link Calvinism to issues of social and political authority. His legitimization of independence signified neither the implicit antiauthori-tarianism and individualism of New Light theology nor an egalitarian, populist, democratic, and ultimately nationalist ethos but foundational convictions about the nature of divine rule and sovereignty.

Bellamy's importance—and the explanation for his prominence as pastor, ecclesiastical leader, author, and teacher—thus lay in how he worked out a transatlantic debate between Calvinists, Arminians, and antinomians in the context of local and colonial affairs. Therein was much of Bellamy's contribution: he gave Calvinism a powerful voice in the midst of New England's crises. Had he lived to see nineteenth-century Ameri-cans reject his teaching, his confidence would not have been shaken. He had merely improved the doctrine to the glory of God; Americans' unbe-lief, he would have asserted, stemmed from narrow and foolish self-interest. In the face of antinomian excess and Arminian obduracy, social faction-alization and armed violence, imperial corruption and the War for Indepen-dence, Bellamy always had held that providence could overrule such sin.

Notes

1. Stiles, *Literary Diary*, III:361 (I have expanded Stiles's contractions and ab-breviations); for further comments on Bellamy's physical decline and visits to New Haven, see Stiles, *Literary Diary*, II:304, 438, 499, 511; and III:4, 75, 226–29. There is no copy of the addresses that Bellamy gave at Yale. Further correspondence regarding Bellamy's last days are contained in Tryon Edwards, "Memoir," xli–li, and Anderson, 160–63, 856–66. In 1791 the Bethlehem church settled Azel Backus as Bellamy's successor; see *HW*, 253–56.

2. Edwards, Job 21:23–27, Mar. 21, 1790, JEHS 76377. Edwards focused the doctrine of this sermon as befit a student of Bellamy's: "Knowledge of God leads to knowledge of his law" and thus "love to men, benevolence to all, [and] com-placency to good."

3. Stiles, *Literary Diary*, III:384–85.

4. Andrew P. Peabody, "Hopkinsianism," *Proceedings of the American Antiquar-*

ian Society, New Series, 5 (1898): 437–61, quotation from 439. Foster's *A Genetic History of the New England Theology* was published in 1907; Haroutunian's *Piety to Moralism* first appeared in 1932.

5. Kuklick, *Churchmen to Philosophers* (1985), 43; Guelzo, *Edwards on the Will* (1989), 137. My other references are to Conforti, *Samuel Hopkins* (1981); Breiten-bach, "Unregenerate Doings" (1982) and "Consistent Calvinism" (1984); Rabino-witz, *The Spiritual Self in Everyday Life* (1989); Weber, *Rhetoric and History* (1988); and Hatch and Stout, eds., *Jonathan Edwards*.

6. Kuklick, *Churchmen to Philosophers*, 47; Guelzo, *Edwards on the Will*, 126–27; Weber, "The Recovery of Jonathan Edwards," in Hatch and Stout, eds., *Jonathan Edwards*, 50–70, quotation from 56.

7. Chauncy to Stiles, June 14, 1771, in Stiles, *Extracts*, 451.

8. As Walzer has written of the Puritan Revolution in seventeenth-century England, "the enthusiasm, the battle-readiness, the confident enmity, the polemi-cal eagerness, the sense of unity" of Calvinism "helped carry men through a time of change. . . . They had been elements of strength in an age of moral confusion and of cruel vigor in an age of vacillation." See Walzer, *Revolution of the Saints*, 320.

9. Wood, *The Radicalism of the American Revolution*, 230; Thompson, "The His-tory of Fundamental Law." For the fate of Edwards at the hands of nineteenth-century evangelicals, see Conforti, "The Invention of the Great Awakening."

10. Stiles, *Literary Diary*, II:274–75 (contractions and abbreviations expanded).

11. For Bellamy's notoriety as far south as Georgia, see John Joachim Zubly, *The Nature of that Faith without which it is Impossible to please God* (Savannah, Ga., 1772), a critique of Bellamy's *Theron, Paulinas, and Aspasio.*

Bibliography

Primary Sources

Manuscript Collections

American Antiquarian Society, Worcester, Mass. Joseph Bellamy Manuscript. Nathan Fiske Papers. Parkman Family Papers. Gay Family Sermons.

Beinecke Library, Yale University, New Haven, Conn. Henry M. Dexter Manuscript Book: Bellamy letters and sermons. Jonathan Edwards Papers.

Bethlehem Congregational Church, Bethlehem, Conn. First Book of the Ecclesiastical Society (1740–1825).

Bethlehem Town Archives, Bethlehem, Conn. Map of tiers and plots. Land Records.

Case Memorial Library, Hartford Seminary, Hartford, Conn. Joseph Bellamy Papers. Jonathan Edwards, Jr., Papers.

Connecticut Historical Society Library, Hartford, Conn. Joseph Bellamy Papers. Levi Hart Papers. Uncatalogued sermons.

Connecticut State Library, Hartford, Conn. Bethlehem, Connecticut, Congregational Church Records, 1738–1850. Connecticut Archives: Colonial Wars; Ecclesiastical Records; Militia Records; Revolutionary War Records. Connecticut Probate Records.

Historical Society of Pennsylvania, Philadelphia. Simon Gratz Collection: Samuel Hopkins Papers; Levi Hart Papers.

Houghton Library, Harvard University, Cambridge, Mass. Joseph Bellamy Manuscripts.

Massachusetts Historical Society, Boston. Andrew Croswell Letterbook.

Presbyterian Historical Society, Philadelphia. Joseph Bellamy letters, tr. Richard Webster. Samuel Davies Papers, tr. Richard Webster.

Sterling Memorial Library, Yale University, New Haven, Conn. Joseph Bellamy Papers. Park Family Manuscripts.

Trask Memorial Library, Andover-Newton Theological School, South Andover, Mass. Jonathan Edwards Papers. Jonathan Edwards, Jr., Papers. Samuel Hopkins Papers.

Woodbury Town Hall, Woodbury, Connecticut. Woodbury Probate Records. Woodbury Land Records. Woodbury Town Records.

Yale Divinity School Library, New Haven, Conn. Miscellaneous Personal Papers:
Joseph Bellamy Papers.

Publications

[anon.]. *The Quarterly Christian Spectator* 2 (1830): 529–40.
Assembly of Pastors of Churches in New England. *Testimony and Advice of an Assembly of Pastors in New-England, At a Meeting in Boston July 7, 1743.* Boston, 1743.
Backus, Isaac. *True Faith Will Produce Good Works.* Boston, 1767.
Barnard, Thomas. *A Sermon Preached Before the Society for Encouraging Industry and Employing the Poor.* Boston, 1758.
Beecher, Lyman. *Autobiography, Correspondence, Etc., of Lyman Beecher, D.D.* 2 vols. Ed. Charles Beecher. New York, 1865.
———. *Dependence and Free Agency.* Boston, 1832.
[Bellamy, Joseph]. *A Letter to the Reverend Author of the Winter-Evening Conversation on Original Sin, from one of his Candid Neighbours.* Boston, 1758.
Bellamy, Joseph. *A Blow at the Root of the Refined Antinomianism of the Present Age.* Boston, 1763.
———. *A Careful and Strict Examination of the External Covenant, and of the Principles by which it is Supported.* New Haven, Conn., 1770.
———. *A Letter to Scripturista.* New Haven, Conn., 1760.
———. *A Sermon Delivered before the General Assembly of the Colony of Connecticut at Hartford on the day of the Anniversary Election, May 13, 1762.* New London, Conn., 1762.
———. *An Answer to a Dialogue concerning the Half-way Covenant.* New Haven, Conn., 1769.
———. *An Essay on the Nature and Glory of the Gospel of Jesus Christ, as also on the Nature and Consequences of Spiritual Blindness, and the Nature and Effects of Divine Illumination.* Boston, 1762.
———. *Early Piety Recommended.* Boston, 1748.
———. *Remarks on the Revd. Mr. Croswell's Letter to the Rev. Mr. Cumming.* Boston, 1763.
———. *Sermons upon the Following Subjects, viz. The Divinity of Jesus Christ, the Millenium [sic], The Wisdom of God, in the Permission of Sin.* Boston, 1758.
———. *That there is but one Covenant, Whereof Baptism and the Lord's Supper are Seals.* New Haven, Conn., 1769.
———. *The Great Evil of Sin, as it is Committed Against God.* Boston, 1753.
———. *The Half-way Covenant: A Dialogue Between a Minister and His Parishioner.* New Haven, Conn., 1769.
———. *The Inconsistence of Renouncing the Half-way Covenant, and yet Retaining the Half-way Practice.* New Haven, Conn., 1769.
———. *The Law, Our School-Master.* New Haven, Conn., 1756.
———. *The Sacramental Controversy Brought to a Point.* New Haven, Conn., 1770.
———. *The Wisdom of God in the Permission of Sin, Vindicted.* Boston, 1760.
———. *The Works of Joseph Bellamy, D.D., First Pastor of the Church in Bethlem, Connecticut, With a Memoir of his Life and Character, by Tryon Edwards.* 2 vols. Boston, 1850.
———. *The Works of the Rev. Joseph Bellamy, D.D. Late of Bethlem, Connecticut.* With

"Funeral Sermon, with an Appendix" by Noah Benedict. 3 vols. New York, 1811–1812.

———. *Theron, Paulinas, and Aspasio, or, Letters and Dialogues upon the Nature of Love to God, Faith in Christ, Assurance of Title to Eternal Life*. Boston, 1759.

———. *True Religion Delineated*. Boston, 1750.

Billings, William. *The Singing Master's Assistant*. Boston, 1778.

[Bolles, John]. *Concerning the Christian Sabbath*. [New London, Conn.], 1757.

Boston Evening Post. Sept. 30, 1742; July 2, 24, 1749; June 23, 1755.

Boston Gazette. Apr. 21, 1747.

Boston Weekly News-Letter. Aug. 14, 1755; July 27, 1758.

Boston Weekly Post-Boy. Apr. 12, 1742.

Briant, Lemuel. *The Absurdity and Blasphemy of Depretiating Moral Virtue*. Boston, 1749.

Champion, Judah. *A Brief View of the Distresses, Hardships and Dangers of our Ancestors*. Hartford, 1770.

[Chauncy, Charles]. *The Opinion of One that has Perused A Summer Morning's Conversation*. Boston, 1758.

Chauncy, Charles. *A Letter to a Friend, Giving A Concise Account of the Ohio-Defeat*. Boston, 1755.

———. *Cornelius' Character*. Boston, 1745.

———. *Earthquakes a Token of the Righteous Anger of God*. Boston, 1755.

———. *Seasonable Thoughts on the State of Religion in New-England*. Boston, 1743.

———. *The Earth Delivered from the Curse . . . A Sermon Occasioned by the late Earthquakes*. Boston, 1756.

———. *The Idle Poor Secluded from the Bread of Charity by the Christian Law*. Boston, 1753.

———. *Trust in God, the Duty of a People in a Day of Trouble*. Boston, 1770.

Churches of the County of Windham. *The Result of a Council of Churches of the County of Windham*. Boston, 1747.

Clap, Thomas. *The Religious Constitution of Colleges, Especially of Yale College in New Haven*. New London, Conn., 1754.

Clark, Peter. *The Scripture-Doctrine of Original Sin Stated and Defended. A Summer Morning's Conversation*. Boston, 1758.

Colony of Connecticut. *Acts and Laws passed by the General Court*. New London, Conn., 1742.

———. *The Public Records of the Colony of Connecticut*. Ed. by Charles J. Hoadly. 15 vols. Hartford, 1850–1890.

Congregational Churches in Connecticut, Saybrook Synod, 1708. *A Confession of Faith*. New London, Conn., 1710.

Congregational Pastors of New England. *Testimony and Advice of an Assembly of Pastors of Churches in New-England*. Boston, 1743.

Connecticut Gazette, Feb. 11, 1758.

Cooper, Samuel. *A Sermon Preached in Boston, New-England, Before the Society for Encouraging Industry, and Employing the Poor*. Boston, 1753.

Croswell, Andrew. *A Letter to the Reverend Alexander Cumming*. Boston, 1762.

———. *What Is Christ to Me if He Is Not Mine?* Boston, 1745.

Cudworth, William. *A Defence of Mr. Hervey's Dialogues against Mr. Bellamy's Theron, Paulinas, and Aspasio*. Boston, 1762.

Davies, Samuel. *Divine Conduct Vindicated, Or the Operations of God Shown to the Operations of Wisdom.* London, 1761.

———. *Religion and Patriotism the Constituents of a Good Soldier.* Philadelphia, 1755.

———. *The Curse of Cowardice.* Boston, 1759.

———. *The State of Religion Among the Protestant Dissenters in Virginia: In a Letter to the Reverend Mr. Joseph Bellamy.* Boston, 1751.

Devotion, Ebenezer. *A Letter to the Rev. Joseph Bellamy, D.D. Concerning Qualifications for Christian Communion.* New Haven, Conn., 1770.

———. *A Second Letter, to the Rev. Joseph Bellamy.* New Haven, Conn., 1770.

———. *The Civil Ruler, a Dignified Servant of the Lord.* New Haven, Conn., 1753.

———. *The Half-way Covenant, A Dialogue between Joseph Bellamy, D.D., and a Parishioner.* New London, Conn., 1769.

———. *The Parishioner having studied the Point . . . on the Half-way Covenant.* Hartford, 1769.

Dewey, Israel. *Letter, By a Layman, to Samuel Hopkins, D.D.* n. p., 1759. 2d ed. Dedham, 1809.

Dickinson, Jonathan. *A Vindication of God's Sovereign Free Grace.* Boston, 1746.

Doddridge, Philip. *A Course of Lectures on the Principal Subjects in Pneumatology, Ethics, and Divinity.* London, 1763.

Edwards, Jonathan. *A Faithful Narrative of the Surprising Work of God.* Boston, 1737.

———. *A History of the Work of Redemption.* Vol. 9 of *The Works of Jonathan Edwards.* Ed. John F. Wilson. New Haven, Conn., 1989.

———. *A Strong Rod Broken and Withered.* Boston, 1748.

———. *An Humble Inquiry Into the Rules of the Word of God.* Boston, 1749.

———. *Apocalyptic Writings.* Vol. 5 of *The Works of Jonathan Edwards.* Ed. Stephen J. Stein. New Haven, Conn., 1977.

———. *Discourses on Various Important Subjects Nearly Concerning the Great Affair of the Soul's Eternal Salvation.* Boston, 1738.

———. *Ethical Writings.* Vol. 8 of *The Works of Jonathan Edwards.* Ed. Paul Ramsey. New Haven, Conn., 1989.

———. *Freedom of the Will.* Vol. 1 of *The Works of Jonathan Edwards.* Ed. Paul Ramsey. New Haven, Conn., 1957.

———. *Jonathan Edwards: Representative Selections, with Introduction, Bibliography, and Notes.* Ed. Clarence N. Faust and Thomas H. Johnson. New York, 1935.

———. *Original Sin.* Vol. 3 of *The Works of Jonathan Edwards.* Ed. Clyde A. Holbrook. New Haven, Conn., 1970.

———. *Practical Sermons: Never Before Published.* Tr. Jonathan Edwards the Younger. Edinburgh, 1788.

———. *Religious Affections.* Vol. 2 of *The Works of Jonathan Edwards.* Ed. John E. Smith. New Haven, Conn., 1959.

———. *Scientific and Philosophical Writings.* Vol. 6 of *The Works of Jonathan Edwards.* Ed. Wallace E. Anderson. New Haven, Conn., 1980.

———. *Selections from the Unpublished Writings of Jonathan Edwards.* Ed. Alexander B. Grossart. Edinburgh, 1865.

———. *Sinners in the Hands of an Angry God.* Boston, 1741.

———. *Some Thoughts Concerning the Present Revival.* Boston, 1742.

———. *The Great Awakening.* Vol. 4 of *The Works of Jonathan Edwards.* Ed. C. C. Goen. New Haven, Conn., 1972.

———. *The Works of Jonathan Edwards in Two Volumes*. Ed. Edward Hickman. London, 1839.

———. *The Works of President Edwards*. 10 vols. Ed. Sereno E. Dwight. New York, 1830.

———. *Two Dissertations, I. Concerning the End for Which God Created the World. II. The Nature of True Virtue*. Boston, 1765.

[Fisk, Joseph]. *A Few Lines on the Happy Reduction of Canada and Sickness at Woodbury*. New Haven, Conn., 1761.

Foxcroft, Thomas. *Grateful Reflexions on Occasion of the Surrender of Montreal*. Boston, 1760.

Frink, Thomas. *A King Reigning in Righteousness, and Princes Reigning in Judgment*. Boston, 1758.

[Gale, Benjamin]. *The Present State of the Colony of Connecticut Considered*. [n. p., 1755].

Graham, John. *The Christian's Duty of Watchfullness Against Error*. New London, Conn., 1733.

Hall, Samuel. *The Legislature's Right, Charge, and Duty in Respect to Religion*. New London, Conn., 1746.

Hart, Levi. *Liberty Described and Recommended*. Hartford, 1775.

[Hart, William.] *A Letter to Paulinas*. New Haven, Conn., 1760.

Hart, William. *Brief Remarks on a Number of False Propositions*. New London, Conn., 1769.

Harvey, Joseph. *A Review of a Sermon, Delivered in the Chapel of Yale College*. Hartford, 1829.

Hervey, James. *Theron and Aspasio*. 3 vols. London, 1755.

Hobart, Noah. *Civil Government the Foundation of Social Happiness*. New London, Conn., 1751.

Holly, Israel. *Old Divinity Preferable to Modern Novelty*. New Haven, Conn., 1780.

[Hopkins, Samuel]. *A Bold Push, in a letter to the Author of "Fair Play"*. Boston, 1758.

Hopkins, Samuel. *A Dialogue Concerning the Slavery of the Africans, Shewing It to be the Duty and Interest of the American States to Emancipate All Their African Slaves*. Norwich, Conn., 1776.

———. *An Inquiry into the Nature of True Holiness*. Newport, R.I., 1773.

———. *Inquiry into the Promises of the Gospel*. Boston, 1765.

———. *Sin, thro' Divine Interposition, an Advantage to the Universe*. Boston, 1759.

———. *Sketches of the Life of the Late, Rev. Samuel Hopkins, D.D.* Ed. Stephen West. Hartford, 1805.

———. *The System of Doctrines Contained in Divine Revelation*. 3 vols. Boston, 1793.

———. *The Works of Samuel Hopkins, D.D.* With "Memoir" by Edwards A. Park. 3 vols. Boston, 1754.

———. *Twenty-one Sermons, On a Variety of Interesting Subjects, Sentimental and Practical*. Salem, Mass., 1803.

Hunn, Nathanael. *The Welfare of a Government Considered*. New London, Conn., 1747.

Hutcheson, Francis. *An Inquiry into the Original of our Ideas of Beauty and Virtue*. 4th ed. London, 1738.

Industry & Frugality Proposed As the Surest Means to Make Us a Rich and Flourishing People, and the Linen Manufacture Recommended. Boston, 1753.

[Johnson, Samuel]. *Ethices Elementa. Or the First Principles of Moral Philosophy*. Boston, 1746.

Johnson, Samuel. *A Sermon Concerning the Obligations We are under to Love and Delight in the Public Worship of God.* Boston, 1746.

Jones, Erasmus. *Luxury, Pride and Vanity the Bane of the British Nation.* London, 1750.

Leach, John. "A Journal Kept by John Leach, During His Confinement by the British, In Boston Gaol, in 1775." *The New England Historical and Geneological Register* 19 (1865): 255–63.

[March, Edmund]. *Fair Play!* Portsmouth, N.H., 1758.

Mather, Cotton. *Concio ad Populum.* Boston, 1719.

———. *Debtor and Creditor.* Boston, 1716.

———. *Magnalia Christi Americana.* Boston, 1702.

———. *Malachi . . . and the Maxims of Piety.* Boston, 1717.

Mather, Moses. *The Visible Church, in Covenant with God.* New York, 1769.

———. *The Visible Church, in Covenant with God, Further Illustrated.* New Haven, Conn., 1770.

Mayhew, Jonathan. *God's Hand and Providence.* Boston, 1760.

———. *Practical Discourses.* Boston, 1760.

———. *Sermons on the Following Subjects.* Boston, 1755.

———. *Seven Sermons upon the Following Subjects.* Boston, 1749.

———. *The Dissolution of All Things.* Boston, 1755.

———. *Two Discourses Delivered October 25th, 1759 . . . A Day of Public Thanksgiving for the Reduction of Quebec.* Boston, 1749.

———. *Two Sermons on the Nature, Extent and Perfection of the Divine Goodness.* Boston, 1763.

Moody, Samuel. *An Attempt to Point Out the Fatal and Pernicious Consequences of The Rev. Mr. Joseph Bellamy's Doctrines Respecting Moral Evil.* Boston, 1759.

New York Gazette or Weekly Post-Boy. Jan. 14, 1762.

Niles, Nathaniel. *Two Discourses on Liberty.* Newbury-Port, Mass., 1774.

North and South Consociations of Litchfield County, Connecticut. *Proceedings in Convention at Litchfield, July 7 and 8, 1852.* Hartford, 1852.

Oliver, Peter. *Peter Oliver's Origin and Progress of the American Revolution.* Ed. Douglas Adair and John A. Schutz. San Marino, Calif., 1961.

Pastors of the Churches in Massachusetts Bay. *The Testimony of the Pastors of the Churches in the Province of Massachusetts-Bay, at their Annual Convention in Boston.* Boston, 1743.

[Peters, Samuel]. *A General History of Connecticut . . . wherein new and the true Sources of the present Rebellion in America are pointed out.* 2d. ed. London, 1782.

Robbins, Philemon. *A Plain Narrative.* Boston, 1747.

Sandeman, Robert. *Letters on Theron and Aspasio.* 2 vols. Edinburgh, 1757.

[Sherman, Roger]. *Caveat Against Injustice, or an Enquiry into the evil Consequences of a Fluctuating Medium of Exchange.* New York, 1752.

Smith, Adam. *The Theory of Moral Sentiments.* London, 1759; rep. 1853. Rep. 1853 ed. New York, 1966.

Stapfer, Johann Frederich. *Institutiones Theologiae Polemicae Universae.* 5 vols. Tiguri [Zurich], 1743–1747.

Stiles, Ezra. *Extracts from the Itineraries and other Miscellanies of Ezra Stiles, D.D., LL.D., 1755–1794, with a Selection from his Correspondence.* Ed. Franklin Bowditch Dexter. New Haven, Conn., 1916.

———. *The Literary Diary of Ezra Stiles, D.D., LL.D., President of Yale College.* Ed. Franklin Bowditch Dexter. 3 vols. New York, 1901.

Stiles, Isaac. *A Prospect of the City of Jerusalem, In Its Spiritual Building.* New London, Conn., 1742.

Stowe, Harriet Beecher. *Oldtown Folks.* Boston, 1869.

Taylor, John. *The Scripture-Doctrine of Original Sin Proposed to A Free and Candid Examination.* London, 1740.

Taylor, Nathaniel. *A Second Dialogue, Between a Minister and His Parishioner, Concerning the Half-way Covenant.* Hartford, 1769.

Taylor, Nathaniel William. *Concio ad Clerum.* New Haven, Conn., 1828.

Thacher, Peter. *Fear of God Restraining Men from Iniquity in Commerce.* Boston, 1720.

Todd, Jonathan. *Civil Rulers the Ministers of God, for Good to Men.* New London, Conn., 1749.

Wadsworth, Benjamin. *Fraud and Injustice Detected and Condemned.* Boston, 1712.

Webster, Samuel. *A Winter Evening's Conversation Upon the Doctrine of Original Sin.* New Haven, Conn., 1757.

Wetmore, Israhiah. *A Sermon Preached before the Honorable Assembly.* Hartford, 1773.

Willard, Samuel. *A Compleat Body of Divinity.* Boston, 1726.

Wilson, David. *Palaemon's Creed Revised and Examined.* Boston, 1762.

Zubly, John Joachim. *The Nature of that Faith without which it is Impossible to please God.* Savannah, Ga., 1772.

Secondary Sources

(All references for *The William and Mary Quarterly* are to the Third Series.)

Ahlstrom, Sydney E. "The Puritan Ethic and the Spirit of American Democracy." In *Calvinism and the Political Order: Essays Prepared for the Woodrow Wilson Lectureship of the National Presbyterian Center, Washington, D.C.* Ed. George Laird Hunt. Philadelphia, 1965.

Akers, Charles W. *Called Unto Liberty: A Life of Jonathan Mayhew, 1720–1766.* Cambridge, Mass., 1964.

———. "Religion and the American Revolution: Samuel Cooper and the Brattle Street Church." *William and Mary Quarterly* 35 (1978): 477–98.

Albenese, Catherine L. *Sons of the Fathers: The Civil Religion of the American Revolution.* Philadelphia, 1976.

Aldridge, A. Owen. "Edwards and Hutcheson." *Harvard Theological Review* 44 (1951): 35–53.

Anderson, Fred. *A People's Army: Massachusetts Soldiers and Society in the Seven Years' War.* Chapel Hill, N.C., 1984.

Anderson, Glenn Paul. "Joseph Bellamy (1719–1790): The Man and his Work." Ph.D. dissertation, Boston University, 1971.

Anderson, Michael P. "The Pope of Litchfield County: An Intellectual Biography of Joseph Bellamy, 1719–1790." Ph.D. dissertation, Claremont Graduate School, 1980.

Appleby, Joyce Oldham. *Economic Thought and Ideology in Seventeenth-Century England.* Princeton, N.J., 1978.

Bailyn, Bernard. "Religion and Revolution: Three Biographical Studies." *Perspectives in American History* 4 (1970): 85–169.

———. *The Ideological Origins of the American Revolution.* Cambridge, Mass., 1967.

Baldwin, Alice M. *The New England Clergy and the American Revolution.* Durham, N.C., 1928.

Banner, James M. *To the Hartford Convention: The Federalists and the Origins of Party Politics in Massachusetts, 1789–1815.* New York, 1970.

Battles, Ford Lewis. "Bellamy Papers." *Hartford Quarterly* 8 (1967): 64–91.

Bercovitch, Sacvan. *The American Jeremiad.* Madison, Wis., 1978.

———. *The Puritan Origins of the American Self.* New Haven, Conn., 1975.

Berens, John F. *Providence and Patriotism in Early America, 1640–1815.* Charlottesville, Va., 1978.

Berk, Stephen E. *Calvinism versus Democracy.* Hamden, Conn., 1974.

Birdsall, Richard D. "Ezra Stiles versus the New Divinity Men." *American Quarterly* 17 (Summer 1965): 248–58.

Bloch, Ruth H. "Religion and Ideological Change in the American Revolution." In *Religion and American Politics: From the Colonial Period to the 1980's.* Ed. Mark A. Noll. New York, 1990.

———. *Visionary Republic: Millennial Themes in American Thought, 1756–1800.* New York, 1985.

Bonomi, Patricia U. *Under the Cope of Heaven: Religion, Society, and Politics in Colonial America.* New York, 1986.

Bouwsma, William J. *John Calvin: A Sixteenth-Century Portrait.* New York, 1988.

Breen, T. H. "'Baubles of Britain': The American and Consumer Revolutions of the Eighteenth Century." *Past and Present* 119 (1988): 73–104.

———. "Narrative of Commerical Life: Consumption, Ideology, and Community on the Eve of the American Revolution." *William and Mary Quarterly* 50 (1993): 471–501.

———. *The Good Ruler: A Study of Puritan Political Ideas in New England, 1630–1730.* New Haven, Conn., 1970.

Breitenbach, William K. "New Divinity Theology and the Idea of Moral Accountability." Ph.D. dissertation, Yale University, 1978.

———. "Piety *and* Moralism: Edwards and the New Divinity." In *Jonathan Edwards and the American Experience.* Ed. Nathan O. Hatch and Harry S. Stout. New York, 1988.

———. "The Consistent Calvinism of the New Divinity Movement." *William and Mary Quarterly* 41 (1984): 241–64.

———. "Unregenerate Doings: Selflessness and Selfishness in New Divinity Theology." *American Quarterly* 34 (Winter 1982): 479–502.

Bridenbaugh, Carl. *Mitre and Sceptre: Transatlantic Faith, Ideas, Personalities and Politics, 1689–1775.* New York, 1962.

Brock, Leslie V. *The Currency of the American Colonies, 1700–1764: A Study in Colonial Finance and Imperial Relations.* New York, 1975.

Brown, Richard D. *Knowledge Is Power: The Diffusion of Information in Early America, 1700–1865.* New York, 1989.

Brumm, Ursula. *American Thought and Religious Typology.* New Brunswick, N.J., 1970.

Buel, Richard, Jr. *Dear Liberty: Connecticut's Mobilization for the Revolutionary War.* Middletown, Conn., 1980.

Bumsted, John M. "Religion, Finance, and Democracy in Massachusetts." *Journal of Social History* 57 (1971): 817–31.

Bumsted, J. M., and John E. Van de Wetering. *What Must I Do To Be Saved?: The Great Awakening in Colonial America*. Hinsdale, Ill., 1976.

Burrows, Edwin G., and Michael Wallace. "The American Revolution: The Ideology and Psychology of National Liberation." *Perspectives in American History* 6 (1972): 167–306.

Bushman, Richard L. *From Puritan to Yankee: Character and the Social Order in Connecticut, 1690–1765*. Cambridge, Mass., 1967; rep. New York, 1970.

———. "Jonathan Edwards and the Puritan Consciousness." *Journal for the Scientific Study of Religion* 5 (1966): 383–96.

———. "Massachusetts Farmers and the Revolution." In *Society, Freedom, and Conscience: The American Revolution in Virginia, Massachusetts, and New York*. Ed. Richard M. Jellison. New York, 1976.

Butler, Jon. "Enthusiasm Described and Decried: The Great Awakening as Interpretive Fiction." *The Journal of American History* 69 (1982): 305–25.

Caskey, Marie. *Chariots of Fire: Religion and the Beecher Family*. New Haven, Conn., 1978.

Cherry, Conrad. *Nature and Religious Imagination: From Edwards to Bushnell*. Philadelphia, 1980.

———. *The Theology of Jonathan Edwards: A Reappraisal*. New York, 1966.

Chitnis, Anand C. *The Scottish Enlightenment: A Social History*. London, 1976.

Clark, Christopher. "The Household Economy, Market Exchange, and the Rise of Capitalism in the Connecticut Valley, 1800–1860." *Journal of Social History* 13 (Winter 1979): 169–89.

Clark, Joseph S. *A Historical Sketch of the Congregational Churches in Massachusetts, From 1620 to 1858*. Boston, 1858.

Conforti, Joseph. "Edwardsians, Unitarians, and the Memory of the Great Awakening, 1800–1840." In *American Unitarianism: 1805–1865*. Ed. Conrad Edick Wright. Boston, 1989.

———. "Joseph Bellamy and The New Divinity Movement." *The New England Historical and Geneological Register* 87 (1983): 126–38.

———. *Samuel Hopkins and the New Divinity Movement: Calvinism, the Congregational Ministry, and Reform in New England Between the Great Awakenings*. Grand Rapids, Mich., 1981.

———. "Samuel Hopkins and the New Divinity: Theology, Ethics and Social Reform in Eighteenth-Century New England." *William and Mary Quarterly* 34 (1977): 572–89.

———. "The Invention of the Great Awakening." *Early American Literature* 26 (1991): 99–118.

———. "The Rise of the New Divinity in Western New England, 1740–1800." *Historical Journal of Western Massachusetts* 3 (1980): 37–47.

Constantin, Charles Joseph, Jr. "The New Divinity Men." Ph.D. dissertation, University of California at Berkeley, 1972.

Corrigan, John. *The Prism of Piety: Catholick Congregational Clergy at the Beginning of the Enlightenment*. New York, 1991.

Cothren, William. *History of Ancient Woodbury, Connecticut from the First Indian Deed in 1659 to 1854*. 3 vols. Waterbury, Conn., 1854.

Crawford, Michael J. *Seasons of Grace: Colonial New England's Revival Tradition in Its British Context*. New York, 1991.

Crowley, J. E. *This Sheba, Self: The Conceptualization of Economic Life in Eigteenth-Century America*. Baltimore, 1974.

Daniels, Bruce C. "Large Town Officeholding in Eighteenth-Century Connecticut." *Journal of American Studies* 9 (1975): 1–12.

———. *The Connecticut Town: Growth and Development, 1635–1790*. Middletown, Conn., 1979.

———. *The Fragmentation of New England: Comparative Perspectives on Economic, Political, and Social Divisions in the Eighteenth Century*. Westport, Conn., 1988.

Davidson, Edward H. "From Locke to Edwards." *Journal of the History of Ideas* 24 (1963): 355–72.

Davidson, James West. *The Logic of Millennial Thought: Eighteenth-Century New England*. New Haven, Conn., 1977.

Delattre, Roland Andre. *Beauty and Sensibility in the Thought of Jonathan Edwards: An Essay in Aesthetics and Theological Ethics*. New Haven, Conn., 1968.

Dexter, Franklin Bowditch. *Biographical Sketches of the Graduates of Yale College, with Annals of the College History*. 9 vols. New York, 1885–1912.

Dickson, P. G. M. *The Financial Revolution in England: A Study in the Development of Public Credit, 1688–1756*. London, 1967.

Ditz, Toby L. "Ownership and Obligation: Inheritance and Patriarchal Households in Connecticut, 1750–1820." *William and Mary Quarterly* 47 (1990): 235–65.

Divinsky, Pamela. "Virtue in Distress: The Discourse on Economy in Eighteenth-Century England." Ph.D. dissertation, University of Chicago, 1990.

Dwight, Sereno E. *The Life of President Edwards*. New York, 1830.

Eggleston, Percy Coe. *A Man of Bethlehem, Joseph Bellamy, D.D., and His Divinity School*. New London, Conn., 1908.

Ellis, Joseph J. *The New England Mind in Transition: Samuel Johnson of Connecticut, 1696–1722*. New Haven, Conn., 1973.

Elsbree, Oliver Wendell. "Samuel Hopkins and His Doctrine of Benevolence." *New England Quarterly* 8 (1935): 539–50.

Elwood, Douglas. *The Philosophical Theology of Jonathan Edwards*. New York, 1960.

Endy, Melvin B., Jr. "Just War, Holy War, and Millennialism in Revolutionary America." *William and Mary Quarterly* 42 (1985): 3–25.

Erdt, Terrence. *Jonathan Edwards and the Sense of the Heart*. Amherst, Mass., 1980.

Eusden, John D. "Natural Law and Covenant Theology in New England, 1620–1670." *Natural Law Forum* 5 (1960): 1–30.

Ferm, Robert L. *Jonathan Edwards the Younger, 1745–1801, A Colonial Pastor*. Grand Rapids, Mich., 1976.

Fiering, Norman S. "Benjamin Franklin and the Way to Virtue." *American Quarterly* 30 (Summer 1978): 199–223.

———. *Jonathan Edwards's Moral Thought and Its British Context*. Chapel Hill, N.C., 1981.

———. "President Samuel Johnson and the Circle of Knowledge." *William and Mary Quarterly* 28 (1971): 199–236.

———. "The First American Enlightenment: Tillotson, Leverett, and Philosophical Anglicanism." *New England Quarterly* 54 (1981): 307–44.

———. "The Transatlantic Republic of Letters: A Note on the Circulation of Learned Periodicals to Early Eighteenth-Century America." *William and Mary Quarterly* 33 (1976): 642–60.

————. "Will and Intellect in the New England Mind." *William and Mary Quarterly* 29 (1972): 515–58.

Fisher, George Park. *A Discourse, Commemorative of the History of the Church of Christ in Yale College*. New Haven, Conn., 1858.

Foster, Frank Hugh. *A Genetic History of the New England Theology*. Chicago, 1907; rep. New York, 1963.

————. "The Eschatology of the New England Divines." *Bibliotheca Sacra* 43 (1886): 1–32.

Foster, Stephen. *Their Solitary Way: The Puritan Social Ethic in the First Century of Settlement in New England*. New Haven, Conn., 1971.

Gambrell, Mary Latimer. *Ministerial Training in Eighteenth-Century New England*. New York, 1937.

Gaustad, Edwin Scott. *The Great Awakening in New England*. New York, 1957.

Gay, Peter. *A Loss of Mastery: Puritan Historians in Colonial America*. Berkeley, Calif., 1966.

————. *The Enlightenment: An Interpretation*. 2 vols. New York, 1967–1969.

Geertz, Clifford. *The Interpretation of Cultures*. New York, 1973.

Geissler, Suzanne. *Jonathan Edwards to Aaron Burr, Jr.: From The Great Awakening to Democratic Politics*. New York, 1981.

Goen, C. C. "Jonathan Edwards: A New Departure in Eschatology." *Church History* 28 (1959): 25–40.

————. *Revivalism and Separatism in New England, 1740–1800: Strict Congregationalists and Separate Baptists in the Great Awakening*. New Haven, Conn., 1962.

Goodrich, Chauncey A. "Narrative of Revivals of Religion in Yale College." *The American Quarterly Register* 10 (1858): 289–310.

Goodwin, Gerald J. "The Myth of Arminianism-Calvinism in Eighteenth-Century New England." *New England Quarterly* 41 (1968): 213–37.

Grant, Charles S. *Democracy in the Connecticut Frontier Town of Kent*. New York, 1961.

Grasso, Christopher. "Between Awakenings: Learned Men and the Transformation of Public Discourse in Connecticut, 1740–1800." Ph.D. dissertation, Yale University, 1992.

Green, M. Louise. *The Development of Religious Liberty in Connecticut*. Boston, 1905.

Greene, Jack P., and J. R. Pole, eds. *Colonial British America: Essays in the New History of the Early Modern Era*. Baltimore, 1984.

Greer, Curtis Manning. *The Hartford Theological Seminary*. Hartford, 1934.

Griffin, Edward M. *Old Brick: Charles Chauncy of Boston, 1705–1787*. Minneapolis, Minn., 1980.

Guelzo, Allen C. *Edwards on the Will: A Century of American Theological Debate*. Middletown, Conn., 1989.

Hall, David D. *Worlds of Wonder, Days of Judgment: Popular Religious Belief in Early New England*. New York, 1989.

Hankamer, Ernst Wolfram. *Das Politische Denken von Jonathan Edwards*. Munich, 1972.

Hankins, Jean F. "A Different Kind of Loyalist: The Sandemanians of New England during the Revolutionary War." *New England Quarterly* 60 (1984): 223–49.

Harlan, David. *The Clergy and the Great Awakening in New England*. Ann Arbor, Mich., 1980.

Haroutunian, Joseph. "Jonathan Edwards: A Study in Godliness." *Journal of Religion* 11 (1931): 400–409.

———. *Piety Versus Moralism: The Passing of the New England Theology.* New York, 1932; rep. 1970.

Hatch, Nathan O. *The Democratization of American Christianity.* New Haven, Conn., 1989.

———. *The Sacred Cause of Liberty: Republican Thought and the Millennium in Revolutionary New England.* New Haven, Conn., 1977.

Hatch, Nathan O., and Mark A. Noll. "From the Great Awakening to the War for Independence: Christian Values in the American Revolution." *Christian Scholar's Review* 12 (1983): 99–110.

Hatch, Nathan O., and Harry S. Stout, eds. *Jonathan Edwards and the American Experience.* New York, 1988.

Heimert, Alan, *Religion and the American Mind: From the Great Awakening to the Revolution.* Cambridge, Mass., 1966.

Heimert, Alan, and Perry Miller, eds. "Introduction" to *The Great Awakening: Documents Illustrating the Crisis and Its Consequences.* New York, 1967.

Helm, Paul. "John Locke and Jonathan Edwards: A Reconsideration." *Journal of the History of Philosophy* 7 (1969): 51–61.

Henretta, James A. "Economic Development and Social Structure in Colonial Boston." *William and Mary Quarterly* 22 (1965): 75–92.

———. "Families and Farms: *Mentalité* in Pre-Industrial America." *William and Mary Quarterly* 35 (1978): 3–32.

———. *The Origins of American Capitalism.* Boston, 1991.

Heyd, Michael. "The Reaction to Enthusiasm in the Seventeenth Century: Towards an Integrative Approach." *Journal of Modern History* 53 (1981): 258–80.

Holbrook, Clyde A. "Original Sin and the Enlightenment." In *The Heritage of Christian Thought: Essays in Honor of Robert Lowry Calhoun.* Ed. Robert E. Cushman and Egil Grislis. New York, 1965.

———. *The Ethics of Jonathan Edwards: Morality and Aesthetics.* Ann Arbor, Mich., 1973.

Howe, Daniel Walker. "The Decline of Calvinism: An Approach to Its Study." *Comparative Studies in Society and History* 14 (1972): 306–27.

Jedrey, Christopher M. *The World of John Cleaveland: Family and Community in Eighteenth-Century New England.* New York, 1979.

Kearney, Flora McLaughlin. *James Hervey and Eighteenth-Century Taste.* Muncie, Ind., 1969.

Kloppenberg, James T. "The Virtues of Liberalism: Christianity, Republicanism, and Ethics in Early American Political Discourse." *Journal of American History* 74 (1987): 9–33.

Knapp, Hugh H. "Samuel Hopkins and the New Divinity." Ph.D. dissertation, University of Wisconsin, 1971.

Koch, Adolph G. *Republican Religion: The American Revolution and the Cult of Reason.* New York, 1933.

Kramnick, Isaac. "Republican Revisionism Revisited." *American Historical Review* 87 (1982): 629–64.

Kuklick, Bruce. *Churchmen and Philosophers: From Jonathan Edwards to John Dewey.* New Haven, Conn., 1985.

Kulikoff, Allan. "The Progress of Inequality in Revolutionary Boston." *William and Mary Quarterly* 28 (1971): 375–412.

————. "The Transition to Capitalism in Rural America." *William and Mary Quarterly* 46 (1989): 120–44.

Laurence, David. "Jonathan Edwards, Solomon Stoddard, and the Preparationist Model of Conversion." *Harvard Theological Review* 72 (1979): 267–83.

Linden, Marshall, and Linton E. Simerl, eds. *250 Years of the First Church of Bethlehem.* Bethlehem, Conn., 1990.

Lockridge, Kenneth A. *A New England Town, The First Hundred Years: Dedham, Massachusetts, 1636–1736.* New York, 1970.

————. *Literacy in Colonial New England: An Inquiry into the Social Context of Literacy in the Early Modern West.* New York, 1974.

————. "Social Change and the Meaning of the American Revolution." *Journal of Social History* 6 (Summer 1973): 409–39.

Lovejoy, David S. *Religious Enthusiasm and the Great Awakening.* Englewood Cliffs, N.J., 1969.

————. "Samuel Hopkins: Religion, Slavery, and the Revolution." *New England Quarterly* 40 (1967): 227–43.

Lowance, Mason I., Jr. *The Language of Canaan: Metaphor and Symbol in New England from the Puritans to the Transcendentalists.* Cambridge, Mass., 1980.

Lucas, Paul R. "An Appeal to the Learned: The Mind of Solomon Stoddard." *William and Mary Quarterly* 30 (1973): 257–92.

————. *Valley of Discord: Church and Society Along the Connecticut River, 1636–1725.* Hanover, N.H., 1976.

MacFarlane, Alan. *The Culture of Capitalism.* New York, 1987.

Maier, Pauline. *From Resistance to Revolution: Colonial Radicals and the Development of American Opposition to Britain, 1765–1776.* New York, 1972.

Main, Gloria L., and Jackson T. Main. "Economic Growth and the Standard of Living in Southern New England: 1640–1774." *The Journal of Economic History* 48 (1988): 27–46.

Main, Jackson Turner. *Connecticut Society on the Eve of the American Revolution.* Hartford, 1977.

————. "The Distribution of Property in Colonial Connecticut." In *The Human Dimensions of Nation Making: Essays on Colonial and Revolutionary America.* Ed. James Kirby Martin. Madison, Wis., 1976.

Mann, Bruce H. *Neighbors and Strangers: Law and Community in Early Connecticut.* Chapel Hill, N.C., 1987.

Mansbridge, Jane J., ed. *Beyond Self-Interest.* Chicago, 1990.

Marini, Stephen A. *Radical Sects of Revolutionary New England.* Cambridge, Mass., 1982.

May, Henry F. *The Enlightenment in America.* New York, 1976.

————. "The Problem of the American Enlightenment." *New Literary History* 1 (Winter 1970): 201–14.

McCallum, James Dow. *Eleazar Wheelock: Founder of Dartmouth College.* Hanover, N.H., 1939.

McCracken, Grant. *Culture and Consumption: New Approaches to the Symbolic Character of Consumer Goods and Activities.* Indianapolis, 1990.

McCusker, John J. *Money and Exchange in Europe and America, 1600–1775: A Handbook.* Chapel Hill, N.C., 1977.

McDermott, Gerald R. *One Holy and Happy Society: The Public Theology of Jonathan Edwards.* University Park, Pa., 1992.

McDonald, Forrest. *Novus Ordo Seculorum: The Intellectual Origins of the Constitution.* Lawrence, Kan., 1985.

McLachlan, James. *Princetonians, 1748–1768: A Biographical Dictionary.* Princeton, N.J., 1976.

McLoughlin, William G. *New England Dissent 1630–1833: The Baptists and the Separation of Church and State.* 2 vols. Cambridge, Mass., 1971.

———. "The American Revolution as a Religious Revival." *New England Quarterly* 40 (1967): 99–110.

———. "The Role of Religion in the Revolution: Liberty of Conscience and Cultural Cohesion in the New Nation." In *Essays on the American Revolution.* Ed. Stephen G. Kurtz and James H. Hutson. Chapel Hill, N.C., 1973.

Mead, Sidney Earl. *Nathaniel William Taylor, 1786–1858: A Connecticut Liberal.* Chicago, 1942.

Meyer, Donald H. *The Democratic Enlightenment.* New York, 1976.

Middlekauff, Robert. *The Mathers: Three Generations of Puritan Intellectuals.* New York, 1971.

Miller, John C. "Religion, Finance, and Democracy in Massachusetts." *New England Quarterly* 6 (1933): 29–58.

Miller, Perry. *Errand into the Wilderness.* Cambridge, Mass., 1956.

———. "From the Covenant to the Revival." In *The Shaping of American Religion.* Vol. 1 of *Religion in American Life.* Ed. James Ward Smith and A. Leland Jamison. Princeton, N.J., 1961.

———. *Jonathan Edwards.* New York, 1949; rep. Cleveland, Ohio, 1959.

———. "Jonathan Edwards' Sociology of the Great Awakening." *New England Quarterly* 21 (1948): 50–77.

———. *Nature's Nation.* Cambridge, Mass., 1967.

———. "Solomon Stoddard, 1643–1729." *Harvard Theological Review* 34 (1941): 277–320.

———. *The New England Mind: From Colony to Province.* Cambridge, Mass., 1953; rep. Boston, 1963.

———. *The New England Mind: The Seventeenth Century.* New York, 1939; rep. Boston, 1963.

Moorhead, James H. "Between Progress and Apocalypse: A Reassessment of Millennialism in American Religious Thought, 1800–1880." *Journal of American History* 71 (1984): 524–42.

———. "Social Reform in Antebellum Protestantism." *Church History* 48 (1979): 416–30.

Morais, Herbert M. *Deism in Eighteenth Century America.* New York, 1934.

Morgan, Edmund S. "The American Revolution Considered as an Intellectual Movement." In *Paths of American Thought.* Ed. Morton White and Arthur M. Schlesinger, Jr. Boston, 1963.

———. *The Gentle Puritan: A Life of Ezra Stiles, 1727–1795.* New Haven, Conn., 1962.

———. "The Puritan Ethic and the American Revolution." *William and Mary Quarterly* 24 (1967): 3–43.

———. *Visible Saints: The History of A Puritan Idea.* Ithaca, N.Y., 1963.

Morgan, Edmund S., and Helen M. Morgan. *The Stamp Act Crisis: Prologue to Revolution.* Chapel Hill, N.C., 1953; rev. ed. New York, 1962.

Nash, Gary B. *The Urban Crucible: Social Change, Political Consciousness, and the Origins of the American Revolution.* Cambridge, Mass., 1979.

Niebuhr, H. Richard. "The Idea of Covenant and American Democracy." *Church History* 23 (1954): 126–35.

———. *The Kingdom of God in America*. New York, 1937.

———. *The Social Sources of Denominationalism*. New York, 1929.

Nissenbaum, Stephen, ed. *The Great Awakening at Yale College*. Belmont, Calif., 1972.

Noll, Mark A. *Christians in the American Revolution*. Grand Rapids, Mich., 1977.

———. "Ebenezer Devotion: Religion and Society in Revolutionary Connecticut." *Church History* 45 (1976): 293–307.

———. "The Church and the American Revolution: Historiographical Pitfalls, Problems, and Progress." *Fides et Historia* 8 (Fall 1975): 2–19.

Olson, Albert Laverne. *Agricultural Economy and the Population in Eighteenth Century Connecticut*. New Haven, Conn., 1935.

Park, Edwards A. *A Memoir of Nathaniel Emmons*. Boston, 1861.

———. *Memoir of the Life and Character of Samuel Hopkins, D.D.* 2d ed. Boston, 1854.

Peabody, Andrew P. "Hopkinsianism." *Proceedings of the American Antiquarian Society*, New Series, 5 (1898): 437–61.

Pettit, Norman. *The Heart Prepared: Grace and Conversion in Puritan Spiritual Life*. New Haven, Conn., 1966.

Pierce, David C. "Jonathan Edwards and the 'New Sense' of Glory." *New England Quarterly* 41 (1948): 82–95.

Pocock, J. G. A. *The Machiavellian Moment: Florentine Political Thought and the Atlantic Republican Tradition*. Princeton, N.J., 1975.

———. *Virtue, Commerce, and History: Essays on Political Thought and History, Chiefly in the Eighteenth Century*. New York, 1985.

Pope, Robert G. *The Half-way Covenant: Church Membership in Puritan New England*. Princeton, N.J., 1969.

Purcell, Richard J. *Connecticut in Transition, 1775–1818*. Washington, D.C., 1918.

Rabinowitz, Richard. *The Spiritual Self in Everyday Life: The Transformation of Personal Religious Experience in Nineteeth-Century New England*. Boston, 1989.

Raphael, David Daiches. *The Moral Sense*. London, 1947.

Richards, Jeffrey H. *Theatre Enough: American Culture and the Metaphor of the World Stage, 1607–1789*. Durham, N.C., 1991.

Robbins, Caroline. *The Eighteenth-Century Commonwealthman: Studies in the Transmission, Development, and Circumstance of English Liberal Thought from the Restoration of Charles II until the War with the Thirteen Colonies*. Cambridge, Mass., 1959.

———. "'When It Is That Colonies May Turn Independent': An Analysis of the Ethics and Politics of Francis Hutcheson (1694–1746)." *William and Mary Quarterly* 11 (1954): 214–51.

Rodgers, Daniel T. "Republicanism: The Career of a Concept." *The Journal of American History* 79 (1992): 11–38.

Rothenberg, Winifred B. "The Emergence of Farm Labor Markets and the Transformation of the Rural Economy: Massachusetts, 1750–1855." *The Journal of Economic History* 48 (1988): 537–66.

———. "The Market and Massachusetts Farmers, 1750–1855." *The Journal of Economic History* 41 (1981): 283–314.

Royster, Charles. *A Revolutionary People at War: The Continental Army and the American Character, 1775–1783*. Chapel Hill, N.C., 1979.

Rudisill, Doris Paul. *The Doctrine of the Atonement in Jonathan Edwards and His Successors*. New York, 1971.

Saillant, John. "Lemuel Haynes and the Revolutionary Origins of Black Theology, 1776–1801." *Religion and American Culture* 2 (1992): 79–102.

Schaefer, Thomas A. "Jonathan Edwards and Justification by Faith." *Church History* 20 (1951): 55–67.

———. "Jonathan Edwards's Conception of the Church." *Church History* 24 (1955): 51–66.

Scheick, William J. "The Grand Design: Jonathan Edwards's History of the Work of Redemption." *Eighteenth Century Studies* 8 (1975): 300–314.

Schmidt, Leigh Eric. "'A Second and Glorious Reformation': The New Light Extremism of Andrew Croswell." *William and Mary Quarterly* 43 (1986): 214–44.

Schmotter, James W. "Ministerial Careers in Eighteenth-Century New England." *Journal of Social History* 9 (Winter 1975): 249–67.

Scott, Donald M. *From Office to Profession: The New England Ministry, 1750–1850*. Philadelphia, 1978.

Scott, Lee Osborne. "The Concept of Love as Disinterested Benevolence in the Early Edwardseans." Ph.D. dissertation, Yale University, 1952.

Selesky, Harold E. *War and Society in Colonial Connecticut.* New Haven, Conn., 1990.

Sen, Amartya K. "Rational Fools: A Critique of the Behavioral Foundations of Economic Theory." In *Beyond Self-Interest*. Ed. Jane J. Mansbridge. Chicago, 1990.

Shalhope, Robert. "Toward a Republican Synthesis: The Emergence of an Understanding of Republicanism in American Historiography." *William and Mary Quarterly* 29 (1982): 49–80.

Shewmaker, William Orpheus. "The Training of the Protestant Ministry in the United States of America, before the Establishment of Theological Seminaries." *Papers of the American Society of Church History*, Second Series, 6 (1921): 71–202.

Shipton, Clifford K., and John Langdon Sibley. *Sibley's Harvard Graduates: Biographical Sketches of those who attended Harvard College*. 14 vols. Boston, 1873–1968.

Simonson, Harold D. *Jonathan Edwards: Theologian of the Heart*. Grand Rapids, Mich., 1974.

Sklar, Robert. "The Great Awakening and Colonial Politics: Connecticut's Revolution in the Minds of Men." *The Connecticut Historical Society Bulletin* 28 (1963): 81–95.

Smith, H. Shelton. *Changing Conceptions of Original Sin*. New York, 1955.

Smyth, Ralph D. "Matthew Bellamy of New Haven, Conn., and His Descendants." *The New England Historical and Geneological Register* 61 (1907): 338–40.

Spohn, William Costello. "Religion and Morality in the Thought of Jonathan Edwards." Ph.D. dissertation, University of Chicago, 1978.

———. "Sovereign Beauty: Jonathan Edwards and the Nature of True Religion." *Theological Studies* 42 (1981): 394–421.

Sprague, William B. *Annals of the American Pulpit; or Commemorative Notices of Distinguished American Clergymen of Various Denominations*. 9 vols. New York, 1857– 1869.

Stein, Stephen J. "An Apocalyptic Rationale for the American Revolution." *Early American Literature* 9 (Winter 1972): 211–25.

Steiner, Bruce E. "Anglican Officeholding in Pre-Revolutionary Connecticut: The Parameters of New England Community." *William and Mary Quarterly* 31 (1974): 369–406.

Stephens, Bruce M. *God's Last Metaphor: The Doctrine of the Trinity in New England Theology.* Chico, Calif., 1981.

Stoever, William K. B. *"A Faire and Easie Way to Heaven": Covenant Theology and Antinomianism in Early Massachusetts.* Middletown, Conn., 1978.

Stout, Harry S. "Religion, Communications, and the Ideological Origins of the American Revolution." *William and Mary Quarterly* 34 (1977): 519–41.

———. *The Divine Dramatist: George Whitefield and the Rise of Modern Evangelism.* Grand Rapids, Mich., 1991.

———. "The Great Awakening in New England Reconsidered: The New England Clergy." *Journal of Social History* 8 (Spring 1974): 21–48.

———. *The New England Soul: Preaching and Religious Culture in Colonial New England.* New York, 1986.

———. "The Puritans and Edwards." In *Jonathan Edwards and the American Experience.* Ed. Nathan O. Hatch and Harry S. Stout. New York, 1988.

Sweeney, Kevin M. "Furniture and the Domestic Environment in Wethersfield, Connecticut, 1639–1800." In *Material Life in America, 1600–1860.* Ed. Robert Blair St. George. Boston, 1988.

Taylor, Robert J. *Colonial Connecticut: A History.* Millwood, N.Y., 1979.

Thompson, E. P. "The Moral Economy of the English Crowd in the Eighteenth Century." *Past and Present* 50 (1971): 76–136.

Thompson, Martyn P. "The History of Fundamental Law in Political Thought from the French Wars of Religion to the American Revolution." *American Historical Review* 91 (1986): 1103–28.

Tracy, Patricia J. *Jonathan Edwards, Pastor: Religion and Society in Eighteenth-Century Northampton.* New York, 1980.

Trask, Kerry A. *In the Pursuit of Shadows: Massachusetts Millenialism [sic] and the Seven Years War.* New York, 1989.

Trumbull, Benjamin. *A Complete History of Connecticut, Civil and Ecclesiastical.* 2 vols. New Haven, Conn., 1818; rep. 1898.

Tucker, Louis Leonard. *Puritan Protagonist: President Thomas Clap of Yale College.* Chapel Hill, N.C., 1962.

Tuveson, Ernest Lee. *Redeemer Nation: The Idea of America's Millennial Role.* Chicago, 1968.

Valeri, Mark. "The Economic Thought of Jonathan Edwards." *Church History* 60 (1991): 37–54.

———. "The New Divinity and the American Revolution." *William and Mary Quarterly* 46 (1989): 741–69.

Vickers, Daniel. "Competency and Competition: Economic Culture in Early America." *William and Mary Quarterly* 47 (1990): 3–29.

Vos, Howard Frederic. "The Great Awakening in Connecticut." Ph.D. dissertation, Northwestern University, 1967.

Walker, Williston. "The Sandemaneans of New England." *Annual Report of the American Historical Association for the Year 1901* 1 (1901): 133–62.

Wallace, Dewey D., Jr. "Socinianism, Justification by Faith, and the Sources of John Locke's *The Reasonableness of Christianity.*" *Journal of the History of Ideas* 45 (1984): 49–66.

Walsh, James. "The Great Awakening in the First Congregational Church of Woodbury, Connecticut." *William and Mary Quarterly* 28 (1971): 543–62.

———. "The Pure Church in Eighteenth-Century Connecticut." Ph.D. dissertation, Columbia University, 1967.

Walzer, Michael. "Puritanism as a Revolutionary Ideology." *History and Theory* 3 (1965): 59–90.

———. *The Revolution of the Saints: A Study in Origins of Radical Politics.* Cambridge, Mass., 1965.

Warch, Richard. *School of the Prophets: Yale College, 1701–1740.* New Haven, Conn., 1973.

Waters, John J. "Patrimony, Successsion and Social Stability in Guilford, Connecticut." *Perspectives in American History* 10 (1976): 131–60.

Weaver, Glenn. *Jonathan Trumbull: Connecticut's Merchant Magistrate (1710–1785).* Hartford, 1956.

Weber, Donald. *Rhetoric and History in Revolutionary New England.* New York, 1988.

———. "The Recovery of Jonathan Edwards." In *Jonathan Edwards and the American Experience.* Ed. Nathan O. Hatch and Harry S. Stout. New York, 1988.

Webster, Richard. *A History of the Presbyterian Church in America, from its Origin until the Year 1760.* Philadelphia, 1857.

White, Morton. *The Philosophy of the American Revolution.* New York, 1978.

Williams, Stanley T. "Six Letters of Jonathan Edwards to Joseph Bellamy." *New England Quarterly* 1 (1928): 226–42.

Willingham, William F. "Deference, Democracy, and Town Government in Windham, 1758–1786." *William and Mary Quarterly* 30 (1973): 401–22.

Wills, Garry. *Inventing America: Jefferson's Declaration of Independence.* Garden City, N.Y., 1978.

Wilson, John F. "History, Redemption, and the Millennium." In *Jonathan Edwards and the American Experience.* Ed. Nathan O. Hatch and Harry S. Stout. New York, 1988.

———. "Jonathan Edwards as Historian." *Church History* 46 (1977): 5–18.

———. *Pulpit in Parliament: Puritanism During the English Civil Wars, 1640–1648.* Princeton, N.J., 1969.

Wilson, Robert J. *The Benevolent Deity: Ebenezer Gay and the Rise of Rational Religion in New England, 1696–1787.* Philadelphia, 1984.

Winslow, Ola Elizabeth. *Jonathan Edwards: 1703–1758.* New York, 1940.

———. *Meetinghouse Hill, 1630–1783.* New York, 1952.

Wolf, Edwin, II. *The Book Culture of a Colonial American City: Philadelphia Books, Bookmen, and Booksellers.* New York, 1988.

Wood, Gordon S. "Rhetoric and Reality in the American Revolution." *William and Mary Quarterly* 23 (1966): 3–32.

———. *The Creation of the American Republic, 1776–1787.* Chapel Hill, N.C., 1969.

———. *The Radicalism of the American Revolution.* New York, 1992.

Worthley, Harold Field. *An Inventory of the Records of the Particular (Congregational) Churches of Massachusetts Gathered 1620–1805.* Cambridge, Mass., 1970.

Wright, Conrad. *The Beginnings of Unitarianism in America.* Boston, 1955.

Wright, Conrad Edick. *The Transformation of Charity in Postrevolutionary New England*. Boston, 1992.

Youngs, J. William T., Jr. *God's Messengers: Religious Leadership in Colonial New England, 1700–1750*. Baltimore, 1976.

Zeichner, Oscar. *Connecticut's Years of Controversy: 1750–1770*. Chapel Hill, N.C., 1949.

Zuckerman, Michael. *Peaceable Kingdoms: New England Towns in the Eighteenth Century*. New York, 1970.

Index